CONTENTIOUS POLITICS

CONTENTIOUS POLITICS

Charles Tilly and Sidney Tarrow

Paradigm Publishers

Boulder • London

Copyright © 2007 by Paradigm Publishers

Published in the United States by Paradigm Publishers, 3360 Mitchell Lane, Suite E, Boulder, Colorado 80301 USA.

Paradigm Publishers is the trade name of Birkenkamp & Company, LLC, Dean Birkenkamp, President and Publisher.

Library of Congress Cataloging-in-Publication Data

Tilly, Charles.
   Contentious politics / Charles Tilly and Sidney Tarrow.
     p. cm.
   Includes bibliographical references and index.
   ISBN-13: 978-1-59451-245-2 (hardcover : alk. paper)
   ISBN-10: 1-59451-245-0 (hardcover : alk. paper)
   ISBN-13: 978-1-59451-246-9 (pbk)
   ISBN-10: 1-59451-246-9 (pbk)
   1. Social movements.   2. Social conflict.   3. Political sociology.   I. Tarrow,
Sidney G.   II. Title.
   HM881.T54 2006
   306.2—dc22

                            2006003610

Designed and Typeset by Straight Creek Bookmakers.

11 10 09 08 07   1 2 3 4 5

Paperback cover: "Procesión del Día de Moscú" Diego Rivera © 2006 Banco de México Diego Rivera & Frida Kahlo Museums Trust. Av. Cinco de Mayo No. 2, Col. Centro, Del. Cuauhtémoc 06059, México, D.F.

To Doug,
Silent Partner

CONTENTS

FIGURES AND BOXES

Figures

Boxes

PREFACE

In recent years, many students of politics and sociology have become interested in this book's two main themes: contentious politics and the explanation of political events by means of well-specified mechanisms and processes. As you will soon see, scholars, journalists, and citizens have been studying one version or another of contentious politics for a long time. But only recently have specialists in the subject tried hard to find a middle ground between general laws of human behavior (of which any sort of political struggle would simply be a special case) and separate sets of generalizations for revolutions, civil wars, social movements, and each other variety of contention. The contentious politics approach looks deliberately for similarities in cause-effect relationships across a wide range of political struggles without aiming for general laws that govern all of politics. It does so through identification of crucial mechanisms and processes—you will, for example, soon meet the mechanism of brokerage and the process of mobilization—that operate in similar ways across a wide variety of conflict and cooperation. This book brings together the basic elements of the two approaches.

A few years ago, we made an earlier attempt to join the two approaches. It only succeeded halfway. We wrote *Dynamics of Contention* (Cambridge University Press, 2001) in collaboration with one of world's great analysts of contentious politics, Doug McAdam of Stanford University. Although that book stirred up a lively scholarly discussion, even specialists who were sympathetic to our approach made three justified complaints about it. First, it pointed to mechanisms and processes by the dozen without defining and documenting them carefully, much less showing exactly how they worked. Second, it remained unclear about the methods and evidence students and scholars could use to check out its explanations. Third, instead of making a straightforward presentation of its teachings, it reveled in complications, asides, and illustrations.

In this new book, we try hard to overcome all three difficulties. We limit the number of mechanisms and processes under study, describing them as clearly and consistently as we can. We stress methods and evidence, summarizing our main points in the book's two appendices. Finally, we present the contentious politics approach step-by-step, starting with the basics and moving on through extensions and applications. We also summarize our findings twice: first in chapter 9 and again in our appendices.

We have not met all the objections of our critics and friends. For example, our book aims mainly at identifying and illustrating the analytical elements in our narratives—elements such as streams of contention, episodes, mechanisms, processes, and outcomes. Confirming their presence empirically would have meant either writing a different book or increasing the size of this one exponentially. Nor have we attempted a balanced coverage of all the world's contentious politics; we prefer to write about regions on which we have done research and some of whose languages we know.

The first-time reader may find the array of concepts in the first part of the book daunting. Do not be discouraged: regard these concepts not as rules but as tools. You should use them to understand the narratives we use to illustrate our explanations. They should also help when it is your turn to examine episodes of contentious politics.

Let us clear away one frequent misunderstanding at once. Both of us work in a field that, for short, many other people refer to as "social movements." Both of us think that social movements exist and have distinctive properties. This book's chapter 6 deals explicitly with social movements. Both of us have even written books about social movements: Tarrow's *Power in Movement* (Cambridge University Press, revised edition, 1998) and Tilly's *Social Movements, 1768–2004* (Paradigm Publishers, 2004). But here, instead of sweeping all popular mobilizations into the bin of social movements, we place social movements in the context of a much wider variety of popular struggles. We note both their common properties and their distinctive characteristics. We hope that students of social movements will read this book together with their favorite studies of social movements. As they read, we hope they will recognize similarities, differences, and connections between social movements and other forms of contentious politics.

We have received indispensable information, advice, help, criticism, and encouragement from Ron Aminzade, Kenneth Andrews, Karen Beckwith, Mark Beissinger, Dean Birkenkamp, Charles Brockett, Angela Carter,

Anne Costain, Donatella della Porta, Mikael Eriksson, Lev Grinberg, Craig Jenkins, Mary Katzenstein, Angela Kim, Bert Klandermans, Karrie Koesel, Hanspeter Kriesi, Jane Mansbridge, Lilian Mathieu, Doug McAdam, David S. Meyer, Maryjane Osa, Dieter Rucht, Sarah Soule, Sarah Tarrow, Peter Wallensteen, and a group of anonymous students who were willing to give of their time to analyze our efforts. We owe our greatest debt to our (not-always) silent partner Doug McAdam. Doug was too busy running the Center for Advanced Study in the Behavioral Sciences to join this particular venture. But he combined the attentions of cheerleader, critic, and friend with the amiable grace for which he has become famous.

1

Circa 1830: A slave auction in America.
(Photo by Rischgitz/Getty Images)

CHAPTER ONE

MAKING CLAIMS

When a young English divinity student named Thomas Clarkson won a Latin Prize with an essay on slavery at Cambridge in 1785, neither he nor his listeners imagined the effect it would have on slavery in the British Empire. But as he sat down at the side of the road on his way to London to take up a career as a Protestant minister, Clarkson reflected that if the horrors he had uncovered about slavery were true, "it was time some person should see these calamities to their end" (Hochschild 2005: 89).

Clarkson turned out to be that person. Together with a small band of antislavery advocates, he became the world's first modern professional organizer. Clarkson wrote thousands of letters, organized petition drives, and helped to launch the world's first successful transnational movement. That movement eventually ended the vicious violence of the slave trade and led to the abolition of slavery around the Atlantic. It allowed English reformers to claim moral superiority over the newly independent but slaveholding United States. The antislavery movement went through many phases, suffered reversals during the repressive years of the Napoleonic wars, and required a savage civil war to end slavery in the United States. But it joined religious evangelicalism, the political emancipation of Catholics, and parliamentary reform to create the pattern of modern social movements in eighteenth-century England.

The movement that Clarkson and his friends started looks decorous and even conservative to us today. But they made their claims much as social movements still do. They stimulated the formation of committees, took out newspaper ads, encouraged the deposing of petitions, gathered evidence, and laid it before the House of Commons. Although the word *boycott* itself would not enter the language for another century, they organized what was in effect a boycott of slave-produced sugar. Britain's antislavery activists also shocked the nation's conscience by presenting instruments of torture the slave owners used. In the process, they forged

1

alliances with parliamentary and literary opponents of slavery such as William Wilberforce and Samuel Taylor Coleridge. They even sent Clarkson to help antislavery forces in France during the brief period when French republicans were interpreting the Rights of Man to include people of color (Drescher 1991).

It took almost twenty years for Britain's antislavery campaign to bring the Atlantic slave trade to an end and another three decades for slavery to end in Britain's colonies. But less than a year after Clarkson and the committee began their campaign, "Britons were challenging slavery in London debating societies, in provincial pubs, and across dinner tables throughout the country" (Hochschild 2005: 213). In the newly independent United States, opponents of the slave trade would eventually persuade Congress to make the trade illegal, though it took a civil war to end slavery in the South. Clarkson, his allies, his enemies, and public authorities on both sides of the Atlantic were engaging in serious politics.

We could tell many different stories about antislavery. We could treat it as a moral tale showing what determination can accomplish in the face of difficult odds. We could think about it as an application of enlightened values, as an expression of religious zeal, or as English capitalists' attempt to promote free labor and free trade. We could see it as an early example of a transnational social movement, a phenomenon that has become important in this age of globalization. Different observers of European and American antislavery campaigns have told all these tales, and more. Here we treat it as a dramatic example of *contentious politics,* of people struggling with each other over which political program will prevail.

For another dramatic episode of contentious politics, fast-forward to the Ukrainian capital of Kiev in 2004. Ukraine's ruler, Leonid Kuchma, was imposing corruption, electoral chicanery, and political crime on a populace that had escaped from Soviet rule only a decade earlier. The regime's agents stole a national election from the opposition party and poisoned its candidate, Victor Yushchenko, with dioxin. In reaction to the stolen election, and supported by foreign observers and neighboring states, outraged citizens poured into the streets of the capital. They sang and chanted through cold November nights, blocked entry to government buildings, and produced what came to be called the "Orange Revolution." The Ukrainian protests followed similar episodes in Serbia during 2000 and in Georgia during 2003. They belonged to a wave of popular protest against electoral fraud that spread throughout the former Soviet Union and adjacent regions.

Yet the Orange Revolution came close to failing. As the protesters filled the streets of Kiev, more than 10,000 Interior Ministry troops scrambled into trucks with the intention of meeting them with force. "As the troops began to move towards the center of the capital," wrote C. J. Chivers in the *New York Times*, "Kiev was tilting towards a terrible clash, a Soviet-style crackdown that could have brought civil war" (Chivers 2005). But the outcome was not what any outsider might have expected. Although the press focused on the highly visible protest in the streets, much more was happening in Ukraine in that month:

- A group of army officers "funneled information to Mr. Kuchma's rivals, provided security to opposition figures and demonstrations, sent choreographed public signals about their unwillingness to follow the administration's path and engaged in a psychological tug-of-war with state officials to soften responses against the protests" (Chivers 2005).
- Throughout the crisis, "an inside battle was waged by a clique of Ukraine's top intelligence officers, who chose not to follow the plan by President Leonid D. Kuchma's administration to pass power to ... the President's chosen successor" (Chivers 2005).
- At the same time, "Police cadets openly agitated in favor of Yushchenko and called upon riot police to switch sides ... when 10,000 Interior Ministry troops were mobilized on November 28 to put down the protests in Independence Square, the SBU [Ukrainian Security Service] had already warned opposition leaders of the crackdown" (Kuzio 2005: 128).
- Senior intelligence officials, told informally what was afoot, frantically worked the phones to persuade the Interior Ministry to turn its troops back. As demonstrators marched, chanted, sang songs, and rubbed their hands against the cold, an undercover agent of the SBU moved among them, warning of the approaching repression.

Not only that: Behind the scenes, the protesters and the army officers who supported them enjoyed quiet approval from many sectors of Ukrainian society, including some of the crooked "oligarchs" who had previously supported Kuchma's corrupt regime.

External actors also weighed in: European election monitors and advocates of democracy supported the opposition. The influence of Russia's president Vladimir Putin weighed on the regime's side; Putin announced his support for the regime-backed candidate even as reports were coming in that the election was rigged. Rather than a bipolar contest between a social movement for progress and the dark forces of reaction, in the "Orange Revolution" we see a many-faceted episode of contention. Allies and enemies, "good" and "bad" actors, insiders and outsiders, participants and bystanders intersected in a process of making claims that we call contentious politics.

Contentious Politics

What do the campaign against the slave trade in eighteenth-century England and the Orange Revolution in Ukraine in 2004 have in common? Although we can identify differences, these campaigns converged in many ways. Both made claims on authorities, used public performances to do so, drew on inherited forms of collective action (our term for this is *repertoires*) and invented new ones, forged alliances with influential members of their respective polities, took advantage of existing political regime opportunities and made new ones, and used a combination of institutional and extrainstitutional routines to advance their claims. They engaged in *contentious politics*.

Contentious politics involves interactions in which actors make claims bearing on someone else's interests, leading to coordinated efforts on behalf of shared interests or programs, in which governments are involved as targets, initiators of claims, or third parties. Contentious politics thus brings together three familiar features of social life: contention, collective action, and politics.

Contention involves making claims that bear on someone else's interests. In everyday life, contention ranges from small matters such as which television show we should watch tonight to bigger questions such as whether your sister Sue should marry the man she is dating. But it also takes place in football matches, rival advertising campaigns, and struggles between cantankerous patients and irritable doctors.

In the simplest version of contention, one party makes claims on another. The parties are often persons, but one or the other can also be a group or even an institution; you can make a claim on your school or file a claim on the government for unemployment benefits. In the elementary version, we can think of one party as a subject (the maker of a claim) and the other as an object (the receiver of a claim). Claims always involve at least one subject's reaching visibly toward at least one object. You (subject) may ask a friend (object) to pay back the money he borrowed from you yesterday. But claims range from timid requests to strident demands to direct attacks, just so long as they would, if realized, somehow affect the object's well-being, the object's interests. Often three or more parties are involved, as when you demand that your friend pay you back the money he was about to hand over to another creditor. Contention always brings together subjects, objects, and claims.

Collective action means coordinating efforts on behalf of shared interests or programs. Football teams engage in collective action, but so do churches, voluntary associations, and neighbors who clear weeds from a vacant lot. When you go to school or to work for a big company, you enter an organization that is carrying on collective action. But most of the collective action involved occurs with no significant contention and no government involvement. The bulk of collective action takes place outside contentious politics.

Most contention also occurs outside politics. We enter the realm of *politics* when we interact with agents of governments, either dealing with them directly or engaging in activities bearing on governmental rights, regulations, and interests. Politics likewise ranges from fairly routine matters such as applying for a driver's license to momentous questions such as whether the country should go to war. But most of politics involves little or no contention. Most of the time, people register for benefits, answer census takers, cash government checks, or show their passports to immigration officers without making significant claims on other people.

The presence or absence of governments in contention makes a difference for three big reasons. First, people who control governments gain advantages over people who don't. Even where the government is weak, controlling it gives you the means of collecting taxes, distributing resources, and regulating other people's behavior. As a result, political contention puts at risk, however slightly, the advantages of those who currently enjoy governmental power.

Second, governments always make rules governing contention: who can make what collective claims, by what means, with what outcomes. Even weak governments have some influence over the prevailing forms of claim making, and they resist anyone else building up competitive centers of power within their territories.

Third, governments control substantial coercive means: armies, police forces, courts, prisons, and the like. The availability of governmental coercion gives an edge to political contention that rarely exists outside the political arena. In political contention, large-scale violence always remains a possibility, however faint. Contention connected to governments does resemble contention in families, sports, churches, and businesses in some regards. We will sometimes call attention to those parallels. But we single out government-connected contention because it has these distinctive properties.

Let us immediately rule out a few possible misunderstandings. Restriction of contentious politics to claim making that somehow involves governments by no means implies that governments must figure as the makers or receivers of contentious claims. On the contrary, as the book proceeds, we will encounter a wide range of contention in which nongovernmental actors are pitted against each other and make claims on religious, economic, ethnic, or other nongovernmental holders of power. Remember the story with which this chapter began? In both England and America, antislavery activists directed their claims first against slaveholders and only then against governments, which were drawn into the action because only they could resolve the legal and physical conflicts that slavery fostered.

As you move through the book, you will read sustained discussions of many such conflicts:

- Struggles between advocates and opponents of slavery in the United States (chapter 2)
- College campus activism against South Africa's apartheid (chapter 2)
- Attempts of prostitutes in Lyons, France, to improve their lives (chapter 5)
- Transformations of American women's lives by participation in feminist organizations (chapter 6)
- Lunch counter sit-ins by African American activists (chapter 9)

All of these conflicts eventually drew governments—local or national—into the action, as did our initial story of the struggle against slavery in England. But they began by pitting nongovernmental actors against each other.

Let us be clear. We do not deny that processes much like those occurring in contentious politics also occur in nonpolitical settings. That is actually the point of distinguishing collective action and contention from politics. We also do not deny that some forms of contention—such as religious movements—aim primarily at internal change. But even these frequently come into contact with governments—for example, when evangelical Christians attempt to incorporate religious values into the public school curriculum. Finally, sometimes a corporation that runs a company

W AREN'T THEY THE SAME THING?. INTERNAL CHANGE? UN POLITICAL?.

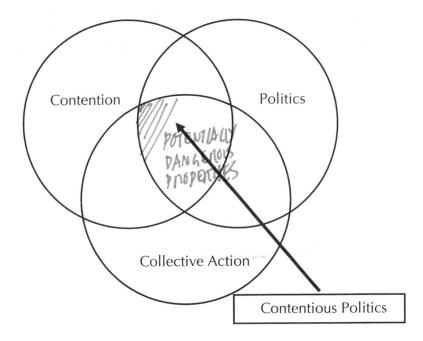

[handwritten: POTENTIALLY DANGEROUS PROPERTIES]

Figure 1.1. Components of Contentious Politics

town, an international military force such as NATO, or an international institution such as the United Nations and the World Trade Organization behaves much like a government. Those cases come close enough to our *[handwritten: ADD]* definition of contentious politics for this book to include them. Still, we *[handwritten: WHY]* focus our attention on the convergence of collective action, contention, *[handwritten: IS IT]* and politics because the area of their overlap has distinctive—and poten- *[handwritten: DEFINING]* tially dangerous—properties.

Figure 1.1 shows how contention, collective action, and politics converge in contentious politics. Many scholars would draw different boundaries—for example, by treating collective action as the fundamental process. In that view, such episodes as antislavery and the Orange Revolution qualify simply as special instances of collective action. Others define politics as consisting of struggles for power however and wherever they occur. They thus take in all of contentious politics, add to it struggles outside the range of government, but treat routine political transactions as something else. In this line of thought, many analysts distinguish between real politics—our contentious politics plus similar struggles outside political arenas—and public administration.

Many students of the subject use the term *social movement* to cover most or all of the overlap between contention and collective action, whether it happens in politics or some other arena. The same analysts often extend the term *social movement* to what we will call *social movement bases*: the social background, organizational resources, and cultural frameworks of contention and collective action. Our book provides plenty of evidence about social movements. But we recommend resisting expansion of the term to embrace most or all of contentious politics, its social bases, and its cultural contexts. Such an expansion has several drawbacks. First, it hampers systematic comparison across different types of contention by collecting them under the same label. Second, if different forms of contention all count as social movements, that expansion makes it difficult to examine transitions among them. Third, it obscures a fundamental fact: that social movements are a *historical*—and not a universal—category.

As our story of British antislavery shows, the social movement we know took shape about two centuries ago, and it only became widely available as a means of popular claim making during the twentieth century (Tilly 2004b). It emerged through episodes such as antislavery, found its feet in the early nineteenth century through labor and other struggles, and eventually became a staple of popular politics across the world's less authoritarian regimes during the twentieth century. American civil rights activism formed a social movement; so did the Gandhian movement for Indian independence.

What qualifies as a social movement? We define a *social movement* as a sustained campaign of claim making, using repeated performances that advertise the claim, based on organizations, networks, traditions, and solidarities that sustain these activities. But most forms of contentious politics are not social movements. Social movements combine: (1) sustained campaigns of claim making; (2) an array of public performances including marches, rallies, demonstrations, creation of specialized associations, public meetings, public statements, petitions, letter writing, and lobbying; (3) repeated public displays of worthiness, unity, numbers, and commitment by such means as wearing colors, marching in disciplined ranks, sporting badges that advertise the cause, displaying signs, chanting slogans, and picketing public buildings. They draw on (4) the organizations, networks, traditions, and solidarities that sustain these activities—our *social movement bases*. As familiar as it has become to citizens of Western countries, this combination of campaigns, performances, and displays only took shape a few hundred years ago, and it is still rare or nonexistent through much of the contemporary world.

The second part of this book compares social movements to other forms of contention. Chapter 6 shows how social movement forms of action figured in Poland's Solidarity movement and the American women's movement. These movements' combinations of public displays of worthiness, unity, numbers, and commitment produced significantly less violent confrontation than the three forms of lethal conflict reviewed in chapter 7: ethnic-religious strife, civil wars, and revolutions. Social movement politics and lethal conflicts often co-occur and intersect in the same places. Chapter 8 highlights the interactions between movements and lethal conflicts in two "composite regimes": the movement of Jewish settlers forced to withdraw from the Gaza Strip in 2005, and the clash between human rights campaigners and human rights violators in Latin America, Spain, and Great Britain.

Our two landmark episodes—British antislavery and the Ukrainian Orange Revolution—also reveal intersections among contention, politics, and collective action. Though buffeted by the varying winds of reaction and reform, antislavery was a true social movement. Over a period of more than thirty years, its participants sustained a powerful campaign of contentious politics both within and against Britain's political institutions. In contrast, though it was more tumultuous than antislavery and teetered on the edge of revolution, the Ukrainian uprising included a short-term movement coalition ranging from masses in the streets to opposition leaders, to figures inside the state's repressive institutions, and to the economic elite. It broke up as soon as it reached its major goal—the reversal of a stolen election.

When contention, politics, and collective action get together, something distinctive happens: power, shared interests, and government policy come into play. Claims become collective, which means they depend on some sort of coordination among the people making the claims. They also become political, at least by assuming the presence of governments as monitors, guarantors, or regulators of collective claim making and often more directly as subjects or objects of claims. In those circumstances, we will speak about groups that sometimes make claims as *political actors*. We will call the collective names that they give themselves or that other people give them—those workers, we citizens, us women, and so on—their *political identities*.

People often make collective claims on governments, and governments make claims on whole categories of people. Governments also involve themselves in how people outside government make claims on each other. Lawmakers make laws banning some kinds of assemblies, police arrest unruly demonstrators, judges try people for seditious claims, and officials intervene when their clients or constituents are fighting collectively. The intersection of contention, politics, and collective action contains events ranging from local ethnic competition to great revolutions.

This book looks hard and systematically at that intersection. It lays out a simple set of tools for describing and explaining contentious politics in all its varieties. The tools consist of concepts and causal connections among the phenomena singled out by those concepts. We make a rough distinction between *description* and *explanation*. *Description* consists of specifying what special properties and variations in contention deserve serious attention. *Explanation* entails showing what produces those special properties and variations.

The distinction between description and explanation remains rough; sometimes one special property or brand of variation helps to explain another. When we compare Ukraine's Orange Revolution with other mobilizations against authoritarian regimes that took place during 2004 and 2005, we actually move toward explanation by identifying relevant differences among the regimes and their oppositions. Chapter 2 takes up explanatory concepts more directly, and chapter 3 combines description and explanation by placing different forms of contention in different forms of regimes and examining the role of contention in regime transitions. But this chapter concentrates on concepts describing the interesting features of contention that deserve explanation.

What concepts? This chapter's concepts show how political actors make claims in the names of their political identities, identify various sorts of collective political performances, describe how contentious performances cluster into repertoires of contention, analyze how repertoires change, and apply those ideas to the United States since World War II. The rest of the book returns repeatedly to the United States. But it also draws on cases from Europe, Latin America, the Middle East, and beyond. As the book moves on, much of our descriptive work will involve connecting these concepts with each other.

How? The book shows how repertoires of contention differ between democratic and undemocratic *regimes.* The book explains what difference it makes whether contention takes place within existing *institutions,* outside them, or against them. It considers how *political opportunity structures* affect which political identities people bring into contention. It describes how social movements combine institutional and extrainstitutional forms of action. It shows that actors build on a broad set of *social bases* but that these bases are not sufficient to explain *contentious interaction,* which depends on the triggering of a finite set of *mechanisms* and *processes.* The book reveals that a similar group of mechanisms and processes—for example, brokerage, certification, mobilization, demobilization, and scale shift—recur in different combinations with substantially different outcomes in revolutions, social movements, ethnic conflict, nationalism, civil war, and other distinct forms of contentious politics. Later chapters will treat all of these elements in detail.

This book presents an *interactive approach* to contentious politics. As Doug McAdam (1999) writes, "a viable model of the individual must take full account of the fundamentally *social/relational* nature of human existence" (xiii). Some students of contention give primary attention to its social bases—for example, to social networks, organizations, cultural predispositions, and the political and ideological traditions that nourish contention. While we give ample space to these bases of contention, we are primarily concerned with the mechanisms and processes that involve challengers, their targets, public authorities, and third parties like the media and the public in sequences of interaction. For example, when we turn to social movements in chapter 6, we focus on the mechanisms and processes that transform the bases of contention into social movement campaigns.

Putting these elements together will help us to resolve a fundamental paradox of contentious politics: its recurring combination of *variations* and *regularities*. Contentious politics features enormous variation in its issues, actors, interactions, claims, sequences, and outcomes from time to time and place to place. But it also displays great regularities in the ways that contention unfolds. We will see how similar mechanisms and processes produce distinctive political trajectories and outcomes depending on their combinations and on the social bases and political contexts in which they operate. We can begin to capture some of the recurrent, historically embedded character of contentious politics by means of two related theatrical metaphors: performances and repertoires.

- *Contentious performances* are relatively familiar and standardized ways in which one set of political actors makes collective claims on some other set of political actors. Among other performances, participants in Ukraine's Orange Revolution used mass demonstrations as visible, effective performances.
- *Contentious repertoires* are arrays of contentious performances that are currently known and available within some set of political actors. England's antislavery activists helped to invent the demonstration as a political performance, but they also drew on petitions, lobbying, press releases, public meetings, and a number of other performances.

Claim Making as Performance

Once we look closely at collective making of claims, we see that particular instances improvise on shared scripts. Presentation of a petition, taking of a hostage, or mounting of a demonstration constitutes a *performance* linking at least two actors: a claimant and an object of claims. Innovation occurs incessantly on the small scale, but effective claims depend on a recognizable relation to their setting, on relations between the parties, and on previous uses of the claim-making form.

Performances evolve over time. Consider how Clarkson and his colleagues used petitions to inundate Parliament with antislavery demands. One of the most traditional forms of making claims, petitions originally came from individual petitioners seeking benefits for themselves. They bowed before their lords to request personal exemption from military service or lowering of their excise tax. The British antislavery group turned the petition into an instrument for *mass* claim making, accumulating thousands of signatures on petitions to demand redress for others.

Now think of the massing of protest in the streets of Kiev against the stolen 2004 elections. In the 1830s, British Chartists adopted the mass demonstration, then a new form, as they demanded political rights for working people (Thompson 1984). In the mid–nineteenth century, during what we remember as the 1848 revolution, demonstrations traversed Europe on the part of workers, nationalists, middle-class reformers, and revolutionary socialists. By 2004, Ukrainians knew exactly how to organize demonstrations that would challenge the rules, reinforce their own solidarity, and gain international support.

All forms of contention rest on performances, but performances range from direct assaults on others to theatricals staged for nearby or distant audiences (Tarrow 1998; Taylor and Van Dyke 2004: 271). In the eighteenth century, people mainly engaged in performances that were specific to their particular claims, such as seizing grain, invading landlords' fields, barricading their streets, and pulling down wrongdoers' houses (Tilly 2005a). Think of the Boston colonists who attacked the home of an official charged with collecting the hated stamp tax in 1765, or of those who dumped tea into Boston Harbor in 1775. Both groups were engaging in particular performances. But by the twentieth century, many contentious performances had spread around the world and become what we call modular performances that could be adopted and adapted across a wide range of conflicts and sites of contention by a broad range of actors. Think again of the quintessential modern performance, the protest demonstration. It grew out of—and at first resembled—the religious procession to a place of worship. It turned contentious as demonstrators moved from a place of assembly to a site from which they could confront the targets of their claims. Later, it became the central form of action, mounted routinely to demonstrate a claim before the public. With the diffusion of mass media, that public expanded from neighbors who witnessed a demonstration passing beneath their windows to a wider range of citizens who could watch it on their television sets. By the twentieth century, it had become the major conventional form of contention used by claim makers across the world.

More recently, reaching people through the Internet has become a favored means of mobilization. For example, "hactivism," the practice of hacking into the computer of a transnational firm or a government to disrupt its routines, is becoming more and more common (Samuel 2004). Yet so far the Internet's major role in contentious politics has been either (1) to assemble people in demonstrations at one site or (2) to coordinate demonstrations in many sites across a broad range of territory. A good example of the Internet's first sort of use for mobilization was the 1999 Seattle demonstration against the World Trade Organization. A major example of the second was the coordination of demonstrations across the globe against the American invasion of Iraq in 2003. Neither has done away with the classical set of contentious politics performances.

The petition, the demonstration, and the Internet-based call to action have become *modular performances*, generic forms that can be adapted to a variety of local and social circumstances. The advantage of modular performances is their dual generality and specificity. Seen generically, they have features that adapt to a wide variety of circumstances and have meaning to a wide variety of potential participants and audiences. American students demonstrate on college campuses, French farmers demonstrate outside the prefecture, Israeli settlers demonstrate beside the Wailing Wall, and Chinese democracy protesters demonstrate at Beijing's Tiananmen Square—all are using some variant of the same modular performance. But seen in particular circumstances, demonstrations offer a variety of facets that can be attached to local knowledge. Skillful organizers adapt the generic form to local circumstances, embedding a modular form such as the demonstration in the languages, symbols, and practices that make them compelling in those circumstances. This is but one specific version of the duality of similarities and differences that will show up throughout our book.

Of course, not all contentious performances are as orderly, theatrical, and peaceful as the demonstration. Take the confrontational forms of

contentious politics that exploded in Western Europe and the United States
during the 1960s. The Cold War between the Soviet Union and the United
States had dominated the early 1950s, restricting protest in general and
confrontational protest in particular. But the African American awaken-
ings of the mid-1950s and the 1960s, the student and antiwar movements
of the late 1960s, the women's and gay rights movements of the 1970s,
the peace and environmental movements of the 1980s, the collapse of
communism at the end of that decade, and the rise of right-wing populism
in the 1980s and 1990s expanded all kinds of protest and particularly of
confrontational and violent contention.

Think of how North African youth inhabiting France's suburban ghettoes burned thousands of cars in 2005 to express their rage at their treatment in French society. They used a performance that hearkened back to
the events of May 1968, when thousands of university students rampaged
through Paris and other large cities (Tilly 1986: 346). These two generations of protesters were unconnected to each other, but the performance
of burning cars during social unrest became a standard part of French
traditions when it came to violent contention.

Dieter Rucht has provided us with a running portrait tracing how different forms of contentious politics developed in one archetypical European
country, Germany, over this period. Rucht and his colleagues examined
contention from major newspapers for the years 1950–1988 for West
Germany and for both halves of Germany over the following decade. His
findings show a dramatic increase in the numbers of protests in the 1960s
and smaller, but still substantial, increases over the next three decades.
Protests rose from a low of just over 1,100 in the 1950s to over 4,000 in
the 1990s. Not only that: The mix of conventional, confrontational, and
violent activities changed dramatically between the beginning of the West
German Republic and the end of the century.

Although no linear trend appeared in the proportion of "demonstrative"
protests (about 50 percent at the beginning and at the end of the period),
a net decline occurred in the percentage of routine expressions of claims,
what Rucht calls "procedural protests" and "appeals." In contrast, Rucht's
evidence shows increases in the proportion of "confrontational" protests
in the 1980s and of "violent encounters" in the 1990s. The declines correspond largely to the tactics of the peace movement, while the later
increases in violence reflect the rise of right-wing anti-immigrant groups
and of the absorption of East Germany (Rucht 2005). Figure 1.2 summarizes these data for West Germany through 1988 and for the country as a
whole between 1989 and 1997.

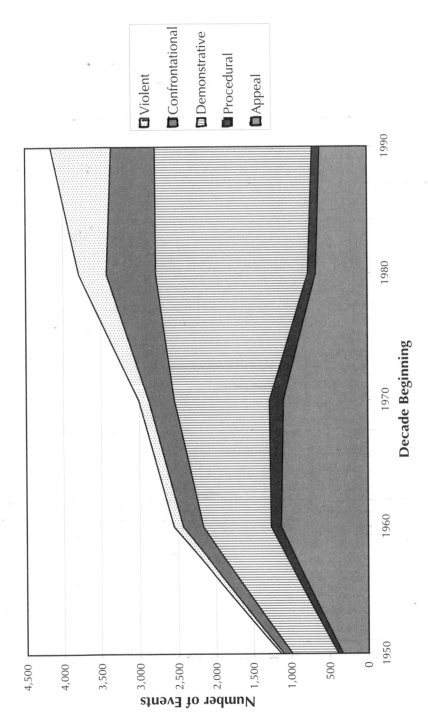

Figure 1.2. Protest Events in Germany, 1950–1997

Notice how Germany's conventional "appeals" rose and fell repeatedly, up to their peak of 44.4 percent of the total in the 1960s to a low of 14.7 percent in the final decade of the century. Violent events, in contrast, remained at modest levels during the "hot" 1960s and 1970s, more than doubled during the 1980s, and exploded to almost one-fifth of the total events in the "skinhead" attacks on immigrants of the 1990s. Different sorts of performances had their own distinctive rhythms in Germany, as they usually do in other places and times (see Kriesi et al. 1995; Tarrow 1989). Later chapters will employ the concepts of contained, demonstrative, confrontational, and violent forms to help us understand contention in Latin America, Italy, the former Soviet Union, and, of course, the United States.

US

Repertoires of Contention

Contentious performances sometimes clump into *repertoires* of claim-making routines that apply to the same claimant-object pairs: bosses and workers, peasants and landlords, rival nationalist factions, and many more. These days, for example, strikes, slowdowns, lockouts, contract negotiations, grievance hearings, and third-party mediation all belong to the claim-making repertoires that connect bosses and workers. The theatrical metaphor calls attention to the clustered, learned, yet improvisational character of people's interactions as they make and receive each other's claims. Claim making usually resembles jazz and street theater rather than ritual reading of scripture. Like a jazz trio or an improvisatory theater group, people who participate in contentious politics normally have several pieces they can play, but not an infinite number (Sawyer 2001). Like familiar jazz tunes, the pieces evoke and express specific emotions, recall memories of previous encounters, and thus establish continuity between political actors' pasts and presents.

Repertoires vary from place to place, time to time, and pair to pair. But on the whole, when people make collective claims, they innovate within limits set by the repertoire already established for their place, time, and pair. Clarkson and his colleagues used the petition, the newspaper campaign, the pamphlet war, and the solicitation of elite support. Most of these forms of claim making had already occurred separately in different eighteenth-century conflicts. The major innovation was to bring them together in an integrated social movement campaign. Similarly, social movement activists in today's European cities adopt some mixture of public meetings, press statements, demonstrations, and petitions, but they stay away from suicide bombing, hostage taking, and self-immolation. Their repertoire draws on a long history of previous struggles (Tilly 2004b).

Exactly how people draw on contentious repertoires varies greatly. We can see the influence of *weak repertoires* when formerly authoritarian regimes give way to semidemocratic or pluralistic regimes. This occurred in the former Soviet Union as its citizens emerged from seventy years of state socialism. There, the tradition of "samizdat" (self-published clandestine writing) and of everyday resistance (Scott 1985) that had grown up in the USSR's repressive conditions had little use in the new conditions of post-Soviet semidemocracy. Remembering the high costs of dissent under the previous regime, most citizens were resistant to mobilization, suspicious of leaders, and reluctant to join political parties in large numbers. Even after a decade of relatively open political life, the routines of organizing sustained collective action remained unfamiliar to most Russians (Fish 1995; Mendelson and Gerber 2005).

At the other extreme from weak repertoires, *ritual political performances* sometimes occur (Kertzer 1998; Muir 1997). Think of May Day, the international day of workers' rights. It began in July 1889, the centenary of the French Revolution, when a congress of trade unionists met in Paris to propose that "a great international demonstration should be convoked, on the same day all over the world, to put governments on notice to reduce the workday to eight hours" (Tartakowsky 2005: 14). Over the next few decades, this contentious claim settled down into a regular and ritualized demonstration of popular power, spread across the globe (except to the United States), and brought millions of workers onto the street and into the parks and squares for what became a ritualized festival of labor.

But when people intervene in such events to make collective claims, they bend them back from ritual toward *strong repertoires*. In Europe, some workers used May 1 to go on strike or to place insurgent demands on the agenda. Similarly, in the United States, student protesters sometimes interrupt the ritual of a college commencement, turning it temporarily into a demonstration. So doing, they generally adapt chants, signs, symbols, and actions that are familiar from other settings. Over the times and places this book examines, strong repertoires have usually prevailed. This is not to say that strong repertoires never change, but only that changes normally occur through innovation at the margins.[7] Nevertheless, some periods of history overflow with new performances and new variants of old ones. Let us review what happened to the United States' repertoire of contention in the half-century between 1955 and 2005.

Repertoire Change in the United States, 1955–2005

The post–World War II years did not begin with the promise of major change in the American repertoire of contention. The Cold War, domestic anticommunism, and satisfactions of the consumer society turned people's attention away from political contention. When innovations in the repertoire of contention emerged, they arrived from a new and unexpected quarter, the black middle class. African Americans did not enter contentious politics all at once or use any single form of collective action. But the civil rights movement that began quietly in the mid-1950s led to a fundamental change in the American repertoire of contention.

Partially released from the grip of southern Jim Crow repression by urbanization, migration to the North, and entry into the middle class, many educated African Americans were growing restive under the effective segregation of American life. The federal government gave them an assist. Concerned about the contradiction between fighting for freedom abroad and abetting discrimination at home, from the late 1940s on, the government took halting steps to combat segregation. African Americans also drew encouragement from the most institutionalized form of contention that Americans possess: bringing lawsuits. *Brown v. Board of Education* and other landmark cases ultimately brought mixed results. But they encouraged black parents to register their children in formerly white public schools and black college students to fight to register in once-white universities. Conventional legal battles offered incentives for the more confrontational contentious politics to come.

Three major developments marked a shift in performances that would culminate in the major cycle of protest of the early 1960s. First was the practice of "marching on Washington" in major set-piece demonstrations culminating in rallies before the Lincoln Memorial. Second came the practice of dedicating a period of time—usually the summer—to a particular campaign. The third spread the disruptive practice of sit-ins, blockages, and building occupations: first at lunch counters, then at bus stations, and finally wherever public segregation was practiced.

The sixties' marches on Washington descended from forms of contention already familiar in the American past. Among other precedents, they stemmed from the veterans' march of the 1930s and from the civil rights march that A. Philip Randolph threatened to organize in 1941, just as the United States was mobilizing for its part in World War II. Mississippi's "Freedom Summer" was the most notable example of the choice of a finite period of time to concentrate the energies of militants on a particular goal—in that event, to register African Americans to vote (McAdam 1988). Other campaigns such as Vietnam Summer and Labor Summer followed.

The third innovation—the sit-in—had a family resemblance to the factory occupations of the 1930s (Piven and Cloward 1977), but it gained power from the presence of a new actor in public life: television. If the public saw spitting thugs brutalizing well-dressed young black men sitting calmly at lunch counters or police hosing peaceful demonstrators, it would be hard to ignore the contradiction between the American claim of freedom and the reality of segregation. "The whole world is watching," wrote Todd Gitlin (1980). (Chapter 9 examines one important episode based on the sit-in.)

The powerful set-piece march and disruptive sit-in attracted plenty of support and media attention. Both forms of claim making spread from civil rights to the campus revolts and anti–Vietnam War protests of the later 1960s. The variations themselves were interesting. African Americans mainly occupied only sites in which public services were unequally enjoyed by whites and blacks. College student activists sat in at their administration buildings. But antiwar protesters sat in wherever they could disrupt routines and gain media attention. The Civil Rights March on Washington stayed contained and ended predictably at the Lincoln Memorial. But antiwar protesters marched across the Potomac to the Pentagon, which they surrounded in a mock levitation, while African Americans sat in on the Triborough Bridge in New York City to block the opening of the 1964 World's Fair.

Over the next two decades, America's protest marches became more contained, but they grew in magnitude and in their "made for television" character. Eventually organizers even provided mobile TV monitors for demonstrators who were too numerous or too far away to see the speakers. Organizers set up port-a-potties for the crowds, and the National Park Police offered organizers seminars in how to run an orderly demonstration (McCarthy, McPhail, and Smith 1996). With the routinization of the March on Washington, what had begun as a disruptive performance became conventional while retaining the trappings of contention: banners, chants, serried ranks moving forward in the face of power.

Sit-ins also diffused widely across American society. From their origins in the civil rights movement, they spread to groups of all kinds who occupied public space on behalf of causes they favored. From students occupying administration buildings in the 1960s, it was a short step to the antinuclear road blockades of the 1970s and the "shantytown" protests of the 1980s (see chapter 2). From there to the "prolife sidewalk vigils" of the 1980s and 1990s, the ideological move was greater, but the logic remained the same: occupying public space so as to disrupt routines and gain media attention.

Two other trends emerged more prominently in the 1980s and 1990s. On the one hand, many social movement organizations transformed themselves into public interest groups and shifted their main forms of mobilization from the streets and campuses to direct mailings, educational campaigns, and "checkbook activism." At the same time, religious groups involved themselves increasingly in contentious politics. These trends came together—or, rather, they clashed—in the growing, rancorous, and apparently endless struggle over abortion. It pitted "choice" advocates largely organized by public interest groups and using direct mail appeals against Catholic and evangelical Protestant congregations employing more effective door-to-door proselytizing on behalf of "life" (Ginsburg 1989; McCarthy 1987). Both trends coincided in the 2004 election, when the enormous outpouring of small contributions to the Democratic Party campaign failed to match the capacity of the Republican Party to mobilize supporters among the religious faithful for George W. Bush's presidential campaign.

As the United States entered the new century, it was clear that a new instrument—the Internet—might be transforming the nature of contentious politics. The 2004 moveon.com campaign on behalf of Governor Howard Dean demonstrated that through skilled use of electronic media, it was now possible to mobilize thousands of people on behalf of a common cause—if only for brief periods of time. This meant that the elaborate mobilizing structures that previous campaigns had mounted to organize major demonstrations might one day become obsolete (Bennett 2005). The Internet also brought once-parochial American activists into greater contact with counterparts abroad—for example, in the simultaneous protests against the launching of the Iraq War.

Violence frequently occurred as a by-product of both conventional and confrontational contention. As the mainstream of the civil rights movement moved into institutional politics and the New Left faded, minorities of militants, outraged at what they saw as the "sellout" of their values by their more moderate comrades, formed military or underground groups such as the Black Panthers and the (mostly white) Weather Underground. Far smaller than the more moderate groups they sought to supplant, these groups used violent performances to catch the attention of the media and add an air of terror to contentious politics. (Most Americans, even today, think of the 1960s as a period of "riots.") Their desperate efforts backfired, because their violent methods gave political elites a justification to meet contention with state violence. Even more violent—and therefore justifying greater repression—were the Islamist movements of the 1990s. The culmination of both trends arrived with the attacks on the World Trade Center and the Pentagon on September 11, 2001, and the Patriot Act, which curtailed Americans' civil liberties on the altar of freedom.

VIOLENCE or REPRESSION

Sources of Repertoire Change

This takes us to the factors that bring about changes in repertoires. We can distinguish two major kinds of processes in repertoire change: the effects of periods of rapid political change and the outcome of incrementally changing structural factors. The first are more dramatic, sometimes produce lasting change, but are more easily routinized and repressed as authorities regain control of contention. Incremental changes are less dramatic, depend on factors that evolve more slowly, but can be more enduring.

With respect to periods of rapid political change, during major cycles of contention, the ordinary preference for familiar claim-making routines dissolves in spurts of innovation. American civil rights activists did not simply use the decorous old social movement forms but deliberately disrupted existing routines. Periods of rapid political change produce sequences of innovation in repertoires, and successive innovations largely account for the ebb and flow of movement activity (Kriesi et al. 1995; McAdam 1983).

During such times of rapid political change, we find both recurrent innovation and frequent misapprehension among parties to contention. As each new round of claim making begins to threaten the interests of (or provide new opportunities for) political actors who had previously remained inactive, a spiral of contention ensues. Social movements engender countermovements. Challengers' allies appear and retreat. The state, at first thrown off balance by new forms of contention, eventually reacts and in some cases turns to repression. We will turn to such "cycles of contention" in chapter 5. The extreme case arrives in a revolutionary situation: a deep split in control of coercive means. During a revolutionary situation, every actor's interest is at risk, and many actors therefore mobilize for action. We saw exactly that shift in the Ukrainian Orange Revolution. When we turn to lethal conflict in chapter 7, we will see it again.

A recent major change is globalization, the increasing economic integration of the planet. We do not predict that globalization will either erase national differences in contentious politics or absorb domestic contention into "global social movements." As we will argue, the major constraints and incentives for contentious politics are *political opportunity structures*, and most of these are local and national. But we think it is important to look beyond the nation-state at processes such as the shift of some kinds of contention to international institutions, the framing of local issues as the results of global problems, and the formation of transnational networks and movement coalitions. In chapter 8, we turn from the local and national patterns of contention that occupy most of our book to transnational diffusion and mobilization.

In contrast to the effects of periods of rapid change, incremental changes in repertoires are less dramatic, but more decisive in the long run. The major causes of incremental change sort into three main categories:

- *Connections between claim making and everyday social organization.* For example, mothers bereft of bread for their children gather around the granary whose owner they suspect of hoarding flour. Land-poor peasants who believe that the landlord stole their land sometimes occupy it. And workers, whose one effective tool is the fact that their labor is necessary to make the wheels of production turn, strike to prevent employers from the successful pursuit of profit.
- *Cumulative creation of a signaling system by contention itself.* For example, over the past two centuries, French claim makers have drawn on a dense experience with contention. Three major revolutions, a revolutionary commune, more than a hundred years of strikes, barricades, marches, and demonstrations all lie under the surface of French contention today, to be drawn on, innovated upon, and replayed in endless permutations (Tartakowsky 1997, 2005; Tilly 1986).
- *Operation of the regime as such.* Regimes sort performances into prescribed, tolerated, and forbidden categories, dispensing threats and penalties to claimants who move onto forbidden ground. When Clarkson and his colleagues perfected the petition into a tool of mass mobilization, they did so in the context of a parliamentary regime that had recognized petitions as legitimate forms of collective action for centuries. But when French radicalism and Napoleonic arms were threatening Britain, reformers paid the penalty with imprisonment and worse. Chapter 3 deals in detail with the relations between regimes and forms of contention.

Repertoires draw on the identities, social ties, and organizational forms that constitute everyday social life. From those identities, social ties, and organizational forms emerge both the collective claims that people make and the means they have for making claims. In the course of contending or watching others contend, people learn the interactions that can make a political difference as well as the locally shared meanings of those interactions. The changing interaction of everyday social organization, cumulative experience with contention, and regime intervention produces incremental alterations in contentious performances. At any given moment, however, that interaction promotes clustering of claim making in a limited number of recognizable performances, a repertoire.

What's Coming

This chapter's comparison of British antislavery with Ukrainian opposition to a corrupt government sent us on a fresh path across bumpy terrain. We have seen how contention, collective action, and politics overlap in *contentious politics*: interactive, collective making of claims that bear on other people's interests and involve governments as claimants, objects of claims, or third parties. Social movements qualify as a form of contentious politics, but so do revolutions, civil wars, and a wide variety of other struggles this book takes up. In all these forms of contention, distinctive claim-making performances and repertoires vary from setting to setting and regime to regime. Some of those performances are modular; as with the street demonstration, they transfer easily from setting to setting and regime to regime. They build on social bases belonging to the setting or regime.

America's changing contentious politics since 1955, for example, often involved some widely recognizable performances such as street demonstrations. But participants, claims, objects of claims, and forms all grew from particular features of the changing American regime. To explain change and variation in repertoires, we must look at the current pace of political change in the regime at hand, identify incremental changes in the regime's social structure, then figure out how the two affect everyday social organization, people's cumulative experience with contention, and current operation of the regime. With those elements in place, we begin the adventure of explaining change and variation in the forms, participants, issues, objects, and outcomes of contentious politics.

What's next? First, a warning about what this book *does not* do. Despite illustrating its points amply from revolutions, social movements, military coups, civil wars, and other forms of contentious politics, it does not catalog these forms one by one and provide a separate set of generalizations concerning each of them. On the contrary, our aim is to identify parallels in the ways that apparently disparate forms of contention work, and show how their differences result from varying combinations and sequences of mechanisms in contrasting regime environments. Even the later chapters on social movements and large-scale lethal conflict serve mainly to show that similar causes and effects operate in these very different political processes.

The next chapter describes how we propose to study contention and contains a number of hints for students who want to carry out their own analyses. Chapter 3 ("Regimes, Repertoires, and Opportunities") connects contention to different types of regimes and the opportunities and threats they proffer, and relates regimes, opportunities, and threats to democratization and dedemocratization. Chapter 4 ("Contentious Interaction") examines how political actors form, change, make claims, and interact with each other. We then move on to political actors' mobilization and demobilization (chapter 5) before applying the analysis to social movements (chapter 6) and lethal conflicts (chapter 7).

Chapter 8 ("Contention in Composite Regimes") returns to the interaction between regimes and contention, focusing first on contention in the composite state of Israel/Palestine. We turn from there to transnational contention, using the transnational legal pursuit of former Chilean dictator Augusto Pinochet as our major example. Chapter 9 ("Contention Today and Tomorrow") returns to the American civil rights movement; it then recapitulates the book's main lessons and shows how our strategy helps to unearth similarities and differences in forms of contention. For convenient reference, the two appendices inventory the concepts, mechanisms, processes, cases, and methods the book employs.

COMPARISON. RISK OF BEING
SIMPLISTIC?
YET FOCUSING IN ONLY ON
SPECIFICS, OR ZOOMING
OUT, BOTH ISOLATE AND
THINGIFY WHAT ARE
(ESSENTIAL(Y) ATMOSPHERE

2

Shantytown protest against apartheid in South Africa on an American college campus. ("Shantytown II [Arts Quad]" © David Lyons)

WHAT?

CHAPTER TWO

HOW TO ANALYZE CONTENTION

Contentious politics involves many different forms and combinations of collective action. It reveals complicated social processes. Vigilante violence, military coups, worker rebellions, and social movements involve very different sorts of contention, but all of them unfold through intricate interactions. Explaining any complicated social process (contentious or not) involves three steps: (1) description of the process, (2) decomposition of the process into its basic causes, and (3) reassembly of those causes into a more general account of how the process takes place. *OH GOD*

Good description, however, never starts from zero. Because contentious politics is complicated, any observer who wants to explain contention needs a reliable guide to description. A reliable guide identifies features to look for, features that clearly belong to what we must explain. The concepts laid out in chapter 1—political actors, political identities, contentious performances, and repertoires—make up our elementary guide to description of the processes we mean to explain. For explanation, we need additional concepts. This chapter supplies four of them: the *events* and *episodes* of streams of contention and the *mechanisms* and *processes* that constitute them. We will define and illustrate all of them as the chapter proceeds.

Using many different examples, we locate contention in its varied sites and sketch conditions at those sites. We single out streams of contention and tag some apparent outcomes of that contention for explanation. We describe contentious processes by means of episodes and decompose those episodes into their causal mechanisms before reassembling the mechanisms into more general accounts of the processes involved. Mechanisms and processes sometimes operate within individuals. But the central mechanisms of contentious politics are interactive. We can see them in the interactions between peasant resistance and state violence in Guatemala before and during its vicious civil war.

Mass Contention and State Violence in Guatemala

"Among the most dreadful aspects of the years of mass contention and state violence in Central America," writes Charles Brockett (2005), "were the many massacres of unarmed civilians." This was especially true in Guatemala, where a major massacre of civilians "took place on May 29, 1978 in the indigenous town of Panzós ... when fifty-three unarmed Q'eqchí Maya were shot down and another forty-seven were injured" (3–4). The Panzós massacre shocked Guatemalan and international public opinion. But it was not an isolated incident. It can help us to analyze the many forms of contentious politics we will encounter in our book.

Brockett first enumerates a series of events that both led to and accompanied the massacre in Panzós. From a string of demonstrations by peasants claiming land in the area starting in 1970, to petitions read on the floor of the national congress, to meetings denouncing the local mayor for complicity with landowners, to peasant resistance against threatened evictions from their lands, he shows how residents of the Panzós valley joined in a wide array of contentious performances (2005: 4–5). Similar demonstrations and denunciations were multiplying in neighboring municipalities at the same time. State actors responded with escalating violence. Altogether, these events were raising the scale of contention as they brought national labor organizations, peasant leagues, and political parties into an ever-widening "cycle of protest" against the state and the landlord class it supported.

How can we best characterize a narrative like the one we have just sketched from Brockett's work? We could be satisfied by retelling the story step-by-step, as a good narrative historian would do. We could reduce it to the motivations of the actors and their calculations of gain or loss, as analytically sharp rational-choice analysts would do. Or we could point to the habitual desire for ownership of the land, as sensitive culturally oriented scholars would do. As useful as these approaches can be in describing peasant resistance, all of them miss the *dynamics of contention.* We can capture dynamics by looking for the mechanisms and processes that drive contention.

Mechanisms and Processes

This book searches for and illustrates the mechanisms and processes through which contentious politics operates. By *mechanisms,* we mean a delimited class of events that alter relations among specified sets of elements in identical or closely similar ways over a variety of situations. Mechanisms compound into processes. By *processes,* we mean regular combinations and sequences of mechanisms that produce similar (generally more complex and contingent) transformations of those elements. Distinct processes involve different sequences and combinations of mechanisms that interactively produce some outcome. Some mechanisms and processes recur frequently in our book; others appear only rarely. This section outlines the logic of the mechanism-process approach, lays out some of the key mechanisms and processes that appear in a wide variety of contentious politics, and illustrates them through cases, both domestic and international.

Many social scientists model their approaches on simple versions of physics or engineering. They ask how output variables such as levels of violence covary with input variables such as ethnic fragmentation, without saying much about the causal chains in between the inputs and the outputs. Mechanism-process explanations come closer in spirit and reasoning to biology. There mechanisms concatenate into small-scale processes such as reproduction or long-term ones such as evolution. Although these processes' outcomes lend themselves to measurement, the processes themselves are often empirically invisible as such; you don't see evolution happening. Biologists can make headway in identifying crucial processes by correlating outputs with inputs. But for detailed explanations, they soon turn to examination of these processes' constituent mechanisms.

Let's take the process of reproduction of a species as an analogy. Species reproduction is a collective process that depends on a number of interactive mechanisms that occur between individuals—mechanisms like courtship, sexual encounter, pregnancy, birth, and, in some species, the nurturing of infants. Biologists cannot directly observe species reproduction, but they can study its mechanisms. First, they can break reproduction into its component mechanisms to better understand its dynamics. Second, they can compare that process in one species to its equivalent in others to see whether or not the same mechanisms are present in all. Third, they can examine which mechanisms co-occur so frequently as to constitute a robust process.

In examining the dynamics of contention, we can follow the same mechanism-process procedures as biologists do:

- We can disaggregate a familiar process, such as mobilization, into its component mechanisms, in order to understand what makes it work.
- We can compare how such a process works in different settings to understand what difference the presence or absence of a particular mechanism makes.
- We can examine whether particular mechanisms coincide so frequently with similar outcomes as to constitute a robust process.
- Larger processes such as democratization or nationalist mobilization can also be examined through a mechanism-process approach (Tilly 2004a).

In contentious politics, similar reasoning applies to performances and repertoires. People transmit performances such as the demonstration in pretty much the same shape from one contentious episode to the next. Nevertheless, minor innovations in performances occur all the time, much as minor variations in morphology lead to changes in biological adaptation. As in some evolutionary changes, some innovations lead to dead ends, either because they fail to inspire people or because they are too easily repressed (Margadant 1979: 267). Other innovations stick either because they produce unexpected successes, because prestigious leaders adopt them, or because brokers forward their transfer from one setting to another.

The strike, for example, began as sailors in the port of London "struck" their sails to protest poor wages (Linebaugh and Rediker 1990). As the tactic of withdrawing labor spread along with mass production, the initial forms shifted, new elements were added (e.g., the "turnout" of entire communities in support of strikers), and some aspects of the strike were lost as others were retained and elaborated. Performances and repertoires change through nongenetic evolutionary processes in which mechanisms of selection, transmission, and retention play crucial parts.

Our narratives will repeatedly reveal mechanisms that combine in different settings and situations of contentious politics. Three of the most common are brokerage, diffusion, and coordinated action:

- *Brokerage:* production of a new connection between previously unconnected sites
- *Diffusion:* spread of a form of contention, an issue, or a way of framing it from one site to another
- *Coordinated action:* two or more actors' engagement in mutual signaling and parallel making of claims on the same object

In contentious politics, no complex outcome ever results from the operation of a single causal mechanism. Brokerage, the production of a new connection between previously unconnected sites, causes important changes in contention. But production of a new connection makes a difference to contentious politics through its activation of further mechanisms such as diffusion. Through the new connection, ideas, practices, and resources flow that affect claim making at both the origin and the destination. Often the new ideas, practices, and resources facilitate coordination between the sites. From the late 1990s onward, for example, brokers in the form of individual activists and mediating organizations played large parts in the coordination of international days of action targeting the World Trade Organization and other global financial institutions. But diffusion of ideas, practices, and resources from one site of action to another made that coordination possible.

To brokerage and diffusion, suppose we add our third mechanism, coordinated action. In that mechanism, two or more actors signal their intentions to each other and engage in parallel making of claims on the same object. Imagine two neighborhood associations simultaneously erecting signs opposing the construction of a freeway between their neighborhoods. A leader from Neighborhood A talks with leaders of Neighborhood B, persuading them to erect hostile signs on the same day and supplying appropriately hostile language for the signs.

Mechanisms combine into processes. When we add coordination to brokerage and diffusion, we get coordinated action and have one version of a process we can call *new coordination* (see figure 2.1).

Coordinated action produces further effects, perhaps including creation of new alliances across neighborhood boundaries, attempts by city authorities to tear down the offending signs, and even second thoughts on the part of city council members from the affected neighborhoods. Sometimes it leads to coordination at a higher level as, for example, when different neighborhood groups combine to lobby the state legislature or march on Washington. We call this process *upward scale shift*. Chapter 5 examines it in detail.

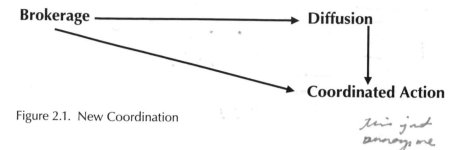

Figure 2.1. New Coordination

this just annoys me

Sites of New Coordination

We recognize the elementary process of new coordination in a wide variety of sites, including the England of 1785 and the Ukraine of 2005. Yet we have other ways to use this mechanism-process analysis of new coordination. Sometimes we will want to work new coordination into our explanation for a particular stream of contention—for example, the search for allies within the elite on the part of the antislavery campaign in England. In that case, we will also have to take initial conditions into account, including such elements as the institution of the petition and the growing role of a free press as a mechanism of communication.

Sometimes, in contrast, we will want to focus on new coordination itself, asking whether it works pretty much the same across a wide variety of sites, and whether it produces dramatically different outcomes depending on the site in which it occurs.

Finally, we might compare different types of regimes (e.g., high-capacity undemocratic and high-capacity democratic) to determine whether new coordination occurs more frequently in one or the other, and if so, why. Mechanism-process explanations serve more than one purpose. We can illustrate the many ways in which new coordination can work from the spread of antielection fraud protests in Europe's formerly socialist countries.

Brokerage and diffusion combined over broad spaces to produce new coordination in the spread of antielection fraud campaigns in former state socialist regimes in Eastern Europe. When dictator Slobodan Milošević tried to steal local elections in Serbia in 1996, opposition was widespread but remained largely uncoordinated. Between that year and 2000, when Milošević tried to steal a national election, the opposition was ready. Inspired by a national student-led movement, Otpor, militants used a variety of performances to oppose the regime. Otpor developed a sophisticated strategy of targeting Milošević using comic and theatrical tactics instead of mass demonstrations that police could target. For nearly two months, demonstrators marched, sang, blew whistles, listened to speeches, alternately heckled and fraternized with the police, and went to court to keep the pressure on Milošević. Otpor, the broker, diffused these tactics across the country to bring down a dictator.

Between 2000 and 2004, the Otpor model diffused from Serbia to Georgia. In November 2003, President Eduard Shevardnadze rigged a parliamentary election to provide a sure victory for the parties that supported him. Shevardnadze was no Milošević. But like the dictator in Serbia, his attempt to foil the electoral process brought down the government. Three weeks of peaceful street protests culminated in a "March of the Angry Voters," led by Mikhail Saakashvili, leader of the opposition coalition and the country's president after Shevardnadze had to step down. For months, activists led by the student group Kmara engaged in graffiti, leaflet, and poster campaigns against corruption and police brutality, and for university reform and media freedom. This was no spontaneous demonstration; it was a coordinated plan for tens of thousands of citizens to converge by buses, cars, and trucks on the capital, Tbilisi.

Where had the opposition learned such tactics? In the months before the election, Saakashvili had traveled to Serbia to contact the former organizers of the anti-Milošević movement. He returned with a plan for nonviolent action modeled closely on the success of Otpor. Ex-Otpor activists traveled to Georgia, where they led training sessions for Georgian reformers. The Georgians, in turn, trained a cadre of grassroots activists. Brokerage combined with diffusion through electronic communication.

An important tool in the Georgian campaign was the American-made documentary on the fall of Milošević, *Bringing Down a Dictator*, which was supported by the Washington-based International Center for Nonviolent Conflict. "Most important was the film," said Ivane Merabishvili, general secretary of the National Movement Party that led the revolt. "All the demonstrators knew the tactics of the revolution in Belgrade by heart because they showed ... the film on their revolution. Everyone knew what to do. This was a copy of that revolution, only louder" (*Washington Post*, November 25, 2003, A22). In Georgia, as in the spread of most new movements, diffusion through the media and brokerage through intermediate agents combined to produce new coordination (Tarrow and McAdam 2005). The spread of antielection fraud campaigns to Ukraine examined in chapter 1 followed a similar path of diffusion and brokerage.

Other Mechanisms

If contentious politics consisted only of diffusion, brokerage, and coordinated action, we would see a great deal of contention but very little continuity. In fact, many episodes of contention do trickle away or suddenly stop because they find little sustenance in society or because little remains to sustain them after their initial claims are made. Think of the American urban riots of the 1960s: They caused tremendous damage and triggered state policies to prevent their recurrence, but they left little behind after the rioters had dispersed.

In many of our episodes, however, additional mechanisms and processes will appear:

- *Social appropriation*: nonpolitical groups transform into political actors by using their organizational and institutional bases to launch movement campaigns. For example, in the 1950s and 1960s, the previously conservative black churches became sites of social appropriation for southern civil rights groups (McAdam 1999; Morris 1984).
- *Boundary activation*: creation of a new boundary or the crystallization of an existing one between challenging groups and their targets. For example, by defining citizens as members of a particular racial or ethnic group, the census acts as an agent of boundary activation (Williams 2006).
- *Certification*: an external authority's signal of its readiness to recognize and support the existence and claims of a political actor. For example, when the state of Israel was proclaimed in 1948, both superpowers, the United States and the USSR, lent it certification by voting to recognize its creation in the United Nations.
- *Identity shift*: formation of new identities within challenging groups whose coordinated action brings them together and reveals their commonalities. For example, in 1956, Martin Luther King Jr. framed the Montgomery bus boycott as the source of an identity shift to what he called "the new Negro" (McAdam, Tarrow, and Tilly 2001: 319).

These four mechanisms all figured in the struggle over slavery of nineteenth-century America. Here, too, as in Clarkson's England, social appropriation of religious and educational institutions occurred in the abolitionist cause. We also see boundary activation when Congress passed an act in 1820 determining that entire territories would be designated "slave" or "free" as they entered the Union (Weingast 1998). While the Supreme Court certified slavery as legal by approving the Fugitive Slave Act, a new coalition of northern and midwestern voters decertified slavery by electing Abraham Lincoln as U.S. president.

Identity shift made a difference through the entire buildup to the civil war. Southerners had long clung to an ideology that glorified a way of life based on ease and gentility (Genovese 1969). As the northern economy expanded, northerners developed an identity based on the virtues of hard work and free labor, and they complained that southern whites' gentility was founded on the exploitation of slaves. In response, southern apologists began to frame northerners as crude and materialistic. For both North and South, identity shift served as the cultural and psychological counterpart of the widening distance between the two regions.

Together with diffusion, brokerage, and new coordinated action, these mechanisms transformed what had been a relatively isolated and mainly peaceful social movement—abolitionism—into the most lethal form of conflict in American history, the Civil War. *peace?*

How did that transformation occur? Traditional historical accounts focus on the injustices of slavery, on the dedication of the abolitionists, and on the evils of the slaveholders. Revisionist accounts emphasize the structural bases of slavery in the cotton economy, the expanding dynamism of the northern economy, and the economic motivation of "free soil" farmers to keep slave-based competition out of the West. Institutionalists add the breakdown of the balance rule in Congress by which, since 1820, the addition of any new slave state required the addition of a free state to the union (Weingast 1998). When that rule lapsed, the balance broke. We do not contest the merits of traditionalist, revisionist, or institutionalist accounts for the coming of the Civil War. Our goal, rather, would be to focus on the dynamics of contentious politics and on how specific mechanisms such as diffusion, brokerage, coordination, social appropriation, boundary formation, identity shift, and certification come together in political processes.

Two major processes recur in our analyses: mobilization and demobilization. By *mobilization*, we mean how people who at a given point in time are not making contentious claims start to do so; by *demobilization*, we ask how people who are making claims stop doing so. The process of mobilization increases the resources available for collective claim making, while the process of demobilization decreases those resources. Our use of the mechanism-process approach will help us in three ways:

- By taking apart mobilization into its constituent mechanisms, we can see how the process is triggered and how central a particular mechanism is to its fruition.
- By comparing different types of contention—such as social movements and civil wars—we can pinpoint which mechanisms are key to the transition from one to the other.
- By examining the co-occurrence of specific mechanisms, we can see under which circumstances they cumulate into larger and perhaps less understood processes.

Episodes of contention will become our main units of analysis; the events that constitute them are our main units of observation.

Episodes and Events

Episodes we define as bounded sequences of continuous interaction, usually produced by an investigator's chopping up longer streams of contention into segments for purposes of systematic observation, comparison, and explanation. These range from relatively simple episodes such as the occupation of a church by a group of prostitutes in Lyons, France (examined in chapter 6), all the way to major cycles of contention, revolutions, and civil wars.

How can we capture the complexity and permutations in such large episodes of contention as the American Civil War? We can learn a lot from what activists say or later write about their activities. But memory tends to be selective. No single activist, however well placed, joins all the activities in an episode of contention. We will learn more by examining what activists *do* during major episodes of contention. This can be done through a variety of methods, some of them sophisticated but most easily available through newspaper records, archives, and online press releases.

Easiest to access—because officials collect them—are records of workers' strikes. Working with such sources, Edward Shorter and Charles Tilly (1974) examined the shape, the size, and the length of strikes in France from 1830 to 1968. At about the same time, scholars such as Seymour Spilerman (1970) and Charles Perrow (1979) and his research team conducted systematic studies of urban riots and protests that had occurred during the 1960s. Their approaches to episodes of contention provided models for the next generation of students. In the 1980s, for example, Doug McAdam (1999) and Craig Jenkins (1986) examined, respectively, the American civil rights and farmworkers' movements. Similarly, Dieter

Rucht (2005) carried out the systematic analysis of German protest events that chapter 1 reviewed. In Italy, Sidney Tarrow (1989) and his team read newspapers systematically for the period 1966–1973. In the early 1990s, Susan Olzak (1992) developed a sophisticated model of ethnic conflict. All of these researchers looked for any episode that qualified as a "conflict event" according to a standard set of definitions.

Also readily available—because officials worry most about this form of collective action—are sources of data on violence. Especially in the wake of 9/11, a whole industry involving studies of organized violence and terrorism has developed (Berman and Laitin 2005; Sageman 2004). Although considerable slippage entered the definition of *terrorism* as a variety of scholars and journalists got into the act, its expansion stimulated a broadening from studies of the statistical incidence of violence and its correlation with other variables to its links to nonviolent contention, its rituals, and its forms of performance (Alexander 2004; Collins 2004; Sambanis and Zinn 2003).

Studies of "waves," "cycles," and particular streams of contention combine attention to strikes, protest demonstrations, sit-ins, organized violence, and even institutional forms of participation, such as referenda. In their study of social movements in France, Germany, the Netherlands, and Switzerland, Hanspeter Kriesi and his collaborators (1995) used a major newspaper in each country to examine the number of contentious events, the magnitude of participation in them, the type of performance involved—demonstrative, confrontational, or violent—the types of organizations that mounted them and their allies, and the dynamics of the episodes. For the fifteen-year period they studied, they complemented their sweeping comparisons by issue-specific analyses of nuclear energy, gay activism, cross-national diffusion, and the outcomes of the movements they studied. In Kriesi and his collaborators' investigation, the division of streams of contention into episodes did three different kinds of analytical work, all of them crucial:

- It drew from a bewildering, tangled series of events a narrower, more manageable set of public interactions that reasonably represented the overall direction of the complicated whole. They could then compare each national profile of contention to the differences in institutional structure and the dominant political strategies of the actors to produce tentative explanations of why some kinds of contention were more prominent in some countries than in others.
- It facilitated comparison of trends and fluctuations in different kinds of contention. In their findings, "demonstrative" events were far and

away the most frequent in all four countries, but marked differences appeared in the incidence of "confrontational" and violent events.

- By distinguishing "new" from "old" actors—mainly the working class—Kriesi and his collaborators could speculate about the directions and dynamics of change.

Suppose you want to do your own study of contentious politics. You need not read newspapers in four different languages, as Kriesi and his collaborators did, to imitate their discipline. Any source that regularly records contentious politics in a relatively uniform way lends itself to the construction of a catalog you can analyze systematically. The next section illustrates two ways of using such event catalogs at opposite ends of the scale of systemic change. First, with Sarah Soule we examine the dynamics and the impact of a single local performance—the building of "shantytowns" on American campuses in the 1980s. Second, based on Mark Beissinger's research, we examine the dynamic of contention that produced the collapse of the Soviet Union.

Building Shanties against Apartheid

In early 1985, news reports described government-ordered beatings and shootings of peaceful South African protesters against that country's repressive system of apartheid, or racial segregation. More than five thousand killings had already occurred in South Africa as the result of political violence. By the end of the apartheid regime in the mid-1990s, there would be thousands more. For her Ph.D. research at Cornell University, Sarah Soule (1995) examined the rise and fall of the protest wave of American college students against their universities' investments in South Africa. Soule's interest in the protests she studied arose from observation of protests on her own campus. She went on to compare Cornell with protests in favor of divestment on many other campuses. She carried out both qualitative and quantitative analyses of the events, their dynamics, and their outcomes of this form of protest (Soule 1997).

The shantytown performance—but not the name "shantytown"—first emerged in an early protest at Columbia University during April 1985. At Columbia, students blockaded Hamilton Hall, the site of the first historic anti–Vietnam War sit-in in 1967. To establish a presence there, they dragged armchairs and sofas from a nearby dormitory. When night fell, they rigged up tarps and brought in blankets. When Reverend Jesse Jackson came to speak, participation in their protest grew to over five thousand. Jackson's presence, the large number of African American demonstrators on campus, and the fact that Columbia had helped to start the 1967–68 protest wave gained national media attention and helped to trigger a diffusion in favor of college divestment in South Africa (Hirsch 1990; Soule 1997: 857).

Columbia's constructions of tarps, blankets, and furniture soon spread with a variety of labels to campuses around the country. At Princeton and Santa Cruz, participants called it a "camp-out"; at Harvard, a "sleep-in"; at Iowa, the students renamed the administration building "Biko Hall," after the murdered South African student leader. A number of other student groups held what they called "sit-outs." It was only in late spring, when the snow melted in Ithaca, that Cornell students collected scraps of wood, tar paper, and plastic to construct a shack in front of the university's administration building. That shack, notes Soule, was the first of what later became known as the *shantytown*, "a performance and a name that eventually spread to similar structures around the country" (Soule 1997: 858; also see Soule 1999).

In all, Soule identified forty-six shantytown protests between 1985, when the campaign against investment in South African firms began, and 1990, when it ended. All of these events used roughly the same performance—student activists' building of a makeshift structure to oppose their universities' investments in firms with ties to South Africa. While some made broader claims, all professed clear statements about the necessity of divestment. Figure 2.2 tracks the shantytown protests that Soule found in her database over this six-year period.

Note the stages of Soule's procedures. From personal observation, she witnessed an event—the Cornell "naming" of the shantytown performance. That experience interested her in learning more. But rather than write up a case study that might have given an exaggerated importance to her own campus and reified the innovation, she turned to a more systematic source: the NEXIS file of hundreds of newspapers. (You will find it in your campus library.) NEXIS offered Soule a search function that made it unnecessary for her to pore over hundreds of newspaper articles as many of her predecessors—including the authors of this book—had done (Soule 1997: 864).

NEXIS also made it possible to construct a time line of the shantytown protests (in Soule's language, an "event history") and relate it to other variables. For example, Soule asked what kind of campuses tended to produce shantytown protests—were they more likely to emerge in large private universities, mostly black or liberal arts colleges, or big state in-

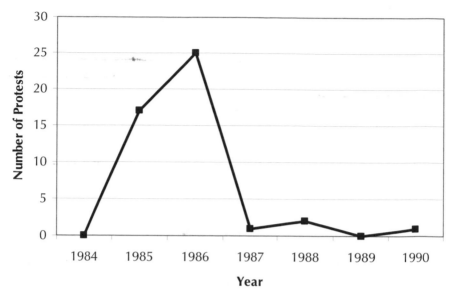

Figure 2.2. "Shantytown Protests" on American College Campuses, 1984–1990
Source: Data provided by Sarah Soule.

stitutions? She could study whether there was a geographic pattern of diffusion from Columbia to nearby campuses in the Northeast, or whether the movement spread through the media, irrespective of location. And she could examine the effect of the protests: Were those campuses in which shantytowns appeared more likely to divest than those that had seen no protests?

Two kinds of results followed from Soule's procedures. On the one hand, by examining her sources carefully, she discovered that the "invention" of the innovation at Columbia was not deliberate and that it only developed a modular identity as it spread. Indeed, it was only after the Cornell events that the student divestment protesters gave a name to their performance and deliberately modeled their actions on it. Looking back, we can see that the innovation was no more than a symbol-laden variant of the sit-in, with a special symbolism related to the conditions of life of black South Africans.

For that reason, the performance petered out at the end of the divestment campaign. It had no symbolic relationship to other types of claims. As a result, unlike the sit-in or the demonstration, it did not become part of the basic repertoire of contention. People now remember it mostly as a failed innovation (Soule 1999). Shantytown protests against divestment failed in another way as well. When Soule carried out an analysis of the co-occurrence of shantytown protests with colleges' investment policies, she found that it was <u>ineffective in forcing divestment</u>. "Colleges and universities that had shantytowns," she concludes, "actually had <u>slower rates of divestment than those that did not have them</u>" (Soule 1999: 121; see also Soule 1995).   *If one of the shantytowns, divestine once expense back us Bite*

Soule's research on the diffusion of the shantytown protests serves as more than the tracking of a "failed innovation." First, it provides a simple model for how students can examine <u>streams of contention</u>, <u>sites of contention</u>, and the <u>diffusion of contention</u>, with data that are easily available. Second, it tells us <u>how a new performance can spread</u>—not randomly in a population, like a contagious disease, but <u>among similar social actors</u>. Third, if we are interested in the mechanisms and processes of contention, her work on a particular performance's "career" helps us to understand <u>how particular paths of diffusion that a performance follows affect its longevity</u>. Will it peter out, trigger a sustained social movement, or explode into revolution? For example, the fact that the shantytown diffused mainly through the media probably meant that <u>activists on different campuses did not know each other</u>, <u>did not coordinate their actions</u>, and, as a result, <u>could not build a national organization</u>. In our language, the shantytown performance diffused but did not produce a shift in the scale of the divestment movement.   *or perhaps a different type of media or use of media*

VT HE EDIA HOULD HAVE USED THIS

The Soviet Union's Collapse

Liberal democracies such as the United States and studies such as Soule's provide the most ready sources of systematic data on episodes of contention, but ingenious and resourceful researchers can carry out similar research in authoritarian regimes too. Using methods very similar to Soule's, Mark Beissinger (2002) traced the contours of what he calls the "tide" of contention in the former Soviet Union between 1987 and 1992, when it imploded. In a massive study that drew some of its inspiration from the work summarized in this chapter, Beissinger used a similar collection of episodes to <u>untangle the disintegration of the Soviet state</u>. As he put it, "<u>The fundamental unit of analysis in this study is the contentious event</u>. Although by no means the only method for dissecting contention, <u>event analysis is widely recognized as a tool for studying waves of mobilization</u>. It is essentially a way of tracking over time the rise and fall of <u>particular types of events and the features associated with them</u>" (42).

An experienced analyst of Soviet politics, Beissinger wanted to explain the enormous rise of separatist nationalism in the Soviet Union after 1986. Successful bids for independence on the part of former Soviet republics blew the union apart by 1991.

Beissinger could have written an interpretive history of the whole process. He chose instead to center his analysis on two large catalogs of episodes from the beginning of 1987 to August 1991: one of 5,067 protest demonstrations with at least one hundred participants, the other of 2,173 incidents in which at least fifteen people attacked persons or property. Beissinger also prepared catalogs of strikes and of demonstrations before 1987, but he concentrated his analysis on the two large files. In preparing those two catalogs, he and his collaborators consulted 150 different sources, including Russian-language newspapers, wire services, compilations by Soviet dissidents, émigré publications, and reports of foreign monitoring services. (Chapters 4 and 5 look at some of Beissinger's results.)

Setting the catalogs against his own knowledge of Soviet politics, Beissinger was able to show how initial demands for internal reforms of the Soviet Union gave way to bids for regional autonomy and independence, by no means all of them successful. In a process parallel to Tarrow's (1989) discoveries concerning Italian contention, early successes of demands for independence in such places as Estonia and Latvia encouraged further demands across a wide range of republics and led to increasing violence as unsuccessful claimants faced competition and repression.

Other Varieties of Evidence and Analysis

Collecting catalogs of contentious episodes serves the analysis of contentious politics well in two different ways. First, it clarifies what you have to explain and therefore what might explain it. Second, it focuses attention on the process of contention itself rather than diverting attention to antecedents and consequences. Still, some investigations properly emphasize antecedents or consequences. Sometimes, for example, we want to know whether certain actions by legislatures regularly generate contentious reactions or under what conditions military coups change the distribution of power outside the military. In either regard, contentious events will mark relevant cases, but large catalogs will probably be less helpful than close case comparisons. At other times, we want to understand what the social bases or organizational bases of a particular movement or episode are. For this purpose, the examination of movement networks would serve our purposes better than the study of events (Diani 1995; Diani and McAdam 2003; Osa 2003a, 2003b).

Mechanism-process accounts facilitate explanation well outside the world of event catalogs. Think back to British antislavery and Ukraine's Orange Revolution. Either one would lend itself to catalogs of contentious episodes. But for many purposes, other methods will serve better. In the analysis of British antislavery, we would learn a great deal by tracing changes in the connections among activists both inside and outside contentious events. We would gain from compiling life histories of many, many activists, to see how their social origins, religious affiliations, occupations, and political memberships varied and changed between 1785 and 1835. Content analysis of parliamentary debates, pamphlets, and news reports concerning antislavery would yield valuable information on splits and shifts in public representation of the issues.

This chapter's general lessons would still apply. You would arrive at better explanations by specifying the sites of contention, describing relevant conditions at those sites, identifying the relevant streams of contention, naming the most important outcomes, looking for crucial mechanisms, compounding those mechanisms into processes, and using analogies or direct comparisons with similar processes elsewhere to combine conditions, mechanisms, and processes into explanations of the outcomes. Chapters to come will often follow exactly that pattern: looking closely at the internal workings of contentious events without chopping them up into episodes for comparison.

As we move on, we will return repeatedly to chapter 1's basic descriptive concepts: political actors, governments, political identities, contentious performances and repertoires, social movements, and so forth. This chapter's basic concepts—mechanisms, processes, events, and episodes—provide a flexible explanatory framework for dealing with such questions as how political actors form, how political identities change, and how streams of contention sometimes congeal into sustained social movements. We will return to some of the mechanisms and processes highlighted in this chapter—in particular, to the mechanisms of brokerage, diffusion, and coordination and to the processes of mobilization and demobilization. Each will serve us well as we move into closer examination of contentious processes. But in order to do this, we will have to place political actors and their forms of contention within their political contexts. We will need to examine political regimes and the different combinations of opportunities and threats they offer or withhold from contentious politics.

3

In Caracas, Venezuela (April 2002), members
of a rally against populist president Hugo
Chávez shout and wave Venezuelan flags.
(Copyright © Reuters/CORBIS)

CHAPTER THREE

REGIMES, REPERTOIRES, AND OPPORTUNITIES

Contentious politics varies and changes in close connection with shifts of political power, and it organizes both inside and outside institutional venues. In this chapter, we examine how different political regimes structure and are affected by contentious politics. *Regimes* consist of regular relations among governments, established political actors, challengers, and outside political actors, including other governments. We will use the case of Venezuela to chart those relations—to map the regime. Our analyses will show that the connections among contention, political power, and institutions appear in both turbulent periods and in the more routine politics of both authoritarian regimes and settled democracies. We develop the key concept of *political opportunity structure* to guide us through these variations. Our central question is: How do the structures of political power and institutions and the character of contentious politics interact? We begin with the turbulent history of Venezuelan contention.

Contentious Politics in Venezuela

Venezuela has had its share of contentious politics. The oil-rich country of twenty-five million people lies between Colombia, Brazil, and Guyana. In that turbulent neighborhood, it has experienced plenty of its own turbulence. What was then "Gran Colombia" declared independence from Spain in 1819, but it split into the separate states of Colombia, Ecuador, and Venezuela in 1830. After that, like many of its neighbors, Venezuela long alternated between warlord competition and military rule. In 1959, however, the country moved into civilian government, after then only occasionally threatened by military intervention. Two elite political parties, one moderately social democratic and the other moderately Christian democratic, then shared power at the national level.

This partial democratization did not calm Venezuela's public politics. For the year 1989, the British political yearbook *Annual Register* reported:

> To obtain further loans from the IMF [International Monetary Fund], the Government of President Carlos Andrés Pérez introduced a new austerity programme on 16 February. Consequential sharp price rises in essential services, designed to reduce national dependence on oil, led to three days of spontaneous rioting in the capital, Caracas, in which 300 died and over 2,000 were wounded when the army mobilized over nine battalions to restore order. Similar riots occurred in provincial areas. (75)

Pérez had campaigned for the presidency on a program of public works and price containment, but after election, he quickly changed direction under pressure from domestic and international financiers.

Caracas's vivid violence of February–March 1989 began with confrontations between commuters and drivers of public transportation who were charging the new prices. It soon extended to sacking and looting of downtown stores. During the first two weeks of March, sixteen Venezuelan cities exploded in similar events. The confrontations gained fame as El Caracazo (the Events of Caracas) or El Sacudón (the Shock). They opened a decade of struggle and regime change. They also provided a marvelous example of the process examined in chapter 2: new coordination. Brokerage connected dissenting populations and directly promoted coordination across multiple cities and multiple sites within the Caracas metropolitan area. Brokerage by various kinds of groups also caused diffusion of ideas and practices from site to site, which further facilitated the new coordination. These effects lasted beyond 1989; connections made during that year's public dissent provided the basis for coordinated action into the 1990s.

Contention did not come only from below. During the early 1980s, a group of nationalist army officers had organized a secret network called the Revolutionary Bolivarian movement. (Simón Bolívar was a hero of nineteenth-century Latin American independence.) Paratroop colonel Hugo Chávez became their leader. In 1992, the Bolivarians almost seized power in a military coup whose failure sent Chávez to prison. He was still in jail when the group tried a second time in November. They captured a TV station and broadcast a video in which Chávez announced the government's fall. For that attempt, Chávez spent another two years in prison.

In 1993, while Chávez languished behind bars, the Venezuelan congress impeached President Carlos Andres Pérez for corruption, removing him from office. But Pérez's successor, Rafael Caldera, soon faced a collapse of the country's banks, a surge of violent crime, rumors of new military coups, and charges of his own corruption. As Chávez left prison and entered politics, popular demands for political housecleaning swelled. By the 1998 presidential elections, the only serious opposition to former coup manager Chávez came from a former beauty queen. She dropped out of the running as the Chávez campaign gained widespread support.

Billing himself as a populist, Chávez won by a large majority. The following year, according to the annual report of the democracy-monitoring organization Freedom House:

> Hugo Chávez, the coupist paratrooper-turned-politician who was elected president in a December 1998 landslide, spent most of 1999 dismantling Venezuela's political system of checks and balances, ostensibly to destroy a discredited two-party system that for four decades presided over several oil booms but has left four out of five Venezuelans impoverished. Early in the year, Congressional power was gutted, the judiciary was placed under executive branch tutelage, and Chávez's army colleagues were given a far bigger say in the day-to-day running of the country. A constituent assembly dominated by Chávez followers drafted a new constitution that would make censorship of the press easier, allow a newly strengthened chief executive the right to dissolve Congress, and make it possible for Chávez to retain power until 2013. Congress and the Supreme Court were dismissed after Venezuelans approved the new constitution in a national referendum December 15. (Karatnycky 2000: 522)

As Chávez came to power in 1999, street confrontations between his supporters and his opponents accelerated. The new president's state visit to Fidel Castro's officially socialist Cuba later the same year dramatized his plan to transform the government and its place in the world at large. Chávez also revived an old, popular Venezuelan claim to a large chunk of western Guyana. Venezuela moved into a new stage of struggle over the country's future.

Histories like Venezuela's make this chapter's main points obvious: Contentious politics varies and changes in close connection with shifts of political power. Contentious politics organizes both inside and outside institutional venues. Even if self-evident in Venezuela's case, the points still deserve attention for several different reasons.

First, the intimate connections among contention, political power, and institutions appear not only in turbulent histories like Venezuela's but also in what seem the more routine politics of authoritarian regimes and settled democracies.

Second, these connections contradict two opposite but equally common assumptions about popular contentious politics: on one side, that it consists largely of expressive, impulsive behavior, letting off steam; on the other, that it results from individuals' short-term pursuit of their interests, with the structure of power simply facilitating or inhibiting realization of those interests.

Third, a whole series of important questions arise as soon as we ask *how*: Exactly how do the structures of political power, established institutions, and the character of contentious politics interact? This chapter lays out some simple tools for posing and answering that question.

Contention within Regimes

In the Venezuelan case, we begin to see the stakes of popular struggle once we trace the history of oil. Venezuela, a major producer and exporter of oil, helped found the Organization of Petroleum Exporting States (OPEC) in 1960. Venezuela nationalized its oil industry fifteen years later, but it gradually let the industry acquire great political autonomy despite periodic efforts of populists and military officers to gain control of its vast revenues. In recent years, oil has accounted for about a third of Venezuela's national income and 80 percent of its export revenues.

Chávez's partly successful attempt to subordinate the oil industry and direct its revenues to popular programs attacked vested interests both abroad and at home. The changing map of Venezuela's regime clarifies such events as the Caracazo of 1989 and the confrontations of 1999. When we turn to comparative analysis later, we will find wide variations in types of regimes.

Before getting much farther, we have to consider *institutions*: established, organized, widely recognized routines, connections, and forms of organization are employed repeatedly in producing collective action within any particular regime.

Some of Venezuela's institutions have already appeared in the story: political parties, election campaigns, political spending programs, and extensive networks among military officers, both retired and active. If we took a closer look, we would also see a relatively free press, an active informal economy, schools and universities with politically energized student bodies, and a system of payoffs to politicians by oil executives. The existence of those institutions shaped the behavior of major political actors, including presidential candidates and their supporters. When we turn to other regimes later in this chapter, we will see how different configurations of institutions shape and partake of contentious politics: legislatures, judiciaries, executives, even local governments.

We can also gain clarity by thinking about the *repertoires* we examined in chapter 1: arrays of contentious performances that are currently known and available within some set of political actors.

For decades, Venezuelans recognized and suffered from the performance called the military coup. In a *coup,* a group of officers rally their troops to seize government buildings, expel existing leaders from their jobs, and take over the government with declarations of patriotism and promises to restore order. As the Caracazo of 1989 showed, city dwellers also knew from previous experience how to protest rising prices by attacking drivers and merchants who adopted the new price schedules. Although the news reports we have looked at so far don't show it, they likewise knew how to conduct electoral rallies, hold street demonstrations, and go out on strike. These familiar performances all became much more common in Venezuela as semidemocratic regimes prevailed after 1958 and a new Venezuelan repertoire emerged. Some elements in the repertoire appear repeatedly in a wide variety of regimes. But, as we will see, some are regime-specific and shift as regimes change.

In addition to regimes, institutions, and repertoires, we use a concept describing the connection between them: political opportunity structure. *Political opportunity structure* refers to features of regimes and institutions (e.g., splits in the ruling class) that facilitate or inhibit a political actor's collective action and to changes in those features. It emphatically includes not only opportunities but also threats, such as the Venezuelan government's repression of the 1992 coup plotters. And it leads us to pay attention to changing opportunities and threats. When these cumulate and combine, they lead to changes in regimes, such as democratization and dedemocratization.

Clearly the Venezuelan political opportunity structure of the late 1990s allowed a wide variety of political actors to intervene directly in national politics, unlike the periods of stark repression that had often arrived with earlier military regimes. Although we will specify elements of opportunity structure more carefully later, it will help to think of political opportunity structure as the framework within which people decide whether to mobilize, make decisions about optimal combinations of performances to use, and are likely to succeed or fail in their efforts.

The chapter's plan is to look systematically at the interplay among regimes, institutions, political opportunity structure, and repertoires, with special attention to the crucial forms of regime change we call democratization and dedemocratization. A return to Venezuela's contentious politics will help the effort along.

Venezuelan Contention, 1983–1999

Venezuelan historian Margarita López Maya and her collaborators have made a valuable contribution to our effort. They self-consciously adopted the same approach to contentious episodes we saw Charles Brockett, Hanspeter Kriesi, Sarah Soule, and Mark Beissinger using for, respectively, Central America, Western Europe, the United States, and the Soviet Union in chapter 2. Reading every issue of the Venezuelan newspaper *El Nacional* from 1983 through 1999, the research team extracted reports describing public expressions of dissent: protests. In detail, they encountered these sorts of episodes:

Legal: asambleas, caravanas, comunicados, concentraciones, huelgas, marchas, mitines, recolección de firmas
Illegal but tolerated: huelgas de hambre, operación morrocoy, paros civicos, paros nacionales
Illegal but tolerated in some circumstances: cierre de vias, invasiones a inmuebles, invasiones de tierras, tomas de establecimientos
Repressed: apredreamientos, disturbios, quemas, saqueos, secuestros
New: apagones de luz, cacerolazos, cadenas humanas, encadenamientos, pitazos, desnudo (López Maya, Smilde, and Stephany 2002: 21)

Much like Dieter Rucht in the German research that chapter 1 described and Sidney Tarrow's Italian research in chapter 2, the Venezuelan researchers regrouped their rich reports of individual episodes into three categories: conventional, confrontational, and violent. Here are the distinctions, as the researchers defined them:

> *Conventional*: protest events well known to the general public which do not provoke fear or feelings of any sense of threat on the part of the authorities or the public, for example meetings and authorized demonstrations

Confrontational: new or illegal types of protest, not characterized by violence but using certain resources in order to provoke surprise, thus generating tensions or feelings of defiance among the authorities and the public, for example street blockages and occupations of public buildings

Violent: involving material or human damage, for example sacking stores and throwing rats at officials. (López Maya 2002: 203; López Maya et al. 2002: 17-19)

Altogether, over the seventeen years from 1983 to 1999, they counted 1,219 conventional events, 1,108 confrontations, and 708 violent encounters. That yielded a total of 3,035 events—178 per year, or 3 to 4 per week. More revealing than the total numbers, however, are fluctuations from year to year. Figure 3.1 traces those fluctuations.

Venezuela's contentious events do not resemble mass phenomena such as weddings and traffic accidents, which generally change little in number from one year to the next. Venezuela's contention comes in waves. More important, as in Italy during the late 1960s and the Soviet Union during the late 1980s, the waves correspond to national political crises. The Venezuelan crisis of 1984-1985 involved widespread unemployment, price rises, and extensive strike activity by organized workers. (Those strikes help to account for the frequency of "conventional" events.) The second peak of 1989 includes the Caracazo-Sacudón. The graph shows a buildup from after the failed coup of 1992 and a slowdown in 1997-1998. For 1999, it then reveals a spectacular rise of violent and especially confrontational episodes combined with a slight decline of conventional episodes.

We have mapped the Venezuelan data cumulatively in figure 3.1 for easier reading. The graph's top line shows the total number of episodes; and the spaces between the lines, the number of episodes in each category. Over the long run of 1983 to 1999, conventional episodes declined greatly both in absolute numbers and as a proportion of all contentious events. They ran between 150 and 200 per year at the start but fell to 50 or 75 per year at the end. Violent episodes became significantly more common absolutely and proportionately during the 1990s, and then they almost disappeared during the election campaign of 1998, only to return with a vengeance in 1999. In each crisis, confrontational episodes rose visibly in absolute number and share of all public contention. Over the long run, they became much more frequent.

Here is another way to think about the changes in Venezuelan contention during the period studied: Some of what had been confrontational performances in 1983 were becoming conventional by the late 1990s.

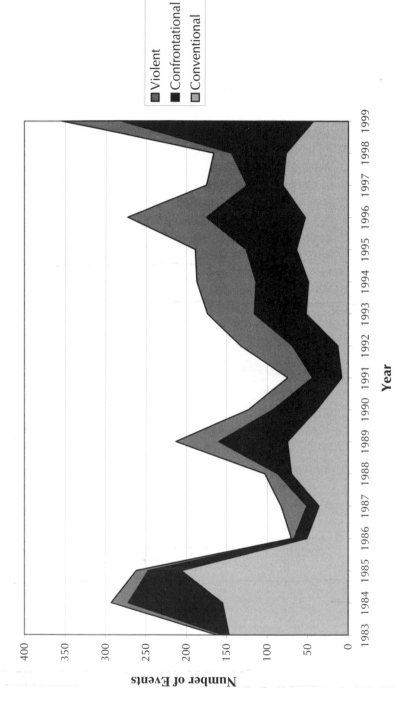

Figure 3.1. Protest Events in Venezuela, 1983–1999
Source: Lopéz-Maya et al. (2002).

Others gave way to violence, which rose spectacularly toward the end of the period. That aspect of the cycle resembles what Donatella della Porta and Sidney Tarrow (1986) found in Italy toward the end of the period they studied. In the dynamics of Venezuelan contention during this period, we are watching repertoire change.

López Maya and her collaborators turned up the magnification for their final year, 1999. They did a close study of that year's street politics in the Caracas metropolitan area. They observed contentious episodes themselves, interviewed participants and other observers of contentious episodes, and did special investigations of five groups that played distinctive parts in contention: neighborhood organizations, pensioners and retired persons, court personnel, university students, and street vendors. This allowed them to go beyond the broad counts of figure 3.1 to specific uses of performances by different political actors.

At first glance, for instance, we might wonder about those land occupations (*invasiones de tierras*). They become much less mysterious, however, when we learn that during the late 1980s the regional governor Abdón Vivas Terán had given street vendors their own space in Caracas's La Hoyada market, that the city had expelled them from the space in 1998 with a promise to give them new quarters nearby, and that the city failed to keep its promise. The vendors' occupation of part of the market made a concrete claim for restitution of their rights. As vendors the research team interviewed put it, the city had put them out of work without compensation and thus threatened their families' survival (López Maya et al. 2002: 174–76). The vendors took action to claim justice for their families. But they used a form that already had precedents in Venezuelan politics.

The evidence from Venezuela shows us that the prevailing mix of claim-making performances—the contentious repertoire—changes over time in response to shifts in the national regime. Between 1983 and 1999, alterations in the Venezuelan regime included the collapse of a once-tight alliance among national rulers organized via two main political parties in collaboration with the oil industry and the army, repeated bids by military officers to take control over the government, and rise to power of a populist coalition led by a former paratrooper colonel. These changes occurred much to the consternation of the U.S. government and major North American oil importers.

In 2002, as Chávez opponents mounted massive protests against his administration, dissident Venezuelan army officers attempted a coup, declared victory, and gained almost instant recognition from the Bush administration. The United States hastily reversed itself when loyalist troops regained control over the streets and brought Chávez back to power. For the next year, Venezuela came close to civil war as oil executives, the oil workers' union, and retail merchants staged a huge strike against the government. Chávez supporters organized a massive countermobilization. External actors including U.S. ex-president Jimmy Carter intervened to help negotiate a settlement. By August 2004, Venezuelans had voted in a referendum that confirmed Chávez as president and helped him to consolidate his power against an increasingly fragmented opposition.

Over and over again, the history of Venezuela shows us the interaction of repertoires, institutions, political opportunities, and regimes. Short-term regime shifts generated both mobilization of existing repertoires and innovation in the forms of claim making. But mobilization and innovation, in their turn, eventually transformed the regime itself. Venezuela's experience between the 1980s and the early twenty-first century shows us mutual causation among changes of government, regime, institutions, political opportunity structure, and repertoires of contention.

Repertoires and Regimes

Regimes do not only change within the same country, as in Venezuela. They also vary from one country to the next. Some regime variations across countries are quite subtle. Think about similarities and differences between the U.S. and Canadian political systems. Both feature federal arrangements (states and provinces), national and regional legislatures, formally independent judiciaries, and forms of common law. Yet the United States has an elected president, while the Canadian chief executive is a prime minister drawn from the parliament's dominant party. The U.S. government exercises priority over natural resources, while Canada cedes extensive control over natural resources to its provinces. These subtle differences in regimes have actually produced significant differences in contentious politics—for example, a more robust tradition of social democracy in Canada as opposed to the more centrist "liberalism" of the American Left.

Regime variations *within* countries also matter. Mainly English-speaking Canada has a major province, Quebec, in which French serves as the dominant official language, and a huge territory, Nunavut, officially run by indigenous people. Canada's regime assigns large political subdivisions to different cultural groups. Despite considerable cultural variation from one U.S. region to another, nothing like those large Canadian units of constitutionally backed cultural distinctiveness exists in the United States. But racial discrimination made the United States between 1890 and the mid-1960s a segmented regime. As these examples show, even broadly democratic regimes differ internally in important ways. Those differences often shape the issues of contentious politics—for example, in struggles over the production, distribution, and revenues of coal and oil or the mobilization of indigenous people. Variations within regimes are sometimes so great as to constitute *composite regimes*, which we turn to in chapter 8.

Two big differences among regimes across the world matter most to contentious politics: governmental capacity and extent (or lack) of democracy. *Capacity* means the extent to which governmental action affects the character and distribution of population, activity, and resources within the government's territory. When a high-capacity government intervenes in population, activity, and resources, it makes a big difference; it raises taxes, distributes benefits, regulates traffic flows, controls the use of natural resources, and much more. Low-capacity governments may try to do the same things, but they have little effect.

Democracy means the extent to which people subject to a given government's authority have broad, equal political rights, exert significant direct influence (e.g., through competitive elections and referenda) over government personnel and policy, as well as receive protection from arbitrary action by governmental agents such as police, judges, and public officials. A regime is undemocratic to the extent that political rights are narrow and/or unequal, consultation of citizens is minimal, and protections are fragile.

Obviously democracy and capacity are relative matters. By these standards, no pure, broad, equal, full-consultation, protective democracy has ever existed on a national scale. Nor has any government—not even those we call totalitarian—had absolute control over the population, activities, and resources within its territory. The distinctions still allow us to separate significantly different types of regimes, as in figure 3.2.

As of the early twenty-first century, here are examples of regimes falling into the four quadrants of this regime space:

High-capacity undemocratic: China, Iran, Morocco
Low-capacity undemocratic: Nepal, Somalia, Sudan
High-capacity democratic: Australia, Japan, Norway
Low-capacity democratic: Belgium, Cyprus, Jamaica

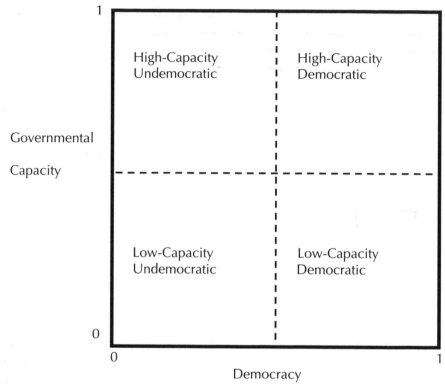

Figure 3.2. Crude Regime Types

By definition, regimes only exist where governments operate at larger than a local scale. Regimes have therefore existed somewhere in the world for about seven thousand years. Over all that human history, regimes have distributed very unevenly across the four types. The great bulk of historical regimes have fallen into the low-capacity undemocratic sector. Many of the biggest and most powerful, however, have dwelt in the high-capacity undemocratic sector. High-capacity democratic regimes have been rare and mostly recent. Low-capacity democratic regimes have remained few and far between.

On the average, very different sorts of contention prevail in the four corners of this regime space. High-capacity undemocratic regimes feature both clandestine oppositions and brief confrontations that usually end in repression. Low-capacity undemocratic regimes host most of the world's civil wars (Fearon and Laitin 2003). Low-capacity democratic regimes

gather more than their share of military coups and struggles among linguistic, religious, or ethnic groups. High-capacity democratic regimes
foster the bulk of the world's social movements. The differences result
from dramatic variation in the sorts of threats and opportunities faced by
potential claim makers in different regime environments.

Political Opportunity Structure

Why do repertoires vary systematically from one kind of regime to another? Some of the difference results from accumulated history. Longer-
lasting regimes also tend to have higher capacities, which is why they
last longer. Over those histories, they accumulate ways of doing political
business that authoritarian leaders borrow from each other and help
each other perform. Despite its multiple twentieth-century revolutions,
China has centuries of experience with centralized rule, and over those
centuries, it has traded influences with its East Asian neighbors Korea,
Japan, and Mongolia.

But a significant part of the systematic variation in contention results
directly from properties of the regimes in the four quadrants of figure
3.2. General features of a regime affect the opportunities and threats im-
pinging on any potential maker of claims, and *changes* in those features
produce changes in the character of contention. We can sum up crucial
features of regimes as political opportunity structure. Political opportunity
structure includes six properties of a regime:

1. The multiplicity of independent centers of power within it
2. Its openness to new actors
3. The instability of current political alignments
4. The availability of influential allies or supporters for challengers
5. The extent to which the regime represses or facilitates collective
   claim making
6. Decisive changes in items 1 to 5

From the perspective of a whole regime, the instability of alignments
and the availability of allies (items 3 and 4) amount to the same thing.
Stable alignments generally mean that many political actors have no potential allies in power. By such a definition, however, political opportunity
structure varies somewhat from one actor to another; at the same moment,
one actor has many available allies, another few.

Threats also vary in different opportunity structures, and most people who mobilize do so to combat threats or risks (Goldstone and Tilly 2001). The prolife movement in the United States sees a threat to Christian values in the legal availability of abortion. The xenophobic National Front in France sees itself struggling against the threat to national integrity represented by North African immigrants. Even Al Qaeda's suicide bombers are responding to the threat of the occupation of their countries by Western forces (Pape 2004). In both democratic and nondemocratic regimes, most people who engage in contentious politics see themselves responding to threats they perceive to their interests, their values, or their identities.

But threats and opportunities co-occur, and most people engaging in contentious politics combine response to threat with seizing opportunities. For example, in Iraq under the American occupation regime, the Sunni population saw construction of a new constitution as a threat to its power. Yet while federalism gave the Shia and Kurdish areas control over Iran's oil revenues—a real threat to the Sunnis—it also provided institutional autonomy to different territorial groups. That autonomy opens up new opportunities. Both threats and opportunities shift with fragmentation or concentration of power, changes in the regime's openness, instability of political alignments, and the availability of allies.

Rapidly shifting threats and opportunities generally move power holders toward rigid repertoires and challengers toward more flexible repertoires. Power holders cling to proven performances, including repression of challengers. Meanwhile, challengers seek new means to outwit authorities and competitors. Rivalry among power holders often leads some of them to form alliances with challengers, which limits the power holders' movement toward rigidity as well as the challengers' move toward flexibility. Since some repertoires link challengers to power holders, rapidly shifting threats and opportunities thus introduce more uncertainties into the relations between claimants and objects of their claims. Programs, identities, and political standing all shift more rapidly.

Opportunity structures shaped contention in many of the episodes of contention we have encountered so far in this book. To recall just a few:

- British antislavery drew guidance in its development from the parliamentary practice of receiving petitions from concerned citizens' groups and gained easier access because of the division within the British elite that resulted from the failed attempt to keep the American colonies in the empire.

- Ukrainian dissidents played skillfully on the divisions within the security services and on the momentum of the election fraud protests that preceded them in Serbia and Georgia.
- American civil rights activists took advantage of the great migration from the South, the growing importance of the black vote, and the onset of the Cold War (see chapter 9) to make more determined attacks on segregation.
- In response to the increasing violence against black demonstrators by South Africa's apartheid regime, American college students in the 1980s took advantage of the open opportunity structure on their campuses to pressure their administrations to divest from South African stocks.
- The minority ethnic groups that Beissinger studied in the Soviet Union used the openings offered by Gorbachev's policies of perestroika and glasnost to place nationalist demands on the agenda.
- The "new social movements" examined by Kriesi and his collaborators in Western Europe responded to different structures of alliance and conflict in France, West Germany, the Netherlands, and Switzerland, resulting in different combinations of conventional, demonstrative, and violent contention.
- In Venezuela between 1980 and 2000, a relatively closed and repressive system run by a well-connected elite broke open.

But on the other side of opportunities lies threats:

- Indigenous groups in the Panzós valley that Brockett examined, faced by troops that had shown themselves willing to massacre unarmed peasants, had to choose between retreat or armed struggle.
- As the Soviet empire imploded and majority ethnic groups in different republics began to assert their hegemony, minorities responded, sometimes with violence, sometimes with migration to regions where they would be in the majority, and sometimes by learning the new hegemonic language.
- On a smaller scale, the Caracas city government threatened local street peddlers' survival by denying their rights to sell their wares on vacant land.

The very character of opportunities and threats varies dramatically from one kind of regime to another. That point takes us to different types of regimes and to the institutions that constrain and condition contentious politics.

Regimes and Institutions

In general, regimes and their institutions grow up together and accommodate to each other. Where kinship groups organize much of social life, for example, they usually intertwine closely with government or even run the government. Where capitalist firms, labor unions, schools, political parties, and private associations prevail, in contrast, they shape the regime to fit their own needs. A given firm, union, school, party, or association may oppose current governmental policies, but on the whole these institutions and others like them depend on a measure of governmental toleration and support. On the other side, no government that runs roughshod over all existing institutions lasts very long.

Yet regimes do shape institutions. Regimes exert significant control over institutional operations in three complementary ways: by *prescribing* institutions (e.g., by requiring people to belong to mass associations or political parties), by *tolerating* others (e.g., by allowing different sorts of religious groups to gather so long as they stay out of public politics), and by *forbidding* still others (e.g., by banning private militias). In a parallel way, regimes prescribe, tolerate, and forbid different sorts of claim-making performances—perhaps prescribing mass pledges of allegiance, tolerating religious processions, but forbidding armed gatherings except for the government's own military forces.

On the whole, high-capacity undemocratic regimes prescribe an exceptionally wide range of institutions and performances. But they tolerate only a narrow range of institutions and performances, while forbidding many institutions and performances. At the opposite end of the range, low-capacity democratic regimes feature extensive toleration of institutions and performances, but they neither prescribe nor forbid very many. Think about differences between Morocco (currently a high-capacity undemocratic regime) and Jamaica (currently a low-capacity but relatively democratic regime).

This variation from one sort of regime to another has an interesting effect on locations of contention. We make a rough distinction between contained and transgressive contention. *Contained* contention takes place within a regime's prescribed and tolerated forms of claim making, even if it pushes the limits, as when participants in a public meeting start shouting seditious slogans. *Transgressive* contention crosses institutional boundaries into forbidden or unknown territory. It either violates standard arrangements or adopts previously unknown forms of claim making. In democratic regimes, we find a great deal of contention, most of it contained by institutions created precisely to structure and contain conflict; in authoritarian regimes, there is much less open contention, but what there is takes largely transgressive forms because the regime regards so many forms of expression as dangerous. In composite regimes, transgressive and contained contention coexist in an uneasy synthesis, as we will see when we turn to the Israeli/Palestinian regime in chapter 8.

Both British antislavery activists and Ukrainian dissidents sometimes transgressed, as the British organized unprecedented boycotts and the Ukrainians employed mass demonstrations united by the opposition color orange. As these examples suggest, contained and transgressive contention influence each other and sometimes flow into each other. But the distinction matters: Transgression challenges the regime, its institutions, and its laws all at once.

The boundary between contained and transgressive contention blurs, yet it embodies an important series of principles:

- Every regime sets limits on acceptable forms of claim making.
- Regimes differ dramatically in the loci and effectiveness of those limits.
- These limits establish three zones: prescribed, tolerated, and forbidden forms of claim making.
- Transgressive politics occurs at the boundary of tolerated and forbidden behavior, sometimes converting forbidden into tolerated forms of claim making.

These are not incidental intersections. But because the study of contentious politics developed independent of the study of political institutions, analysts of contention often forget that contention helped to shape institutions and vice versa. The co-occurrence of social movement development and institutional development in the democracies of the West, for example, produced movement-style claim making within institutions; movement-style claim making against institutions; institutionalization of some movements, participants, and organizations, accompanied by radicalization of other movements, participants, and organizations.

Democratization and Dedemocratization

To look more precisely at democratization and dedemocratization, we can borrow a leaf from the New York–based democracy-monitoring organization Freedom House. Since 1972, Freedom House has been re-cruiting experts to rate all the world's independent regimes along two dimensions: political rights and civil liberties. (Although we have never done so ourselves, our colleagues and former students have often served as experts or advisers on the rating process.) The raters fill in two question-naires for each regime they examine. The political rights questionnaire includes such items as these:

> Is the head of state and/or head of government or other chief authority elected through free and fair elections? Do the people have the right to organize in different political parties or other competitive political group-ings of their choice, and is the system open to the rise and fall of these competing parties or groupings?

The civil liberties questionnaire asks, among other things:

> Is there freedom of assembly, demonstration, and open public discussion? Are property rights secure? Do citizens have the right to establish private businesses? Is private business activity unduly influenced by government officials, the security forces, or organized crime? (Karatnycky 2000: 584–85)

An elaborate scoring system groups answers to such questions in two sets of seven rank levels, from low to high political rights, and from low to high civil liberties.

Roughly speaking, Freedom House's political rights scale covers our breadth, equality, and consultation, while its civil liberties scale rates protection. The two scales actually smuggle in some judgments about governmental capacity as well: Higher ratings on political rights assume that the government can actually enforce those rights, and higher ratings on protection assume that the government actually delivers promised pro-tections. Without some hidden judgments about capacity, the whole rating process would fail, since almost every government in the world declares itself democratic on paper. With that qualification, the Freedom House ratings provide a convenient worldwide look at degrees of democracy.

Figure 3.3 locates nine regimes in the Freedom House space of politi-cal rights and civil liberties as of 2003. The diagonal dotted line marks a rough distinction between democratic and undemocratic regimes, with Venezuela just making it into democratic territory. In the diagram's lower left-hand corner, we see Cuba with the lowest possible ratings on both political rights and civil liberties. Others in that corner (but not in the

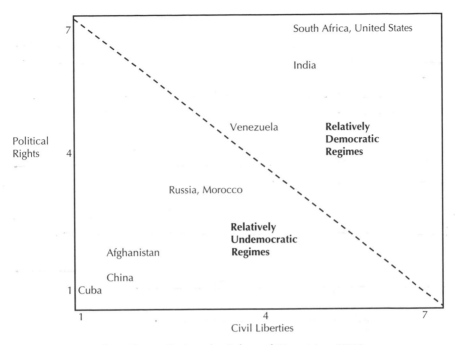

Figure 3.3. Freedom House Ratings for Selected Countries, 2003
Note: We have inverted the actual Freedom House ratings, which run from 1 (high) to 7 (low).
Source: Piano and Puddington (2004: 720–21).

diagram) are Burma, Libya, North Korea, Saudi Arabia, Sudan, Syria, and Turkmenistan. All of them clearly qualify as undemocratic regimes. Most of them also qualify as high-capacity regimes. In 2003, our now-familiar Venezuela stands close to the diagram's middle, in the third rank on political rights and the fourth rank on civil liberties.

The United States anchors the diagram's upper right-hand corner, with the highest possible ratings on political rights and civil liberties. It has plenty of company in the corner: Andorra, Australia, Austria, Bahamas, Barbados, Belgium, Canada, Cape Verde, Chile, Cyprus, Denmark, Dominica, Finland, France, Germany, Iceland, Ireland, Italy, Kiribati, Liechtenstein, Luxembourg, Malta, Marshall Islands, Micronesia, Nauru, Netherlands, New Zealand, Norway, Palau, Portugal, San Marino, Slovenia, Spain, Sweden, Switzerland, Tuvalu, the United Kingdom, and Uruguay.

In this set appears a mixture of very high-capacity democracies (e.g., Germany and Iceland) with some relatively low-capacity democracies (e.g., Barbados and Cyprus). Although any of these countries could dedemocratize under some conditions, we would expect the high-capacity and low-capacity democracies to do so differently. In the case of high-capacity democracies, a vast shock to governmental capacity, military conquest, or ruthless internal takeover of the existing governmental apparatus might do it. In the case of low-capacity democracies, undermining of the regime by criminal activity, externally supported subversion, military coup, or intergroup conflict would be more likely to produce dedemocratization.

A number of composite regimes occupy a position such as Israel/Palestine and South Africa: highest rating on political rights, but civil liberties somewhat compromised by substantially unequal protections for different segments of the citizenry. Postsocialist regimes Bulgaria, the Czech Republic, Estonia, Hungary, Latvia, Lithuania, Poland, and Slovakia all join South Africa in the same position. In all of them, at least one minority surviving from socialist days suffers some sort of legal handicap. Thinking about these cases, however, reminds us that democracy is a matter of degree. Despite its high ranking, the United States still fails to offer equal protection to all its ethnic and racial groups. Plenty of citizens in the other 7 + 7 countries listed earlier also have justified complaints about inequality of rights, consultation, and protection. Freedom House ratings simply tell us that on the whole India doesn't provide as much democracy as, say, Finland and Uruguay.

One feature of the diagram that immediately strikes the eye is the clustering of regimes along the diagonal from 1 + 1 (Cuba) to 7 + 7 (United States). Regimes that receive high ratings on political rights also tend to receive high ratings on civil liberties, while low ratings also go together. Some of the correlation probably results from raters' "halo effects"; that is, if a regime's civil liberties look good, raters most likely give it the benefit of the doubt on political rights. But on the whole, political rights and civil liberties really do go together. They reinforce each other. When a regime dedemocratizes, denial of protection to targeted minorities also undermines the breadth and equality of political participation and consultation.

For a last look at Venezuela's history, figure 3.4 traces Freedom House ratings for the regime from 1972 to 2000. The later years of that period include the regime transitions we examined earlier. In Freedom House experts' view, Venezuela never entered the 7 + 7 corner of highest ratings on political rights and civil liberties. But it moved a great deal. Between 1972 and 1976, according to Freedom House ratings, political rights expanded in Venezuela. The elite two-party system continued to operate, but with some opening in political opportunity structure. In that period, the government of Carlos Andrés Pérez was simultaneously benefiting from

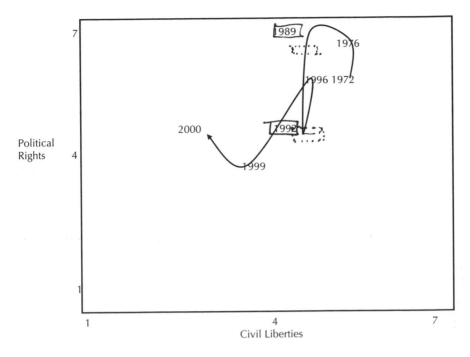

Figure 3.4. Freedom House Ratings for Venezuela, 1972–2000
Note: We have inverted the actual Freedom House ratings, which run from 1 (high) to 7 (low).
Source: Freedom House (2000).

OPEC-backed price rises, taking steps toward nationalization of the oil industry, engaging in large public works projects, and making significant concessions to organized groups of workers and peasants. A small incre-ment of democratization resulted.

Over the long period from 1976 to 1988, Freedom House raters contin-ued to place Venezuela at 7 + 6: extensive political rights compromised by unevenness in civil liberties. The peak of contention during the 1984-1985 price-employment crisis, in this light, looks like a democratic response to faltering government performance rather than a threat to democracy itself. On the whole, Venezuela's high democratic ratings for the period jibe with our account of popular contention.

Then came the Shock of 1989. From that point onward, Freedom House raters observed serious assaults on Venezuelan civil liberties. The graph also identifies a rapid decline in political rights between 1989 and 1992, the year of Chávez's failed coup attempts. A slight revival in political rights (but not in civil liberties) appears between 1992 and 1996, holding through 1997 and the election year of 1998. After that, strife-ridden 1999 marks a low point for Venezuelan democracy before the split recovery of 2000. In that year, according to Freedom House, civil liberties declined to a record-low 3, even if political rights climbed slightly to a 5. (Freedom House ratings for 2001–2004 ran 5 + 3, 5 + 4, 5 + 4, and 5 + 4, which indicates a modest improvement in civil liberties once Chávez outlasted his opposition.)

Regimes and Contention

What does all this mean for contentious politics? As we will see in chapter 6, social movements become more frequent with democratization and tend to concentrate in democracies. Why should that be? Think again about the elements of democracy: broad, relatively equal political participation combined with binding consultation of political participants on governmental personnel, resources, and policy plus protection of political participants from arbitrary action by governmental agents. Broad, equal participation does not qualify as democratic in itself. After all, high-capacity authoritarian regimes such as the European fascist regimes of the 1930s and state socialist regimes before the 1980s commonly institutionalized broad, equal, even compulsory political participation.

When breadth and equality combine with consultation in the form of elections, referenda, opinion polls, press discussion, and interest group formation, however, the combination gives citizens both incentives and means to band together for demands and complaints. Effective breadth, equality, and consultation also depend on protection from arbitrary governmental action, especially when it comes to minorities. When breadth, equality, consultation, and protection join in the same regime, they provide a favorable environment for social movement activity. In general, they guarantee a more open political opportunity structure than their opposites.

An across-the-board increase in breadth, equality, consultation, and protection counts as democratization. On the whole, low-capacity regimes face serious obstacles to democratization. In those regimes, the opening of political opportunity structure provides too many opportunities for ruthless opportunists such as warlords to seize control of the government and turn its activity to their own advantage. High-capacity regimes regularly resist democratization because it means that whoever currently runs the government must share power, and runs the risk of losing it entirely.

Still, a high-capacity regime that democratizes at least has the means of providing protection and enforcing the results of binding consultation.

Dedemocratization occurs when a regime moves toward narrower, more unequal, less binding forms of consultation and protection. Nothing guarantees that democratic institutions will stay in place forever. European governments that lost capacity through losses in World War I became especially vulnerable to dedemocratization. With losses in war, disciplined strongmen could seize the instruments of government and even gain popular appeal by comparison with their discredited predecessors. Many of Europe's fascist and state socialist regimes overturned relatively extensive democratic institutions on their way to high-capacity undemocratic rule. The histories of Italy, Germany, and Hungary after World War I all illustrate strongman dedemocratization.

Increases in state capacity can tilt the balance of largely democratic regimes toward composite regimes. When war, terrorist threat, or natural disasters creates the conditions for expanding state capacity, even established democratic regimes may erode guarantees of protected consultation by expanding state capacity. Think of the passage of legislation allowing the U.S. government to invade people's privacy after the September 11 massacres or the expansion of the British government's power to curtail speech in the wake of the London Underground bombings of 2005. Dedemocratization can occur by lethal coup, as it did in Venezuela, or by an incremental growth in state capacity. With dedemocratization, political opportunity structure generally narrows, and overall levels of contention usually decline after the new regime overcomes resistance to its rule.

Here is the most general point: A regime's relations, institutions, opportunities, threats, and repertoires combine to shape its popular contention. The deep processes of democratization and dedemocratization strongly affect relations, institutions, opportunities, threats, and repertoires. Contention feeds back. It also reshapes political relations, institutions, opportunities, threats, and repertoires, and thereby promotes democratization or dedemocratization. Only a dynamic analysis of contentious politics will capture these connections.

or absolutes

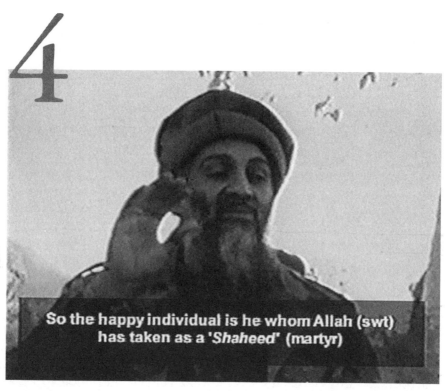

4

So the happy individual is he whom Allah (swt) has taken as a '*Shaheed*' (martyr)

A video (probably from March 2002) shows Osama bin Laden speaking, thus proving that he had survived the United States–led assault on his Afghanistan headquarters. (Copyright © Reuters/CORBIS)

CHAPTER FOUR

CONTENTIOUS INTERACTION

As we pointed out in chapter 1, this book takes an interactive approach to contentious politics. Instead of studying only "protest," "collective action," or "social movements," we examine contentious politics as the interaction among challengers, their opponents, interested third parties, the media, and more. So far, we have focused on the forms of collective action that people use (performances and repertoires), the contexts of their action (different regimes), and the opportunity structures that encourage or constrain them. We have also introduced some key mechanisms, including brokerage, diffusion, and coordination, that link challengers to others. But we have not yet delivered on our promise to connect challengers to the other actors in contentious politics. This chapter begins that task. We begin where many people have found the heartland of contentious politics—in the city of Paris.

Parisian Contentious Interaction

In any given year, writes Olivier Fillieule (1997), Parisians protest over practically everything, from war, civil rights, and racism to wages, employment, and working conditions, all the way to the weight of the *baguette* produced by neighborhood bakers. Although Parisians' repertoire is wide and deep, the street demonstration—*la manifestation*, in French—is their favored instrument. Regularly, but most often on weekends, Parisians assemble in habitual venues such as the square in front of the Gare de l'Est. Organized by the parade marshals of their *services d'ordre*, they array themselves behind colorful banners proclaiming the names of their organizations and their goals. Often chanting, they march down a broad avenue to a prearranged destination where prestigious speakers stir them.

Well-organized marchers representing parties, interest groups, and particular localities are not alone among the demonstrators. Although most demonstrations organize around a central claim, they often attract sympathizers, makers of cognate claims, curious onlookers, occasional opponents, and others with private axes to grind. From their interactions within the enthusiasm and solidarity of the demonstration, a unified "we" may even emerge.

Interaction doesn't only occur among those who demonstrate. On the margins of demonstrations appear onlookers, sympathetic, hostile, or indifferent. In an important sense, the task of the demonstrators is to turn sympathizers into participants, neutralize opponents, and turn indifferent onlookers into sympathizers. At a discreet distance, and often in civilian clothes, stand the police. Snapping photos and taking interviews are reporters from the press and television. Leading the parade are often celebrities, local officials, and party leaders. Bringing up the rear are lines of bright green garbage trucks sent to clean up the debris of pamphlets, handouts, and fast food that participants and spectators will leave behind. Officials of the prefecture who are responsible for public order and public officials at whom demonstrators direct their claims remain out of sight but keep themselves informed.

Pierre Favre (1990) made the demonstration the subject of his book, *La Manifestation*. The book offers an interactive portrait of the demonstration; the actors include not merely the demonstrators but those who join them, oppose them, and observe their progress. Figure 4.1 reproduces Favre's schematic map of the actors in and around a typical demonstration. Favre's diagram separates those on the side of the demonstrators (e.g., organizations, ordinary participants) from those who oppose them (e.g., the targets of protest, the forces of order) and from various third parties (e.g., unaffiliated groups, the press). The important point is that, for Favre, the demonstration is not just an action but a collective *inter*action among all these different actors. The same is true of contentious politics in general. That is this chapter's organizing theme.

As in the demonstration, other sorts of contentious episodes often bring together actors who know little or nothing of one another at the outset, yet they sometimes emerge from their participation as a unified actor, with an identity, with boundaries separating them from others, and with a set of unified claims that they put forward against significant targets. In doing so, they become collective political actors (McAdam et al. 2001: chap. 11). This constitution of collective actors is the most remarkable feature of contentious politics.

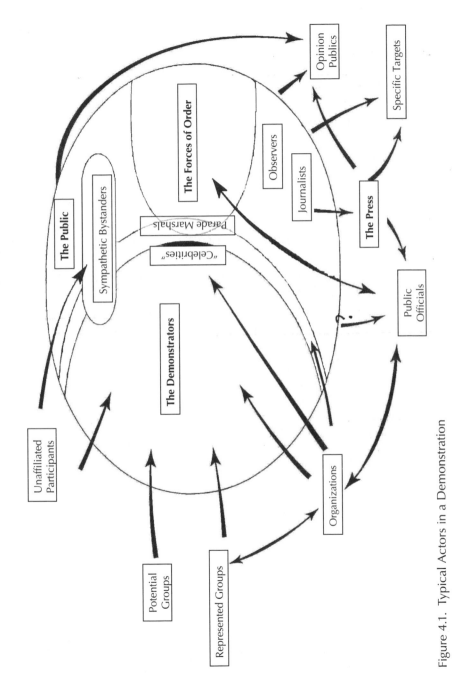

Figure 4.1. Typical Actors in a Demonstration
Source: Favre (1990: 19).

How do such things happen? Let us unpack that big question into five smaller, more manageable questions:

- How do political actors form, change, and disappear?
- How do they acquire and change their collective identities?
- How do they interact with other political actors, including holders of power?
- How do existing institutions promote, inhibit, or shape all these processes?
- What kinds of effects do collective claims produce, and how?

This chapter answers the five questions.

Actor Constitution in Chiapas

On New Year's Day 1994, a previously unknown group startled Mexico by announcing a program of liberation for Mexico's indigenous people. Soon people all over the world were paying attention to the Zapatista Army of National Liberation (EZLN in Spanish). Led by a masked man calling himself Subcomandante Marcos, the group had seized the governmental palace in San Cristóbal, Chiapas. From the palace's balcony, they read a vivid declaration to the Mexican people. It declared that a long-suffering people had suffered centuries of oppression and deprivation, but, finally, *hoy decimos basta!* (today, we say enough). At various points in the declaration, the authors identified themselves in these terms:

- A product of five hundred years of struggle
- Poor people like us
- People used as cannon fodder
- Heirs of our nation's true makers
- Millions of dispossessed
- "The people" as described in Article 39 of the Mexican national constitution
- The Zapatista Army of National Liberation
- Responsible, free men and women
- Patriots

They denied that they were "drug traffickers, or drug guerrillas, or bandits, or whatever other characterization our enemies might use." They opposed themselves explicitly to these groups:

- The dictatorship
- The political police
- A clique of traitors who represent the most conservative and anti-national groups
- The Mexican federal army
- The party in power (PRI) with its supreme and illegitimate leader, Carlos Salinas, installed in the federal executive office (Salinas was then president of Mexico)

Announcing a revolution on behalf of Mexico's poor, dispossessed, indigenous people of Mexico, they called for "us" to rise against "them."

The revolution did not take place. But the Zapatistas soon made an impact on Mexican politics. Within Chiapas, they held off threatened suppression by the army and forced the national government to start negotiations over peasant property rights. On a national scale, they started a much more general campaign for indigenous rights. During the spring of 2001, they staged a colorful march from Chiapas, Mexico's southernmost state, to Mexico City itself. The march publicized demands for enforcement of the local autonomy laws the legislature had passed in response to concerted pressure from organizations of indigenous people, backed by international activists.

The Zapatistas quickly acquired an impressive international reputation and following. Electronic Web sites and mailing lists, operated mainly by foreign supporters, broadcast their messages across North America and Europe. Those connections brought activists, funds, and enthusiastic statements of solidarity to Chiapas from as far away as Western Europe (Hellman 1999). Many outsiders interpreted the Zapatista mobilization as a form of resistance to the recently enacted North American Free Trade Agreement (NAFTA). For that reason, they saw it as a welcome addition to worldwide antiglobalization efforts. In 1996, the Zapatistas drew thousands of supporters to a "First Intercontinental Encounter for Humanity and against Neoliberalism" in the jungle of Chiapas. One observer argued that "the interest and attraction generated by the EZLN beyond its national borders is matched by no other movement in the post–Cold War period" (Olesen 2005: 12).

Constitution of a Zapatista identity did not come out of the blue; it built on what chapter 1 called a social base. Indigenous identity is hardly a new idea in a country such as Mexico, which has literally hundreds of indigenous groups. Many of its military and political heroes came from indigenous roots. Its 1905 revolution was, in part, the struggle of indigenous peasants to assert their rights to the land. It was no accident that the leaders of the Chiapas rebellion named their organization after revolutionary leader Emiliano Zapata (Womack 1971). Though of mixed background, Zapata became best known as the representative of indigenous peasants.

But the mobilization of an identity does not follow automatically from the existence of a social base to which it corresponds; if it did, indigenous uprisings would have occurred constantly throughout Latin America. The fact that such uprisings are sporadic and usually short-lived turns our attention from their social bases to their constitution as actors.

Mexico's native peoples have still not achieved the liberation their Zapatista advocates called for in 1994. Still, they have gone from near-invisibility to significant political prominence. They have become a weighty interest in national politics, an internationally recognized model for political mobilization, and frequent participants in contentious interaction. They had created a significant political actor on regional, national, and international stages. Their success in doing so leads us to the first of our five questions: How do political actors form, change, and disappear?

Formation, Change, and Disappearance of Political Actors

Remember how chapter 1 described *political actors*: recognizable sets of people who carry on collective action in which governments are directly or indirectly involved, making and/or receiving contentious claims. Political actors include governments and agents of governments such as presidents and police. But they also include a wide range of nongovernmental actors, from neighborhood groups to worldwide organizations. They qualify as political actors by making claims, receiving claims, or both. Political actors regularly form, change, and disappear. How does that happen?

The most general answers are quite simple. Political actors form through mobilization, by increasing the resources available for collective making of claims. They change by participating in contention. They disappear by demobilizing. Of course, the complexities start there—in exactly how mobilization, participation, and demobilization work and produce their effects.

Chapter 2 introduced the simple process of *new coordination*, in which the mechanism of brokerage activates the mechanism of diffusion, and the two mechanisms jointly produce coordinated action. Zapatista brokers brought together a motley coalition of indigenous communities, religious activists, urban radicals, and guerrilla fighters in a coordinated large-scale actor that announced itself as the unitary Zapatista Army of National Liberation. Its language, symbols, and practices then diffused widely among opponents of the current Mexican regime. The new actor then collected allies elsewhere in Mexico for even larger-scale making of collective claims. The Zapatistas of 1994 and afterward combined brokerage with diffusion, ultimately creating a coalition of participants, supporters, and sympathizers at a much higher scale than the jungles of Chiapas (Olesen 2005; Tarrow 2005: chap. 7).

The Zapatistas benefited from a mechanism we met briefly in chapter 2: certification. *Certification* occurs when a recognized external authority signals its readiness to recognize and support the existence and claims of a political actor. If the authority has international visibility and heft, its signal broadcasts the likelihood that the authority would intervene to support the new actor in future claims. Certification thus changes both the new actor's strategic position and its relation to other actors that could become its oppressors, rivals, or allies. (The opposite process of decertification withdraws recognition and commitments of future support, while often threatening repression.) The Zapatistas gained leverage within Mexico both from the country's long *indigenista* tradition and from their extensive certification by external organizations—nongovernmental organizations, the foreign press, even some governments urging the Mexican government to avoid a bloodbath. Those external organizations could and did exert pressure on that government to recognize and bargain with the Zapatistas.

Here is another way of seeing the same point. Remember the components of political opportunity structure from chapter 3: (1) the multiplicity of independent centers of power within the regime, (2) the regime's openness to new actors, (3) the instability of current political alignments, (4) the availability of influential allies or supporters for challengers, (5) the extent to which the regime represses or facilitates collective claim making, and (6) decisive changes in items 1 to 5. Changes in political opportunity structure shape the ease or difficulty of mobilization, the costs and benefits of collective claim making, the feasibility of various programs, and the consequences of different performances in the available repertoire. In all these ways, changes in political opportunity structure affect the attractiveness of different collective action strategies.

Changes in opportunities and threats affect activist groups such as the Zapatistas strongly and immediately. Activist groups rise, fall, and change as a function of political opportunity structure, of their programs' success or failure, and of their effectiveness in mustering support from patrons, allies, and social bases. As a result, political actors spend some part of their time and energy doing other things than making collective claims. They build on existing resources and gather new ones, maintain solidarity, manage internal disputes, recruit followers, provide services to members, and so on, through a wide variety of sustaining activities. Even ferociously activist groups devote plenty of effort to building, maintaining, and repairing their organizations.

Making collective claims always depletes available resources in the short run, even if it attracts new resources in the longer run. Because of that, political organizers necessarily balance two kinds of activity that sometimes contradict each other: on one side, making collective claims; on the other side, building up their organization and its access to sustaining resources. Struggles among activists often spring up over precisely that division of labor: Are our leaders spending too much time raising money for themselves and too little on forwarding our interests? On the contrary, have they destroyed our activist group by spending all their energy making claims and not enough energy on recruiting new members and drumming up financial support? The split in the AFL-CIO in 2005 turned on exactly this issue.

By identifying different kinds of political actors, you can untangle complicated contentious episodes. You can detect the arrival and departure of actors from contention, trace how their claim making changed, look for coalitions and divisions among them, and see whether they moved up or down the continuum from intermittent actors to established interests to activist groups. You can even understand why groups that appeared to be insignificant at one point in time seem unstoppable at the next and shrink to a small cadre at a third. Changes in political opportunity structure often return intermittent activists to their ordinary lives, give pause to established interests, and turn activists into a small but militant sect. In the simplest version, you make a list of the major political actors at point 1 in time, sketch connections and divisions among them, do the same thing for point 2 in time, and then try to explain the appearances, disappearances, and realignments from time 1 to time 2.

Here is a simplified example from Mark Beissinger's (2002) work on nationalist activism in the former Soviet Union. Between 1987 and 1991, many regionally organized nationalities across the USSR began to make collective claims for autonomy or independence. By 1992, fifteen of them had managed to secede from the union and gain international certification as sovereign states. When Beissinger was analyzing event catalogs to help explain the Soviet Union's disintegration, one of the many things he did was to chart the frequency with which members of different Soviet nationalities staged protest demonstrations month by month from 1987 through 1991 (84). For the most active, these were the peak months:

Armenians	May 1988
Estonians	November 1988
Moldavians	February 1989
Russians	January 1990
Crimean Tatars	April 1990
Ukrainians	November 1990
Latvians	December 1990
Lithuanians	December 1990
Azerbaijanis	December 1990
Georgians	September 1991

The Soviet Union had built these categories and their boundaries into its governing structure, for example by treating Ukraine and Lithuania as distinct units of rule with some degree of autonomy on such questions as language and cultural expression. As a result, all existed as established interests. They easily created activist groups claiming to speak for all Ukrainians, all Lithuanians, and so on, down the list. Brokerage brought together different clusters within a given nationality into a temporarily unified actor.

Other political actors were also at work in the disintegrating Soviet Union: Soviet leader Mikhail Gorbachev, Russian leader (and later president) Boris Yeltsin, emerging industrial tycoons, the government's security service, and more. Yet by itself this simple chronology tells an important tale about the sequence of flight from the USSR. On the union's edge and supported by powerful neighbors, Armenians and Estonians acted early and successfully, securing quick outside support for their claims to become independent states. Then the rush began. It peaked at the end of 1990. Of these major actors, all but the Tatars of the Crimea (who ended up inside Ukraine) eventually won independence.

If we looked closer, we would distinguish many more actors and begin to see crucial realignments among them. Within Estonia, for example, we would find a group of ethnic Russians who feared and resisted Estonian independence. We would also see multiple alliances and divisions. Starting in 1987, before either Armenia or Azerbaijan came close to independence, Armenians and Azerbaijanis were engaging in violent confrontations over the disputed territory of Karabakh, geographically inside Azerbaijan but with about three-quarters of its population ethnically Armenian (Beissinger 2002: 64–69, 342–47, 375). In 1992, newly independent Armenia invaded the territory between its border and Karabakh. A 1994 cease-fire left Armenia in de facto control of the territory, but without international certification of its claims. This takes us to our second key question: How do actors acquire and change their collective identities?

Political Identities

Once we turn the magnification up far enough to see individual episodes, we begin to notice that crude categories such as "Armenian" and "Azerbaijani" do not capture the self-presentations of the actors or their relations to each other. In Karabakh alone, activists of Armenian heritage did not simply identify themselves as Armenians but as Karabakh Armenians. In order to deal with that complication, we need a better understanding of political identities and the boundaries on which they build. Us-them boundaries play crucial parts in contention. Boundaries themselves commonly take shape outside contentious politics, as a result of a complex, consequential process we call, accordingly, *boundary formation*. Once they exist, however, political actors regularly use them as part of contentious politics. Then the mechanisms of boundary activation and boundary deactivation come into play.

You bump into social boundaries every day. You observe or participate in boundaries that separate news vendors from newspaper buyers, students from teachers, owners from employees, and patients from doctors or nurses. Every one of these boundaries identifies a social relationship you have little trouble recognizing and, if necessary, negotiating. In all these cases, the combination of a boundary with relations inside and across it always generates some shared sense of the boundary's meaning on one side and the other. Workers and bosses may not see eye to eye on the meaning of the boundary between them, but they negotiate some common recognition of the boundary's existence and importance.

When activated, the combination of boundary, relations, and understandings attached to them constitutes a social identity. Seen from one side of the boundary or the other, it provides varying answers to the questions "Who am I?" "Who are we?" "Who are you?" and "Who are they?" The political identities that concern us here always involve plurals, especially "us" and "them."

The word *identity* sounds tones from very interior to quite exterior. At the interior extreme, we find your sense of yourself as someone unique, complicated, and secret, not completely known by anyone else. At the exterior extreme, we discover the identity of data banks and identity theft, where some stranger needs no more than a name and number to place you. In contentious politics, most of the social identities that count lie between these extremes. They depend on and give meaning to relations with other people. Political identities include boundaries, relations across the boundaries, relations *within* the us and within the them, plus accumulated meanings assigned to the boundaries and relations.

Identities center on boundaries separating us from them. On either side of the boundary, people maintain relations with each other: relations within X and relations within Y. They also carry on relations across the boundary: relations linking X to Y. Finally, they create collective understandings about the boundary, about relations within X and Y, and relations between X and Y. Those understandings usually differ from one side of the boundary to another, and they often influence each other. Together, boundary, cross-boundary relations, within-boundary relations, and shared understandings make up collective identities. Changes in any of the elements, however they occur, affect all the others. The existence of collective identities, furthermore, shapes individual experiences—for example, by providing templates for us "good" Karabakh Armenians and distinguishing us from those "bad" Karabakh Azerbaijanis.

Identities, then, have four components: (1) a boundary separating me from you or us from them, (2) a set of relations within the boundary, (3) a set of relations *across* the boundary, and (4) shared understandings of the boundary and the relations. Through the Soviet Union's history, Karabakh Armenians and Karabakh Azerbaijanis had maintained distinctive everyday identities despite sometimes settling together, working together, and intermarrying. As the USSR fell apart, however, the paired identities politicized. As of 1992, Karabakh Armenians and Karabakh Azerbaijanis each had extensive internal relations, fought each other across the boundary between them, and offered competing accounts concerning the history of their region as well as the territorial rights that history implied.

Identities become *political* identities when governments become parties to them. In Karabakh, the governments of Armenia and Azerbaijan backed the people they claimed as their countrymen and denied the opposing claims. They manipulated and controlled permissible answers to the questions "Who are you?" "Who are we?" and "Who are they?"

These questions do not arise in remote corners of the former Soviet Union alone. After the Al Qaeda attacks of September 2001, the U.S. government activated a boundary that already existed but had now become more salient. Identities of Americans as patriotic or subversive became even more political as the U.S. government became a party to us-them boundaries separating patriots from terrorists and their sympathizers. Europeans maneuvered around similar questions, not only in deciding whether to align with U.S. military policy but also in deciding whether Turks are Europeans and whether Muslims in general lie on the opposite side of the us-them boundary. The November 2005 French wave of riots triggered by youths of North African Muslim origin deepened that boundary. The war against terror, European Union expansion, and mass immigration have activated new boundaries and deactivated others.

Boundaries change and new boundaries form largely as a result of processes outside contentious politics—for example, the reorganization of work and the migration of major populations. Most contention does not create and activate new boundaries. On the contrary, most contentious politics activates or deactivates existing boundaries. Everywhere in identity politics we find the mechanism of *boundary activation* that we introduced in chapter 2, in which an existing boundary becomes more salient as a reference point for collective claim making.

Boundaries between social classes, ethnic groups, religious faiths, neighborhoods, and other categories already exist. They organize some of routine social life. But contention typically activates one of these boundaries while deactivating others that could have been relevant. The Zapatista rebellion activated the broad boundary of indigenous identity while deactivating boundaries of the distinct ethnic groups that uneasily cohabit in the state of Chiapas (Hellman 1999). That activation also brought ethnicity into play, while pushing other differences, such as gender, locality, class, or occupation, into the background. Once that happens, conflicts between ethnic groups are almost sure to follow. As the savage wars in the Balkans and the Caucasus after the collapse of communism showed, nonethnic identities commonly give way as ethnicity X and ethnicity Y begin attacking each other.

The overthrow of Saddam Hussein's regime in Iraq had a similar effect. As long as the dictator and his Baath Party were in power, religious and ethnic conflicts remained mainly in check within Iraqi society. Once coalition forces had destroyed the repressive regime that had Iraq in its grip and had launched the process of constitution making, the identities of Shia, Sunni, and Kurds were activated both in institutional politics and through intersectarian violence.

Many people regard identity claims primarily as a form of self-expression or even self-indulgence—what others do when they are too comfortable, too confused, or too distressed for serious politics. On the contrary, identity claims and their attendant stories constitute serious political business. At various points in U.S. history, social movements helped to establish opponents and supporters of slavery, teetotalers, women, African Americans, gays, Vietnam veterans, survivors of 9/11 victims, families of children with cancer, and indigenous peoples as viable political actors. When they mobilized effectively and made successful claims, they received certification from authorities and from other political actors. Throughout American history, the shift toward established interests and activist groups promoted the emergence of general, indirect, and modular claim-making performances.

Political analysts often describe identities as if they were essential properties of individuals, but other scholars reject this essentialism. They see identities as infinitely malleable. We, too, think identities shift, as should by now have become obvious. But individuals cannot adopt a new identity as simply as they put on a new suit of clothes or change their hairstyles; identities appear and mobilize through interaction. This takes us to our third key question: How do political actors interact with other actors, including holders of power?

Contentious Interactions

Political identities take their meaning from contentious interaction: we make claims on them. They (whomever "they" are) often respond with counterclaims. We demand our rights, but the government replies that we have no such rights and, in fact, that we do not even constitute a recognized identity. Karabakh's Armenians claimed they had rights to political autonomy or even to annexation by the Armenian state. But Azerbaijan's leaders replied that Karabakh and its populations belonged to sovereign Azerbaijani territory. Later, the Armenian army bid up the claim making by occupying the part of Azerbaijan between Armenia and Karabakh. It remains there under the terms of the 1994 cease-fire, with both countries claiming ownership of the border strip and of Karabakh. At the Armenia-Azerbaijan border, contentious interaction continues.

Collective claims fall into three categories: identity, standing, and program. *Identity* claims, as we have seen, declare that an actor exists. That actor may have existed as a recognized actor before the episode began (e.g., the category of indigenous groups is a traditional one in Mexican politics), or it may be *constituted* in the course of the episode. Actor constitution is a crucial part of contentious politics (McAdam et al. 2001: 315–21).

Standing claims say that the actor belongs to an established category within the regime and therefore deserves the rights and respect that members of that category receive. The Zapatistas made a number of standing claims, but the most salient was to be valid representatives of Chiapas's indigenous people. (In fact, some indigenous leaders in Chiapas itself later disputed that claim.) They underlined their standing claims, furthermore, by denying that they were "drug traffickers, or drug guerrillas, or bandits, or whatever other characterization our enemies might use."

Program claims call for their objects to act in a certain way. The Zapatistas called on the Mexican government not only to recognize their identity and their standing as valid representatives of indigenous people but also to change its policy toward indigenous people by protecting their land and defending them against rapacious outsiders. In other kinds of contentious politics, programs range across an enormous variety of claims, such as the following:

- Overthrow the present government.
- Support our candidate for city council.
- Don't build that road through our neighborhood.
- Give our starving people food.
- Make our bosses pay us a living wage.
- Exterminate our enemies.

Headlines from any year's press reports illustrate the wide range of program claims. In 2005, for example, they included Iraqi insurgent groups' warnings against voting in the January parliamentary elections, Israeli settlers protesting their evacuation from their settlements in Gaza, guerrilla attacks on Colombian peasants for collaborating with right-wing militias, Indian tsunami victims' assault of an official who had not delivered food and water, French immigrants protesting the fires that ravaged four immigrant hostels, and the mother of an American soldier who was killed in Iraq demanding an audience with George W. Bush outside his Texas ranch.

Although political actors often emphasize one type of claim over others, we see few "pure" cases of identity politics, a politics of standing, or programmatic politics. The Zapatistas first caught international attention by their simple claim to existence. In the elaborate declaration of New Years Day 1994, they said, in effect, "Pay attention to us, because we're a new actor, we mean business, and the boundary between you and us matters." Soon they were also making standing and program claims. But, of course, they made all those claims by speaking concretely—and often negatively—about Mexican institutions. Claims and counterclaims do not occur randomly; they take their shape from surrounding regimes, cultures, and institutions. They respond to a regime's opportunities, threats, and constraints. This takes us to our fourth key question: How do existing institutions promote, inhibit, or shape processes of actor constitution, identify activation, and contentious interaction?

Institutions and Contention

Every regime limits possible claims in three ways. First, political opportunity structure affects what claims are possible. It does so by determining whether established political actors are or are not available as allies for new political actors such as the Zapatistas. If multiple independent centers of power exist within a regime (which means that political opportunity structure is more open in that regard), the chances increase that at least one power center will support and certify a set of identity, standing, or program claims. If political alignments are changing fast, a claimant has more opportunities to join coalitions and to escape repression.

Second, every regime divides known claim-making performances into prescribed, tolerated, and forbidden. A regime's government and other authorities enforce the prescribed performances, facilitate or at least do not block the tolerated performances, and act to suppress forbidden performances. Contained contention occurs within the limits set by prescribed and tolerated performances. Transgressive contention breaks out of those institutional limits into forbidden or previously unknown territory. Like the Mexican state, almost any state of medium or high capacity forbids the formation of actors having autonomous military power such as warlords' militias and guerrilla bands.

In most regimes in most periods, any group that decides to make independent claims by force of arms soon faces vigorous repression. Regimes also channel claims at the prescribed end of the range. Any government that makes its citizens assemble for patriotic ceremonies, for example, runs the risk that some hardy soul will disrupt the proceedings by shouting seditious slogans or assaulting a political leader. Since regimes also vary greatly in what forms of claim making they tolerate and forbid, top-down channeling of claims occurs all the time.

Third, from the bottom up, the available repertoire strongly limits the kinds of claims people can make in any particular regime. No one knew how to stage a street demonstration before social movements became standard forms of contentious politics. Although these days the news media have made the demonstration a familiar image across most of the world, even now suicide bombing only belongs to the repertoires of very small terrorist circles in a few world regions. Like the demonstration, suicide bombing depends on shared knowledge of a complex set of relations and routines.

The same holds for other performances and repertoires elsewhere, even the kidnapping, bombing, and guerrilla warfare of today's Chechnya and Colombia. Participants in Chechen and Colombian contention have learned these routines but not—at least not yet—street demonstrations and suicide bombing. Every contentious repertoire everywhere excludes most forms of claim making that would be technically possible in their settings. Contentious interaction takes place within limits set by political opportunity structure, regime controls, and available repertoires.

Political strategists themselves do not think in terms of political opportunity structure, regime controls, and available repertoires. But they do commonly take existing institutions into account. Within any particular regime, institutions include established, organized, widely recognized routines, connections, and forms of organization employed repeatedly in producing collective action. If you initiate politically contentious interaction in a parliamentary democracy such as France or Japan, you will almost certainly have to consider the presence of a legislature, an executive, and a judiciary, but also think about the relation of your claim making to political parties, labor unions, voluntary associations, economic organizations, religious congregations, and educational institutions, as well as to such routines as electoral campaigns, national holidays, television watching, and sporting events. Every one of them establishes some kind of audience, opportunity, or threat for your contentious claims.

In a religiously run regime such as today's Iran, in contrast, potential claim makers face a quite different institutional environment. There, they have to make their way through complex religious hierarchies and divisions but give less weight to voluntary associations and labor unions. Still other institutions prevail and channel contention in oil sheikhdoms such as Kuwait, military regimes such as Myanmar (formerly Burma), and fragmented warlord regimes such as Somalia. Both inside participants and outside analysts need institutional maps to navigate a regime's contentious politics.

Identity, standing, and program claims and their certification all vary tremendously as a function of prevailing institutions within one regime or another. In Iran, Baha'is once constituted a substantial religious minority. The Muslim victors of the 1979 revolution slaughtered some of them, sent others into exile, and drove the rest underground. These days some Iranian Baha'is surely exist and connect in private. But in a regime dominated by Shiite Muslims, Baha'i activist groups would have no chance of recognition for their distinctive identity, much less opportunity to firm standing within the regime or advancement of programs for religious reform.

The institutional context for identity, standing, and program claims looks quite different in the United States. In the United States, the (partial) successes of women's rights and civil rights advocates institutionalized the recognition of excluded populations as being deprived of rights to equal treatment. That model facilitated identity and standing claims on behalf of gay and lesbian rights, Indian rights, rights of the disabled, and rights of those not yet born. It also promoted program claims on behalf of remedial action in recognition of minority rights. To be sure, in the United States, programs based on rights claims never succeed fully, often fail, and sometimes generate fierce counterclaims. Today, claims to abortion rights and rights to life clash every day. The point is not that regimes automatically grant certain kinds of identity, standing, and program claims. Instead, what sorts of identity, standing, and program claims are even possible varies remarkably from one regime to another. This variance occurs because institutional contexts differ so dramatically from regime to regime. Now we can address our fifth question: What kinds of effects do collective claims produce, and how?

How Claims Produce Effects

Identity, standing, and program claims produce their effects in different ways. In each case we must distinguish between immediate and longer-term effects.

Identity claims announce a boundary, a set of relations within the boundary, a set of relations across the boundary, plus some meanings attributed to relations and boundaries. Contentious interaction frequently triggers attempts to change those boundaries. The American civil rights movement did not simply produce a wave of policy changes; it also triggered a process of identity reassessment in the black community. After the Montgomery bus boycott, Martin Luther King Jr. asserted a new definition of Montgomery's "Negroes." Said King, "In Montgomery we walk in a new way. We hold our heads in a new way" (Burns 1997: 244). This was but the first in a broad process of claiming not only new boundaries between whites and blacks, but creating a new African American identity distinct from old white-enforced stereotypes.

The implication was clear: The civil rights movement was more than an instrumental effort to change bus seating laws, establish voting rights, or improve educational access for African Americans; it was the expression of a new collective identity among southern blacks, a clear and highly consequential example of identity shift as an outcome of contentious interaction (McAdam et al. 2001: 319–20).

Standing claims generally produce their effects on a smaller number of actors who have some power to certify. Members of the general public may have opinions about the claims of an actor to membership in an established political category, and individual politicians may oppose or support those claims, but in most cases a very limited number of courts, legislatures, committees, or organizations actually have effective power to certify—to say not only that X has an authentic claim to be a Y but also that we, the certifying authority, will act to support the claim.

Since World War II, for example, thousands of self-identified spokespersons for different peoples have made standing claims for recognition of their populations as distinctive nations deserving political autonomy. But only about a hundred of them have actually received certification from the United Nations as recognized independent states. As state recognition illustrates, successful standing claims can produce serious effects, including authorization in such weighty matters as creating armies and contracting international loans.

Program claims take very diverse forms. For that reason, tracing their effects takes us into the heart of analyzing contentious politics in general (Giugni, McAdam, and Tilly 1998, 1999; Meyer et al. 2005). The effectiveness of program claims depends in part on the prior effectiveness of identity and standing claims: Is this a recognizable, credible actor that has the right to make such demands? If the answer is yes, the struggle has just begun. Could and would the objects of program claims actually make the changes or yield the resources the contentious actor is demanding? How will third parties, including governments, react to the claims? These questions take us into the thick of contentious negotiation.

Notice what has been going on in this chapter. It has provided more detail on the basic descriptive concepts of political actors and political identities, which you first met in chapter 1. At the same time, it has brought into play all the other descriptive concepts: government, contentious performances, contentious repertoires, social movements, regimes, institutions, and political opportunity structure. From the book's basic explanatory concepts, it has drawn especially on mechanisms and processes, such as certification and mobilization. But it has also connected these concepts with

- sites of contention—for example, Armenia and Azerbaijan;
- conditions—for example, relations of Armenia and Azerbaijan to the disintegrating Soviet Union;
- streams of contention—for example, interactions among the Zapatistas, their domestic allies, their international supporters, and the Mexican government between 1994 and 2001;
- outcomes—for example, the success of the Zapatistas in maintaining a previously forbidden form of organization;
- episodes—for example, the occupation of western Azerbaijan by Armenian troops.

In a very preliminary way, this chapter has also tried out the basic steps in the mechanism-process approach to explaining contention: describing sites of contention by means of the major descriptive concepts, describing conditions at those sites in the same terms, identifying the streams of contention that need explaining, specifying which outcomes of those streams deserve attention, breaking the streams into episodes of contention, searching the episodes for crucial mechanisms, reconstructing the processes containing those mechanisms, and (using analogies or comparisons with similar processes elsewhere) combining conditions, mechanisms, and processes into explanations of the specified outcomes. The small sketches of Parisian demonstrators, of Mexico's Zapatistas, of nationalist mobilizations in the disintegrating Soviet Union, and of Armenian-Azerbaijani struggles over Karabakh give no more than a forecast of the more extended explanatory work of later chapters. But at least they recall our basic explanatory strategy.

Two opposite processes have repeatedly shown up in the chapter's analyses: mobilization and demobilization. They matter so much to contentious politics, however, that they deserve a special discussion of their own. That is the next chapter's mission.

5

In 1956, Hungarian soldiers prepare for a Soviet attack
as the Soviet Union gets ready to crush a Hungarian bid
for more freedom. (Copyright © Bettmann/CORBIS)

CHAPTER FIVE

MOBILIZATION AND DEMOBILIZATION

We begin this chapter with a little-known episode: occupation of a church in the French city of Lyons by a group of irate prostitutes whom the police were badgering. We use it to describe the most central process in contentious politics—mobilization—taking that process apart to examine its component mechanisms. We then turn to mobilization's mechanisms, especially interactive ones that connect challengers to opponents, third parties, and the public. Next we turn to more complex episodes of contention: first to the protest cycles of Italy and Guatemala in the 1960s and the 1980s, and then to the revolutionary upsurge in the former Soviet Union after 1989. In between, we take up a key process that distinguishes these major episodes of contention from local ones like the prostitutes' protest in Lyons—*scale shift*. We conclude the chapter with an examination of the counterpart of mobilization: *demobilization*. Here too, we find many differences in the scale, the impact, and the outcomes of contention. But despite the differences, we find a surprising number of common mechanisms among (1) simple episodes of contention like the Lyonnais protest in France, (2) cycles of contention like those that occurred in Italy and Guatemala, and (3) major tides of contention like the one that destroyed the Soviet Union.

A Failed Occupation in Lyons

Prostitutes would seem to be an unlikely group from whom to expect mobilization into contentious politics. Working illegally and under the "protection" of procurers, they maintain tense relations with the police and public authorities. Much of the public, furthermore, shuns them.

Indeed, even when they organize on behalf of their claims, prostitutes remain vulnerable to repression and defection—and ultimately to demobilization. Lilian Mathieu's (2001) analysis of the occupation of a church in Lyons emphasizes the unusual properties of prostitutes' protests, but it also reveals modal patterns of contentious trajectories that we have found elsewhere.

Following the exposure of a clamorous case of police corruption involving prostitution in Lyons in August 1972, French police ratcheted up the level of suppression of prostitutes and closed down the *hôtels de passe* to which they took their clients, some of which were owned by corrupt police officers. In response, a small group of prostitutes organized a march against the penalties, which they claimed had more to do with cleaning house in a corrupt police force than protecting the morals of the public. In a hallowed routine from the Lyonnais repertoire, the march was supposed to end at the state prefecture. But the unsuspecting women, led by an apparently friendly squad of police, allowed themselves to be led to the police station instead. Dispersion, recrimination, and humiliation at the hands of the media followed (Mathieu 2001: 110).

For several reasons, it was hard for the Lyonnais prostitutes to gear themselves up for public protest. First, like many other unpracticed actors, they suffered from what economist Mancur Olson (1968) calls the "collective action problem." Olson holds that, except in small groups, most people with claims prefer to leave it to those with a larger stake in those claims to represent them. This phenomenon produces the paradox that many claims with genuinely strong support will remain unrealized because the mobilization needed to gain satisfaction for them is missing. It takes strong organization (McCarthy and Zald 1978), determined leadership, or the onset of new opportunities and threats for ordinary people to overcome their collective action problem. The Lyonnais prostitutes possessed none of these.

Second, many social actors face cultural, economic, and social impediments to engaging in public politics. Think of the Saudi Arabian women who tried, and failed, to gain the right to drive a car by actually doing so after the Gulf War of 1991. Police sent them home and warned their husbands to keep their women under tighter control. Prostitutes work in the shadow of the law, their profession frequently hidden from families and friends, and their lives closely controlled by their procurers. Participating in a public march or demonstration would expose them to the ridicule of the press, the condemnation of public authorities, and possibly beatings from their pimps.

Nevertheless, when police pressures on the Lyonnais sex trade intensified after the failed protest, a group of prostitutes formed an informal collective. They gained the support of a progressive Catholic group, "Le Nid"—what John McCarthy and Mayer Zald (1978) would call "conscience constituents." By this term, McCarthy and Zald mean those who support another group or a cause—not because they would profit if its claims were realized, but out of sympathy, solidarity, or ideological commitment. Le Nid offered the prostitutes legal services and helped to legitimate and publicize their cause. Encouraged by the recent appointment of two prominent women to the national government, they also sought the support of France's fledgling feminist movement. Braced by the support of these allies and by the more favorable publicity it brought them, the Lyonnais prostitutes moved from contained to transgressive contention.

That transition occurred gradually. Like many claim makers, the prostitutes first approached public authorities with a letter. But the Prefect of the Rhône rebuffed them. When some of their number received prison sentences, a small group decided to abandon institutional channels and chose a more transgressive performance—the occupation of a church (Mathieu 2001: 115). For members of a despised and competitive constituency, occupying a closed church had two advantages. First, it provided them with a "free space" in which to build solidarity (Evans and Boyte 1992). Second, it allowed them to demonstrate their claims without revealing their identities. Such a performance had achieved success in France when illegal migrants used it a few years before. (It would later become a standard part of the French contentious repertoire.)

Nevertheless, the occupation of the church of Saint-Nizier failed. Breaking with long-standing precedent, the police burst into the building without the prior permission of the local bishop and escorted the occupiers out. Once outside the "free space" of the church, demobilization came rapidly and bitterly. Despite efforts at concealment, the identities of many of the occupants became known, tensions with their pimps rose, and several of the leaders used their newfound notoriety to leave the profession. The episode also divided the fledgling feminist movement between those who wanted to defend the rights of exploited women, whoever they are, and others who opposed prostitution as the exploitation of women. Soon the allies who had sustained and guided the occupation moved off into more conventional causes, and most of the women were back on the street. As in many episodes of contention, what began with enthusiasm and solidarity ended in disillusionment and recrimination (Mathieu 2001: 129; Zolberg 1972).

Yet the occupation of the church of Saint-Nizier did not fail completely. First, the campaign diffused to other cities. Then a national conference on the rights of sex workers took place in a renowned Parisian meeting hall, and prostitutes met with a magistrate who had been charged by the government to write a report about their problems. What was really new was the prostitutes' newfound capacity to frame their status as exploited workers instead of as social parasites. In doing so, they slightly shifted the boundary that divided them from the rest of society. Subsequent protests on the part of prostitutes in France and elsewhere would all be framed as claims on behalf of workers' rights (Jenness 1993).

Mobilization and Its Mechanisms

We begin this chapter with a prostitutes' protest to underscore the underlying messages of our book: that contentious episodes are all around us; that they involve contentious interaction among claim makers, their allies, their opponents, the government, the media, and the mass public; and that their rise and fall describe a trajectory of mobilization and demobilization involving interactions among these actors. These broad processes decompose into a number of constituent mechanisms, some of which we have already encountered. Together they help to explain the emergence of mobilization, how it tips into demobilization, but also how it sometimes rises into major cycles of contention or even revolutions.

The occupation of the church of Saint-Nizier was a simple episode. In contrast, cycles of contention consist of many such episodes, some of them intersecting, but many responding to the same changes in opportunities and threats. In most such cycles, contention begins moderately and in interaction with institutions. It leads to heightened conflict and greater intensity of interaction across the social system; diffuses rapidly from more mobilized to less mobilized sectors; produces flurries of innovation in the forms of contention; broadens issues as new actors enter the fray; and can produce new identities as aggregates of actors merge in the course of contentious interaction (Brockett 2005; Klandermans 1991; Koopmans 2004; Kriesi et al. 1995; Mueller 1999; Tarrow 1989). We can see all these dynamics and others in the cycle of contention that broke out in Italy in the late 1960s.

By the early 1960s, as its supply of cheap labor from the South dried up, Italy's postwar political-economic model was imploding (McAdam et al. 2001: chap. 2; Tarrow 1989). When Cold War tensions eased and secu-

larization eroded Catholic political dominance, the contradictions built
into the growth model began to sharpen. A spurt of industrial conflict in
the early 1960s warned leaders that changes had to be made. They won
a brief reprieve by bringing the socialists into the government, leaving
their Communist allies isolated in opposition (Ginsborg 1990: chap. 8).
Reforms followed, but each attempted reform either triggered a conservative backlash (as did the nationalization of electricity) or opened the
floodgates to broader contention (as did the passage of a modern industrial
relations law).

When the explosion came in the late 1960s, it surprised those who
had feared a Communist-led working-class onslaught. The first mobilization came from a social actor *outside* the Communist Party's traditional
subculture: the middle-class student population. It was significant of
the new identities emerging in the student population that the earliest
outbreaks took place in both the secular Universities of Turin and Pisa
and at Catholic centers of learning in Milan and Trento. Reflecting the
remaining potency of Italy's Marxist subculture, the insurgents framed
their demands in workers' terms. But their links to the industrial working
class remained weak. The wave of student contention did spread to the
high schools as many college students returned home and told younger
siblings what they had done. But by 1969, the main force of university-
based rebellion had subsided (Tarrow 1989).

A second wave of contention began even before the first had spent itself.
Stimulated by the students' example, by the new industrial relations law,
and by Vietnam-era inflation, contention spread to the factories (Franzosi
1995). The Hot Autumn of worker insurgency first stayed concentrated
within the North's large factories. Then it became especially violent among
the new wave of semiskilled mass workers who had entered the workforce in the miracle years of the 1950s. Skilled and white-collar workers
who had enjoyed higher wages responded to the successes of these mass
workers by demanding the preservation of wage differentials. Militant
workers used a variety of new forms of contention that the unions had
not dared to employ. The unions, anxious not to be outflanked, quickly
took hold of working-class insurgency and moved sharply to the left in
their demands and their ideology.

In the Italian cycle, we find many of the mechanisms of mobilization
we saw on a smaller scale in the occupation of the church in Lyons: challengers perceiving and seizing political opportunities, appropriating organizations and social networks, and innovating in the inherited repertoire.
They also formed alliances across the secular/religious divide, shifting

boundaries and forging new collective identities. New organizations, such as Potere Operaio and Lotta Continua, tried to broker ties between worker and student contention. Occupation of university buildings mimicked performances that the students had observed in Berkeley and at Columbia, but it also revived an Italian tradition of factory occupations. When students went home on vacation in the summer of 1968, they diffused the message of their claims to others, including younger brothers and sisters in the secondary school system, who started their own acts of protest during the following year.

Of course, students and workers interacted in different ways within the structure of political opportunities. For both, splits in the elite created opportunities for contention. And the presence of allies within and outside government helped to convince both groups that their claims might be well received: The Socialist Party in government restrained police repression, while the Communists in opposition tried to profit from the new climate of contention by putting reform proposals on the agenda. For the students, however, the Vietnam War and debates about educational reform opened up opportunities. For the workers, inflation and full employment expanded their leverage.

But these factors alone do not explain why contention in Italy rose to the national level and lasted as long as it did. Why, for example, did it not remain at the local level as the occupation of the church of Saint-Nizier had? Our concept of "scale shift" helps us to see the differences between a simple episode of contention (e.g., the occupation of the church of Saint-Nizier) and more substantial cycles of contention (e.g., the Italian one and the ethnic and nationalist movements that caused the Soviet Union to implode).

Scale Shift

Most episodes of contention begin locally. If some process were not expanding contention upward, there would be no national or international waves of contention. Scale shift is a complex process that not only diffuses contention across space or social sectors, but creates instances for new coordination at a higher or a lower level than its initiation. *Downward scale shift* is the coordination of collective action at a more local level than its initiation. A good example is when civil rights groups responded to the Supreme Court's striking down of racial discrimination at the national level by registering African American voters in Mississippi (McAdam 1988).

In contrast, *upward scale shift* involves coordination of collective action at a higher level (whether regional, national, or even international) than its initiation. A general strike touched off by a dramatic or successful local action is a common example of upward scale shift. Another is the expansion of suicide bombing in the Middle East from a hidden tactic of insurgents in Lebanon to the basic weapon of Islamist militancy (Pedahzur and Perliger 2006). We also saw upward scale shift in the British antislavery campaign when thousands of local petitions were forwarded to Parliament.

Upward scale shift is one of the most significant processes in contentious politics. It moves contention beyond its local origins, touches on the interests and values of new actors, involves a shift of venue to sites where contention may be more or less successful, and can threaten other actors or entire regimes. In the France of May 1968, arrest of a small group of student activists from the University of Nanterre triggered a major national explosion of strikes and protests that threatened the stability of the republic. Chapter 8 will show us scale shift from the national to the international level when former Chilean dictator Augusto Pinochet was accused of human rights violations by a Spanish judge and held for a time in Britain.

Figure 5.1 describes two main routes through which upward scale shift can operate: a *direct diffusion* route that passes through individuals and groups whose previous contacts or similarities become the basis of their mobilization, and a *mediated route* through brokers who connect people who would otherwise have no previous contacts. We saw an example of the first route in Venezuela, when a group of nationalist army officers organized a secret network and tried to seize power. We saw the second route when Clarkson connected local antislavery groups in England into a national movement. Both examples of scale shift began with local actions; each ended with coordination at higher levels of the polity (Tarrow and McAdam 2005).

Scale shift involves many of the mechanisms we have met before: diffusion, as people learn about episodes of contention elsewhere; brokerage, as movement missionaries or opportunistic political entrepreneurs make connections among groups that would otherwise be isolated from one another. It also involves emulation, as people imitate the performances that early risers have invented, and it can create an attribution of similarity among people who did not know one another earlier or may have seen each other as strangers. In other words, cycles and revolutions can create new identities.

Upward scale shift makes a big difference to contention. It leads to new coordination at a different level. We see a major difference between

Figure 5.1. Alternative Routes to Upward Scale Shift
Source: Tarrow and McAdam (2005: 128).

single episodes of mobilization such as the occupation of the church of Saint-Nizier and the cycle of mobilization that burst on the scene in Italy in the 1960s. Contentious actors often deliberately "venue shop" in order to seek coordination at a level more favorable to them. This was the strategy of the National Association for the Advancement of Colored People (NAACP) in taking school discrimination to the Supreme Court in the 1950s. In Italy, as wildcat strikes spread from large factories in the North to smaller ones and to central and southern Italy, coordination shifted upward to collective bargaining within entire sectors and to the national level. As student occupations spread from major universities in the North to the rest of the country and to the high schools, the parties of government and opposition pieced together a new educational reform. As police and demonstrators clashed in a number of different cities, a new practice of protest policing was adopted, along lines that had already emerged in the United States (della Porta, Fillieule, and Reiter 1998).

Many of these shifts in scale had the effect of institutionalizing contention. Even the innovative forms of contention that emerged in 1967–1969—the factory occupation, the university sit-in, the assembly in the place of work—were eventually routinized. But some trends within the movement organizations engendered by the 1967–1969 period escalated the scale of contention and exacerbated conflicts between groups. To understand the mixture between institutionalization and violence, we turn to the mechanisms of demobilization.

Mechanisms of Demobilization

From decades of research on social movements, we know a great deal about the conditions and dynamics of mobilization, but we know far less about how contentious actors demobilize. Do they simply disperse after their claims are made, from either satisfaction or disillusionment? Do governments repress them or co-opt them into tranquility? Or do internal divisions lead to factional splits and polarization? How inevitable is demobilization? Do claim makers inevitably give up when the enthusiasm of the struggle wanes or when political opportunities disappear? Or do they turn to more institutional forms of participation when the initial flush of enthusiasm has passed (Piven and Cloward 1977)?

Most mobilization processes eventually reverse themselves. How they do so depends on the initial conditions of mobilization, on the strategy of elites and authorities in response to challengers' claims, and on the degree to which they provide themselves with enduring structures to maintain their solidarity. Remember what happened to the occupiers of the church of Saint-Nizier? After the initial excitement of their mobilization, some lost heart and returned to the street, others used their experience to leave the sex trade, and the state, in the form of the Lyons police, broke up the occupation.

In that story, we see a number of mechanisms and processes that led to demobilization:

- *Competition* among different sources of support—the feminist movement and the Catholic social activists—and the diverging goals of the main actors and their supporters

- *Defection,* as some leaders used the experience as a channel to leave the sex trade
- *Disillusionment,* as others—both leaders and followers—became embittered by their experience with collective action
- *Repression,* both direct, as the police evacuated the church, and indirect, as authorities worked to suppress prostitution by imposing fines on those who were arrested
- A modest degree of *institutionalization,* as the state invited them to meet with the magistrate investigating their problems.

We will see competition, defection, disillusion, repression, and institutionalization combining to different degrees in a number of episodes of contentious politics to produce demobilization. The Italian case illustrates them with particular force because of the great degree of scale shift that the cycle of contention had reached by the early 1970s.

Italian Demobilization

Three facts about the Italian student and worker mobilization made a difference to demobilization, especially when compared to the contemporary French Events of May:

- The Italian May started earlier, lasted longer, caused greater mayhem, and brought about more death and destruction than the French one.
- While the French Events of May had the indirect effect of eroding the republic's tight central control and ushered in the fall from power of the Gaullist Party, Italy's more volatile and longer period of disorder left the Christian Democratic Party in power until it lost out in the political earthquake of the 1990s.
- By the mid-1970s, little was left of the initial enthusiasm, solidarity, and utopianism typical of initial episodes of contention.

What explains this pattern of longer duration and less political impact? When Tarrow disaggregated the Italian cycle into its component performances, he discovered some striking differences in the incidence of different kinds of performances over the near-decade from 1966 to 1974. The majority of the events he uncovered were *conventional.* They included routine performances of petitions, audiences, strikes, marches, and demonstrations—the latter often performed in ways calculated to

REMEMBER THE INSTITUTIONALIZATION OF DEMONSTRATIONS

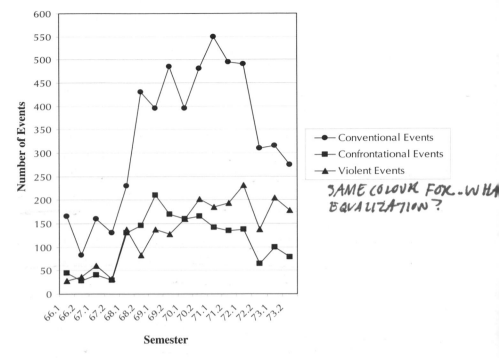

Figure 5.2. Italian Contention, 1966–1973
Source: Tarrow (1989: 70).

attract the attention of the media (Tarrow 1989). But systematic analysis of Italian events over a period of years also showed that large minorities of the events were *confrontational*—direct actions intended to inhibit or upset the lives of targets, objects, and third parties. Another minority was deliberately *violent*—attacks on property, opponents of the claimants, state actors, or third parties.

Figure 5.2 traces the trajectories of these three forms of Italian contention through the years of the Italian "stretched-out May." It shows data on all forms of contention gathered from Italy's major newspaper of record, the *Corriere della Sera,* from 1966 through 1973. Notice how, at its emergence in 1968-1969, the Italian protest cycle contained a relative majority of disruptive events—creative, "in your face" performances designed to draw attention to the protesters, enhance their solidarity, and gain new adherents. The typical disruptive protest was the faculty or factory occupation—exactly the sort of eye-catching performance we saw in Lyons during 1975. This was the period in which students and workers attempted to construct new collective identities, formed loosely coupled informal organizations, and challenged authorities with demands that could not easily be negotiated but also could not be ignored (Pizzorno 1978).

The disruptive part of the cycle soon gave way to a wave of more conventional events and to the routinization of the innovative performances of 1968. Conventional events reached a peak of more than five hundred events during the first half of 1971, only to fall off significantly during the next two years. Many involved the heirs of the 1967–1968 period, but they were more organized, more routinized, and aimed at achieving specific programmatic claims. This infuriated the more extreme sectors of the former student movement, which led them to form new extraparliamentary groups that sought new identities competing with the institutional parties of the Left. It also outraged right-wing groups, which began to organize clandestinely to oppose what they saw as the threat from the left. Violent clashes between extreme left-wing and extreme right-wing groups resulted from this mutual radicalization.

The tempo of these violent events started slowly but reached over four hundred per year by 1970. Violence first appeared in clashes with the police and wars over turf between rival groups of left-wing and right-wing students. The extraparliamentary groups' "services of order," created to discipline marchers and fend off opponents, spawned militant cells that specialized in violence. Out of these experiences came the organized "armed struggle" of the 1970s and such militarized groups as the Red Brigades (della Porta 1995). Once police began to pursue them, their only possible form of action was "the propaganda of the deed." By 1973, the number of violent events had declined. But they had become ever more lethal, shifting from street fights between rival left-wing and right-wing gangs to organized terror.

Just as extremist groups were outbidding each other with violent attacks and confrontations and giving the impression that public order was breaking down, most of the events in the catalog were actually conventional: ordinary strikes, assemblies, and demonstrations that soon institutionalized. The dynamic of the protest cycle lay exactly here: Enthusiastic students and workers began the cycle with creative—but nonviolent—disruptive protests. Conventional collective actions soon surpassed them in frequency and lasted longer. Competition, repression, and escalation led to violence and to organized terror.

In the face of so much violent contention, how did the cycle end? The answer turns on the interaction between institutionalization and violence. Responding to this puzzle, della Porta and Tarrow (1986) traced the pathways from mobilization to demobilization through two contradictory yet mutually dependent processes: *escalation* and *institutionalization.* Combining Tarrow's protest event data set with della Porta's data on organized terrorism, they developed the following explanation:

> Masses of ordinary people who erupt into the streets and out of the factories are soon discouraged by the boredom, repression, and desire for a routine life that eventually affects most protesters. Those who lead them respond to this decline in demand and enthusiasm in one of two opposing ways:
>
> * By *institutionalization:* the substitution of the routines of organized politics for the disorder of life in the streets, buttressed by mass organization and purposive incentives
> * By *escalation:* the substitution of more extreme goals and more robust tactics for more moderate ones in order to maintain the interest of their supporters and attract new ones
>
> Repression exacerbates these two processes and links them. Repression accelerates the demobilization of those with a low level of involvement, and it isolates those whose involvement is most intense into a clandestine world in which their only means of expression is violence.

The opposite pathways intersect: Institutionalization turns off those whose interest in public life is unsatisfied by the routines of everyday politics, leading to alienation from politics or defection to the extremes. Escalation scares off timid souls and motivates them to move into institutional politics or the relative safety of private life. The result is *polarization*—increasing ideological distance between the wings of a once unified movement sector, divisions between its leaders, and, in some cases, terrorism. The Italian protest cycle ended in a paroxysm of organized violence but also in the routinization of contention. In Italy, escalation and institutionalization, fed by repression, formed two sides of demobilization's coin.

Do cycles of contention leave nothing behind but disillusionment and defection? Critics of the 1960s like to tell stories about former activists who turned into pillars of the establishment. But major cycles of contention do not always end in disillusionment and defection. First, many who have earned their spurs in the "high-risk activism" of these cycles enter more conventional activist careers, such as the veterans of the Mississippi Freedom Summer campaign that McAdam studied (1988). When McAdam sought them out in the 1980s, many had moved from civil rights to the women's movement, peace activism, and environmentalism.

Second, the themes of a cycle often imprint the routines of future activists, much as once-innovative performances become part of the repertoire of contention. David Snow and Robert Benford (1992) traced such "master frames" in cycles of protest like the American 1960s. They found that master frames both encapsulate existing frames (e.g., the traditional American "rights frame") and leave a heritage for future movements. Thus, in the United States, the rights frame around which African Americans mobilized in the 1950s and 1960s eventually reappeared in campaigns by Native Americans, women, gays, and lesbians and even in campaigns on behalf of animals and the unborn.

Other Cycles, Different Outcomes

The American cycle of contention began much as the Italian one did—in conflicts within institutions, such as the judiciary's processing of the educational claims of African Americans or the conflict over the denial of the vote for that racial group in Congress. That cycle, too, expanded into broader claims that could not, without significant conflict and reform, be processed within American institutions. And, as in Italy, it ended in a combination of escalation and institutionalization.

Think about the transformation of the Students for a Democratic Society (SDS) into the Weather Underground during the anti–Vietnam War period, just as many other activists were forming public interest groups or entering the Democratic Party. Consider how radical offshoots of the nonviolent civil rights movement gave rise to the Black Panthers and the Symbionese Liberation Army as former civil rights leaders were running for Congress. Here, too, successful challengers filled available niches in the regime while repression put down latecomers and unruly makers of claims.

Not all cycles stay within the existing regime, filling existing niches or suffering repression, as the Italian and American ones of the 1960s did. In some cases, what begins as a cycle of mobilization spirals upward into civil war in response to weak regimes that respond to contention with indiscriminate repression (Sambanis and Zinn 2003). Charles Brockett's (2005) study of Guatemalan and Salvadoran contention reveals this process dramatically. Between 1974 and 1981, as we saw in chapter 2, a cycle of protest arose across Guatemalan society, culminating in a major rural insurgency and in organized violence by and against the Guatemalan regime. Figure 5.3 shows the trajectory of contention in Guatemala during these years.

Figure 5.3 combines Brockett's data for four broad types of contention: strikes and student strikes, peaceful demonstrations, occupations

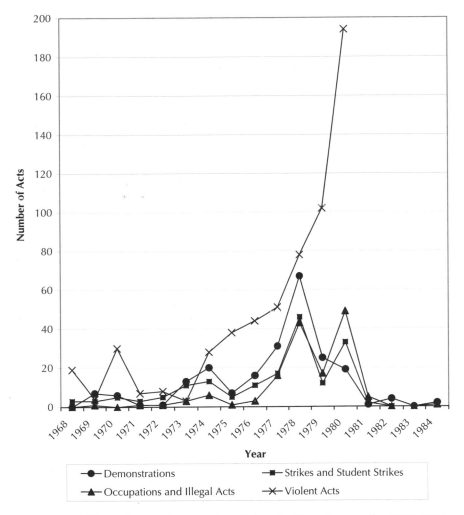

Figure 5.3. Different Forms of Contentious Politics by Year, Guatemala, 1968–1984
Source: Brockett (2005: 176–83).

and other illegal acts, and organized violence. (Note that the record of organized violence that Brockett traced cuts off in 1980, because the conditions of civil war in that decade made it impossible to collect even approximate data.) Brockett's data show that what resembles a cycle of mobilization can escalate into a civil war under some conditions. In still other conditions, even these boundaries are broken as new or resurgent political identities developed in the course of contention give rise to waves of contention that combine to destroy the existing polity. We call these major waves of contention *revolutions.* This is what happened in the Soviet Union between the late 1980s and early 1990s.

Mobilization and Demobilization in the Soviet Union

Nationalism is a political program, or rather two competing programs. From the top down, rulers insist that because they run the state, they have the right to decide what definition of national culture will prevail, who will define the national interest, and when the national interest should trump parochial interests. From the bottom up, leaders of distinct ethnic categories or formerly independent states claim that because they constitute distinct nationalities, they deserve political autonomy or even states of their own.

For several centuries, an expanding Russian empire conquered and incorporated dozens of previously distinct nationalities—for example, Poles, Belarussians, and dozens of Siberian populations. With the Bolshevik Revolution of 1917, many regional leaders tried to escape Russian control. Finland, for example, established its precarious independence from Russia after a civil war. By the early 1920s, however, V. I. Lenin and Leon Trotsky had managed to recapture most of the fugitive territories. From that time on, top-down Soviet nationalism prevailed. It sustained massive transformation of the national economy and an amazing military effort during World War II.

It prevailed, however, with an interesting difference. In general, the Soviet Union assigned a titular nationality to each non-Russian region. In the Kazakh Republic, for example, Kazakhs became the titular nationality despite the region's majority of non-Kazakhs. Moscow's rulers made Russian the Soviet Union's dominant language. But they also tolerated or even promoted the teaching of the titular nationality's language in its region, celebration of its cultural history, and recruitment of its talented members into the USSR's political, economic, and intellectual elite. (Georgia-born

Joseph Stalin, after all, was bilingual in Russian and Georgian, speaking Russian with a Georgian accent.) Heads of regional governments and Communist parties commonly came from members of the titular nationality who had proven their competence and loyalty in Moscow.

Soviet ethnic tolerance had its limits. Jews, for example, had been an important component of the original Bolshevik Party. They received linguistic and cultural rights after the 1917 revolution. Yet as a titular nationality they found themselves relegated to a small, poor republic near the Chinese border, Birobaijan. More cruelly, Jews also saw their synagogues closed down and suffered increasing repression after World War II. But Jews were not alone in suffering from repression. During World War II, Stalin had almost the entire population of the Chechen Republic deported to Kazakhstan because he suspected them of disloyalty. Nevertheless, on the whole, Soviet rulers governed outside Russia by means of assigned national identities (Garcelon 2001; Kaiser 1994; Khazanov 1995; Laitin 1998, 1999; Martin 2001; Olcott 2002; Suny 1993; Tishkov 1997, 1999, 2004). That arrangement strongly affected what happened as central control weakened in the Soviet Union.

The arrival of reformer Mikhail Gorbachev at the head of the Soviet Communist Party (1985) touched off an enormous expansion of claim making—not just mass demonstrations, but also special-purpose associations, strikes, press campaigns, and appeals for international support. Although the earlier claims of Soviet dissidents focused on political and economic reform, nationalist demands soon predominated. Russians themselves sometimes demanded special recognition within the Soviet Union; Boris Yeltsin first came to power as a Russian nationalist. But the bulk of the demands centered on recognition, autonomy, or independence for ethnically labeled subdivisions of the Soviet Union such as Estonia, Armenia, and Chechnya.

As we saw in chapter 2, Mark Beissinger (2002) collected a massive body of evidence on Soviet claim making from 1987 to 1992. From a wide variety of sources, he cataloged two sorts of events: public demonstrations of one hundred persons or more, and "mass violent events" in which fifteen or more people gathered to attack persons or property (462-65). Beissinger points out that demonstrations and attacks did occur occasionally in the Soviet Union before Gorbachev began his reform programs. In April 1965, for example, one hundred thousand people gathered in Yerevan, Armenia, to commemorate victims of the Ottoman expulsion and massacre of Armenians fifty years earlier (71).

Under that repressive regime, however, both demonstrations and collective attacks by anyone other than state authorities remained very rare. The script ran differently after 1985. Once such Soviet republics as Estonia and Armenia started edging toward independence with foreign support, leaders of titular nationalities across the Soviet Union began making demands for autonomy or independence. Figure 5.4 describes monthly changes from 1987 through 1992.

What began as a largely peaceful process soon radicalized and escalated. In principle, a straightforward cycle could have occurred, as in Italy or the United States in the 1960s: A decentralized USSR could have granted partial autonomy to a certain number of titular nationalities, incorporated them into its governing structure, repressed the more unruly and threatening claimants, and returned to a revised version of Soviet business as usual. At one point, Gorbachev actually tried to do just this but failed. Instead, fifteen nationalities gained total independence, others acquired rights they had never enjoyed under Soviet rule, and what Beissinger calls a "tide of nationalism" emerged. In the process, the polity known as the Soviet Union disappeared.

Beissinger explains the sequence as a consequence of a modified political cycle. Early risers, on average, either gained some advantages or demobilized peacefully. But those who persisted despite previous failures or arrived on the scene late encountered rising resistance and engaged increasingly in claim making that incited or entailed violence. If the latecomers' program centered on political autonomy or independence, violence from both sides occurred more often. Thus, Beissinger's "tide," which had begun through the same mechanisms of mobilization we encountered earlier, produced a dramatically modified version of the dynamics we observed in more contained cycles of contention.

Beissinger's evidence stops at the end of 1992. By then, some demobilization had already occurred among the early risers that gained the autonomies they were seeking. For the full story of mobilization and demobilization in Soviet space, however, we would have to follow newly independent countries such as Ukraine, Georgia, Kazakhstan, Estonia, Armenia, Azerbaijan, and Ukraine separately. As we saw in chapters 1 and 2, most of these regimes mounted new waves of mobilization and demobilization in their post-Soviet phases. Struggles for power within titular nationalities did not end with the Soviet collapse. In fact, the great wave of mobilization that swept over the Soviet Union after Gorbachev's arrival in power provided models for renewed claim making through most of the post-Soviet space.

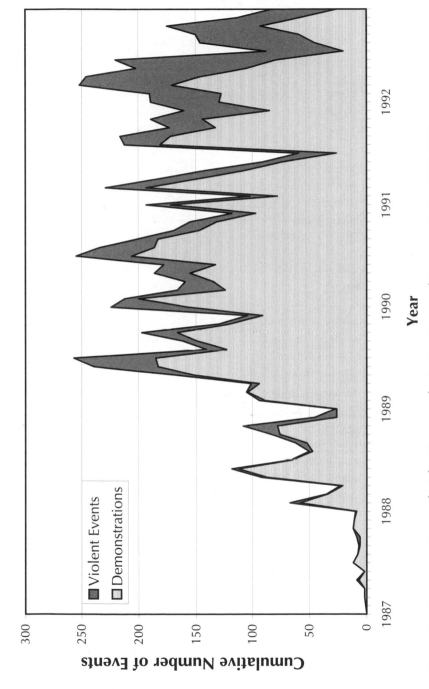

Figure 5.4. Demonstrations and Violent Events in the Soviet Union and Successor States, 1987–1992

Source: Data supplied by Mark Beissinger.

Conclusion

Let us pause briefly to summarize the broad range of cases and many mechanisms we have seen in this chapter. First, we saw that a number of the same mechanisms appeared in contentious episodes of increasing scope and significance. Minor episodes such as the occupation of the church of Saint-Nizier, major cycles such as the Italian protest wave, and continental cataclysms such as the collapse of the Soviet Union resembled each other in many ways. In all three, people used preexisting networks and developed new ones to express their claims, build solidarities, and challenge opponents. In all three, we saw diffusion, brokerage, and new coordination. In all three, demobilization combined escalation, institutionalization, defection, disillusion, and repression.

Do not mistake our message: These were very different contentious phenomena. Elites responded very differently to the occupation of a church in Lyons, the cycle of student and worker protests in Italy, and the tide of nationalism in the Soviet Union. The nature of the claims varied enormously, from the demand to be left alone by Lyons's sex workers, to the much broader but still negotiable claims of most students and workers in Italy, to the call for secession from the USSR on the part of many of the nationalities that now possess their own states.

In all three cases, however, people perceived and seized opportunities, identified and framed claims, mobilized consensus, formed coalitions, and adopted forms of collective action. In all three, elites responded with different combinations of repression and facilitation. If these episodes ended differently—failure for the Lyonnais prostitutes, reintegration for Italian students and workers, revolution in the Soviet Union—that was because their claims making interacted with very different regimes.

Note the implications of our discovery. It means that regularities in trajectories lie elsewhere than in standard sequences, whether scripted episodes, protest cycles, or otherwise. Regularities lie in the mechanisms that bring in new actors, eliminate old ones, transform alliances, and shift the strategies of critical actors. By identifying which mechanisms and processes put an episode of contention in motion and where they take it, we can better understand why some episodes are brief while others are protracted and lead to implosion of regimes and the creation of new ones.

A key combination of mechanisms in our cases is the process we called *upward scale shift*. It largely determined the relative capacity of the actors to create broader social movements out of initial episodes of contention. Even simple episodes sometimes spread widely; recall that prostitutes in other French cities soon copied the occupation of the Saint-Nizier church. Our cycles of contention diffused more broadly. In the Italian case, contention diffused from a few major universities and large factories to provincial universities and high schools as well as to smaller firms throughout the economy.

Contention shifted in scale most broadly in the Soviet Union's spreading tide of nationalism, from Georgia and the Baltic states to Ukraine and Central Asia, and eventually to the national level, as orthodox elements in the Communist Party and the army tried to prevent the disintegration of the regime through a coup d'état in the capital. The protests and demonstrations of each Soviet nationality threatened the position of others, triggering competitive and ultimately system-destroying claims that led the system to implode.

Not all contentious episodes give rise to such scale shift, and few of those that do so endure beyond the end of the cycle. The ones that are most likely to survive draw on preexisting networks or create self-sustaining organizations. Those networks and organizations sustain their claims and recruit new supporters. When those claims involve sustained campaigns, concerted displays of identity, and such means as demonstrations and public meetings, they qualify as social movements. Chapter 6 looks closely and directly at social movements.

During the great strike led by Solidarity at the
Lenin Shipyard in Gdánsk, Poland (August
1980), a priest blesses one of the strikers.
(Photo by Keystone/Getty Images)

CHAPTER SIX
SOCIAL MOVEMENTS

Not all episodes of contention constitute social movements, and not all social movements endure. Remember the definition of the *social movement* from chapter 1: a sustained campaign of claim making, using repeated performances that advertise the claim, based on organizations, networks, traditions, and solidarities that sustain these activities. The first episode we examine in this chapter—Poland in 1956—shows that contention can be widespread and threatening to its regime but fail to survive repression and disorganization. The second episode—Poland's Solidarity in 1980—provides a key by introducing the crucial distinction between social movement bases and social movement campaigns. The shape of institutions and regimes always affects movements. Our third episode shows how the American women's movement interacted with American institutions. We close the chapter with observations on what happens to social movements after their major campaigns end.

Poland's 1956

The year 1956 was a bad one for the Soviet empire that had run East-Central Europe since the end of World War II. In 1953, Soviet leader Josef Stalin had died. The disappearance of the longtime dictator of the USSR left a void that was filled by an unstable "troika" of Communist Party bosses. Nikita Khrushchev was one of them. When Khrushchev emerged at the top of the heap, he tried to consolidate his power by attacking Stalinism. In a dramatic "secret speech" to the delegates of the Twentieth Communist Party Congress, Khrushchev enumerated Stalin's crimes. To underscore how different his own rule would be, Khrushchev called for more pluralism within the party and the bloc.

Announcing Stalin's crimes at a meeting attended by non-Soviet Communist elites was actually a strategy of upward scale shift. If it percolated through the international Communist movement, it would be harder for Khrushchev's Stalinist enemies in the USSR to suppress. Member parties' reactions ranged widely. They ran from rejection in China and uneasy quiet in France, to the embrace of pluralism in Italy, and to an outright revolt in Hungary. More than that, the speech divided many Communist parties internally. That helped to open new and wider opportunities for dissent among the weak and divided oppositions in East-Central Europe, just as it threatened the authoritarian traditions of the ruling parties of these countries.

This combination of opportunity and threat promoted explosions of contentious politics across the Soviet bloc's restive populations. The tragic Hungarian revolution of 1956 attracted the most attention in the West. Hungary was the most "liberal" Communist state in Eastern Europe, and its reform Communists used Khrushchev's secret speech as an opportunity to move gingerly toward a more pluralistic system of government. Even this action was too much for the Soviet Union, which brought tanks into the center of Budapest and smothered the sparks of reform.

Khrushchev's secret speech exacerbated existing internal conflicts between reformers and Stalinists in the Polish Communist Party, the PZPR. Disunity deepened when the relatively liberal Warsaw Party Committee circulated the speech both in Poland and in the West (Osa 2003b: 29). With Stalinists in the leadership thrown off balance, reformers seized the advantage to increase the powers of parliament, replace Stalinist officials, and rehabilitate reform Communist Wladislaw Gomulka. Gomulka soon emerged as party secretary. Divisions within the PZPR led to an opening for dissident groups—a classical case of the opening of political opportunities. "In short," concludes Maryjane Osa (2003b), "de-Stalinization in Poland created an opening for political mobilization" (29-30).

Contention broke out locally in June. A group of workers from the Cygielski factory in Poznan sent a delegation to Warsaw to complain about their working conditions. When the delegation received a runaround in Warsaw and police detained them on their return, angry coworkers organized a march to Poznan's city center. As other workers, students, and local citizens joined them, clashes with authorities ensued. When some of the demonstrators stole arms and stormed party headquarters, the party responded by sending in the troops. But Poland's protest episode in 1956 had no more success than Hungary's revolt. Faced by repression and lacking a solid basis in society, it rose and fell rapidly. Though it raised the hopes of opponents of Communism in Poland and beyond, it lacked the bases for a sustained social movement.

Osa's study of oppositional networks in Poland supports this conclusion. In the period just before 1956, she could identify only three organizations with a significant presence in what she calls "the oppositional domain" (2003b: 45–47). Encouraged by Khrushchev's call for pluralism and by the divisions in the PZPR, Catholics, intellectuals, radical youth, and secular left-wing reformers in 1956 began to organize. The events of 1956–1957 expanded the domain of independent Polish groups fivefold, both increasing the number of active organizations and creating new links among them. But in the conditions of Cold War Poland, such a dense network of organizations couldn't endure, and demobilization soon set in.

In response to the flowering of oppositional groups in 1956–1957, Communist authorities employed a combination of repression and reform: repression of the Poznan workers and reform inside the party (Osa 2003b: 38–39). By 1960, Poles had returned to the state of surly but largely silent dissent characteristic of the pre-1956 period (Osa 2003b: 55). As popular humor put it, "We pretend to work and they pretend to pay us." By the late 1950s, most of the organizations created in the wake of the 1956 events had disappeared from Osa's network maps. No sustained social movement formed in response to the events of 1956.

Social Movement Bases and Social Movement Campaigns

Why begin a chapter on social movements by recalling a protest wave that failed to create a sustained movement? The story of Poland's response to Khrushchev's "secret speech" tells us a number of things.

First, it shows that in authoritarian regimes, social movements are hard to construct, even when contention is widespread. This would change as the regime weakened and new bases for contention appeared.

It also shows how, even in authoritarian regimes, political opportunities grow out of the interaction between contentious and institutional politics. Conflicts and reforms within the ruling party triggered both contention and new forms of organization, which in turn led to grudging reform within the regime and repression against its enemies.

Third, despite its particular properties, Poland in 1956 demonstrates many of the mechanisms of mobilization and demobilization we saw working in chapter 5: response to the opening of opportunities, innovation with different performances, and radicalization in the course of the mobilization. But this combination of mechanisms was not sufficient to produce a social movement.

Why not? In this chapter, we return to a distinction introduced in chapter 1 that will help us to understand the dynamics of social movements both in Poland and wherever they occur: the distinction between a social movement base and a social movement campaign.

- A *social movement base* consists of movement organizations, networks, participants, and the accumulated cultural artifacts, memories, and traditions that contribute to social movement campaigns.
- A *social movement campaign* is a sustained challenge to power holders in the name of a population living under the jurisdiction of those power holders by means of concerted public displays of worthiness, unity, numbers, and commitment, using such means as public meetings, demonstrations, petitions, and press releases.

Some scholars use the term *social movement* to cover most or all of the overlap between contention and collective action, whether it happens in politics or some other arena. In popular usage, it often describes all major changes in society and culture, including scientific, intellectual, and cultural movements (Frickel and Gross 2005). But for purposes of explanation, expansion of the term *social movements* to embrace most or all of contentious politics has three serious drawbacks.

First, such broad definitions make systematic comparison across types of contention difficult. In order to describe and explain contentious politics adequately, we need to identify the special properties of revolutions, military coups, peasant revolts, industrial conflict, and social movements before discovering what they have in common.

Second, so broad a definition makes it difficult to examine transitions between different forms of contention. The conditions that lead an isolated protest to become a social movement are impossible to determine if we raise the umbrella label "social movement" over both. Conversely, we can only understand the failure of contentious episodes like the 1956 events in Poland to generate a sustained movement if we begin with clear boundaries around the concept of movements.

Third, such a broad definition obscures the difference between the bases on which contentious politics builds and the campaigns that launch those politics. While there is a general correlation between the existence of social movement bases and the strength and duration of a campaign, the transition from bases to campaigns is not automatic. It requires the triggering of the sorts of mechanisms and processes we have been presenting in this book.

Remember the British antislavery campaign with which the book began? That campaign built on bases ranging from reformist religious groups—especially the Quakers—to the local newspapers that popularized the cause, to manufacturing towns like Manchester, and to influential elites and members of Parliament. But the campaign depended on Clarkson's writing an essay on slavery, deciding to commit his life to its demise, and forging ties with the Quakers. It also depended on interactions among campaigners, their targets, and influential third parties.

While movement bases tell us when a social movement is possible, a movement campaign is claim making *in motion.* Our distinction between social movement bases and social movement campaigns helps us to sort out the organizations, networks, participants, and traditions that make up a social movement and constitute a movement campaign. It helps to understand why Poland's struggles of 1980, unlike those of 1956, produced a successful social movement.

From Poznan to Solidarity

In the summer of 1980, a strike broke out at the Lenin shipyard in the Baltic port of Gdansk. Like previous outbreaks, it began over largely economic issues. Like other episodes, it escalated to a conflict over the right of the workers to form an independent union (Laba 1991). It also triggered the familiar combination of repression and compromise that Polish authorities had used successfully since 1956 to stalemate, divide, and repress the workers. But, unlike these largely local events, it spread across the country rapidly, paralyzed the government temporarily, led to the recognition of a free trade union, and, ultimately, brought an end to state socialism in East-Central Europe.

The Solidarity strike of 1980 differed from previous Polish episodes of contention in four main ways. First, it enjoyed the certification of the country's most authoritative institution, the Catholic Church. The strike's leaders built an explicit linkage between Poland's national/Catholic heritage and the material demands of workers. Not only had the Polish pope, John Paul II, recently visited the country, but the organizers self-consciously merged Catholic symbols with claims for workers' rights (Kubik 1994).

Second, rapid diffusion moved claim making outward from Gdansk, and a shift in scale upward to the national level occurred. The strike at the Lenin shipyard spread not only to other factories along the Baltic coast but also to industrial centers around the country and into Poland's vast peasant population. In fact, when the shipyard workers voted to accept a management proposal, delegates on the interfactory committee from outside the factory convinced them to hold fast. The rapidity of diffusion and the organization of a solidarity network around the strike center in Gdansk rapidly lifted the scale of the conflict into a national struggle.

Third, repression was more contained in 1980 than in 1956. Polish authorities offered the usual compromises and employed standard divide-and-conquer tactics. But, much to the frustration of Poland's "fraternal" allies in the Soviet Union, the Polish leaders applied only limited repression. This happened in part because the strike paralyzed many different parts of Polish society at once—including parts of the state apparatus—but also because of Poland's growing ties with Western bankers. The government feared that sending tanks in to suppress the strikers would lead to the government's loss of credits from the West.

More than anything, Solidarity's success resulted from expansion of the oppositional domain—its social movement base—in the years after 1956. Since that episode, the oppositional domain had become denser, more diverse, and more centralized—with a few key "nodes" at the heart of a broader map of independent groups. These groups did not start the Gdansk strike or spread the strike to other industrial centers. Many of them, under the rubric of "building civil society," explicitly denied the desire to attack the state (Ost 1990), which helped to protect them from repression. But in 1980, they were ready to swing into action in response to the strike, diffusing it, certifying it, and raising its scale to the national level. Figure 6.1, which reproduces Osa's (2003a) findings, maps the extensive oppositional networks in Poland at the time of the Solidarity strike in 1980.

Do not attempt to memorize the groups in figure 6.1. Use the figure to see how dense the number of Polish oppositional groups and their connections had become by 1980, even in the stifling atmosphere of an authoritarian polity. Osa's corresponding map from 1956, not shown here, displays much less density with many fewer connections. Her 1980 map reveals that when Solidarity emerged on the scene in 1980, it could connect to a dense *social network* of groups and organizations.

Since the 1970s, many social scientists have recognized the importance of social networks in triggering collective action (Diani 1995;

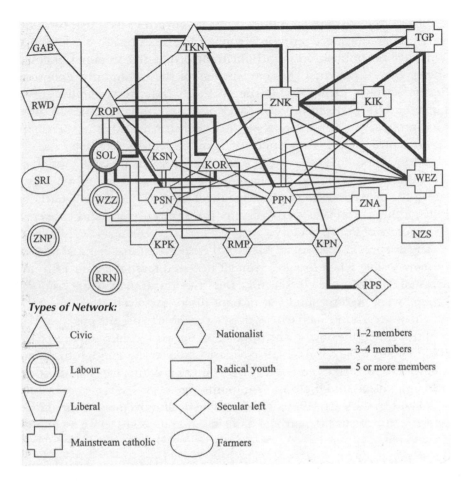

Figure 6.1. Oppositional Networks in Poland, 1980
Source: Osa (2003a: 99).

Diani and McAdam 2003; McAdam 2003). In settings as diverse as the 1848 revolution in Paris (Gould 1995), Republican and Communist China (Perry 1993; Zhao 1998), the 1980s Italian environmental movement (Diani 1995), and post-1960s America (McAdam 1988, 1999), social networks have been shown to be the crucial building blocks of social movements. If the Solidarity strike in Gdansk triggered a national movement, it was largely because, in the intervening years, a broad network of oppositional groups provided its leaders with a social movement base on which to build.

Note three specific factors that Osa's figure reveals. First, by 1980, workers' and farmers' groups belonged to the oppositional network. This gave the opposition a foothold in the productive trenches of Polish society and threatened the mainsprings of the Communist economy. Second, a civic group, KOR (the Worker's Defense Committee), occupied a central position in the network, with brokerage ties to other civic groups, workers, nationalists, and mainstream Catholics (Bernhard 1993). Third, in the years since 1956, and especially following the celebration of the Polish "Great Novena" in the 1960s (Osa 2003b: chap. 2), a dense network of Catholic organizations had formed, which we see in the cluster on the right-hand side of figure 6.1. In heavily Catholic Poland, these groups helped to certify the opposition in many conservative sectors of Polish society.

The deep and broad social bases of the campaign that erupted in 1980 became visible when the government declared martial law in 1981 and arrested Solidarity's leaders. Unlike the situation after 1956, oppositional groups went underground but did not disappear. Even after the crackdown, underground Solidarity activists were able to use the postal system to diffuse their messages. The opposition network continued to expand (Osa 2003b: 163–65). By 1989, Solidarity was strong enough to mount a new wave of strikes and defeat the ruling party in a national election, bringing Poland into the post-Communist age.

Poland in the early 1980s produced a social movement campaign in which many of our familiar mechanisms and processes came together:

- *Social appropriation*: Solidarity built on the country's most legitimate and most powerful institution—the Catholic Church.
- The organizers *certified* their campaign through identification with Catholic symbols and with the memory of the "martyrdom" of victims of past episodes of contention.
- Their movement *diffused and shifted upward in scale* as other organizations that had grown up after the 1956–1957 defeat took up a local conflict on the Baltic coast.

But these mechanisms appeared in many episodes of contention examined earlier that did we not qualify as social movements. What made Polish Solidarity's a *social movement campaign*? Let us see how such campaigns work.

Social Movement Campaigns

The social movement is a particular historical form of contentious politics. As it developed in the West after 1750, movements emerged from an innovative, consequential synthesis of three elements: campaigns, forms of association and action, and public self-representations. Before we turn to an important contemporary exemplar of that form—the new American women's movement—let us specify what these terms mean and illustrate them from the case of Polish Solidarity.

Movement Campaigns

A *campaign* is a sustained, organized public effort making collective claims on targeted authorities. Unlike a onetime petition, declaration, or mass meeting, a *campaign* extends beyond any single event—although social movements often include petitions, declarations, and mass meetings. A campaign always links at least three parties: a group of self-designated claimants, some object(s) of claims, and a public of some kind. The claims may target governmental officials, but the "authorities" in question can also include owners of property, religious functionaries, and others whose actions (or failures to act) significantly affect the welfare of many people.

Even if a few zealots commit themselves to the movement night and day, furthermore, the bulk of participants move back and forth between public claim making and other activities, including the day-to-day organizing that sustains a campaign. The attempt on the part of Solidarity to gain the right to an independent union for Polish workers was a campaign, one that centered on the strike committee in Gdansk but coordinated with strikes throughout the country, attempted to influence public opinion on the part of KOR and other groups, and employed the vast cultural force of the Catholic Church. We call that process *social appropriation.*

Public Self-representation

Movement participants make concerted public representations of their worthiness, unity, numbers, and commitment on the part of themselves and/or their constituencies. For example:

- *Worthiness*: sober demeanor; neat clothing; presence of clergy, dignitaries, mothers with children or, alternatively, signs of militancy such as wearing army uniforms or carrying the tools of a trade
- *Unity*: matching badges, headbands, banners, or costumes; marching in ranks; singing and chanting; symbols of solidarity such as a signature color
- *Numbers*: head counts, signatures on petitions, messages from constituents, filling the streets
- *Commitment*: braving bad weather; visible participation by the old and people with disabilities; resistance to repression; ostentatious sacrifice, subscription, and/or benefaction

The most dramatic element in the self-representation of the Solidarity strikers was their identification with the "martyred workers" of previous suppressed strikes. The very symbol of Solidarity—a silhouetted group of people supporting one another and carrying a banner—reflected workers' unitary commitment and their ties to the general population. Certification by association with Catholic faith was also a key factor. No sooner had the occupation of the factory begun than the local bishop negotiated an agreement with the local party secretary: Priests could say Mass outside the factory gate and symbols of Christian faith went on display where the media could record them.

Associational and Action Repertoires

Movements employ combinations from among the following forms of political action: creation of special-purpose associations and coalitions; public meetings; solemn processions; vigils; rallies; demonstrations; petition drives; statements to and in public media; pamphleteering. We call the variable ensemble of performances the *social movement repertoire*.

The social movement repertoire draws from the general repertoire of contention. But it differs from most forms of collective action we encountered earlier in the *modularity* of its performances: employment of similar forms of collective action by a wide variety of social actors around very different goals against similar actors. As movements developed around a wide range of claims, they elaborated forms of action that could be adopted and adapted in a variety of settings against a wide range of objects: the strike against any kind of employer; the petition on behalf of a wide variety of claims; the street march and demonstration (Favre 1990; Fillieule 1997; Grimsted 1998; Kinealy 2003; Pigenet and Tartakowsky 2003; Tartakowsky 1997, 2004).

Solidarity activists employed traditional tools of working-class insurgency such as strikes and factory occupations. But they also mounted marches, demonstrations, religious processions, and a host of supportive activities such as the handing of food into the factory by family members and friends. The strike committee's meetings with party officials and management around a table in the Lenin works accomplished two things: It achieved certification of the union and symbolized the equal status of union, management, and state actors. Though separated by eight years, the talks of 1980 prefigured the politically important "round table" negotiations of 1988–1989, which brought Solidarity into power. The form of the round table then spread across East-Central Europe. One by one, Communist parties negotiated the end of their regimes in 1989.

Campaigns, public self-representations, and associational and action repertoires vary enormously from one movement to another, but movements connect those properties in logical ways. Consider the American antislavery movement. Beginning in the 1830s abolitionists launched a long and varied campaign against both slaveholders and public authorities. They used forms of association and public action that drew heavily on the evangelical revival of the previous decade, presenting their movement as rightcous, unified, numcrous, and stalwart (Young 2006). That movement interacted by fits and starts with institutional politics. By the 1850s, many with abolitionist leanings had joined the mainstream parties and were present in Congress. Then one branch converged with the "free soil" movement. Together with opportunity-seeking politicians from the old Whig Party and breakaway Democrats, that branch formed the Republican Party. The party elected a little-known reformer, Abraham Lincoln, as president in 1860.

We see a similar transformation of a movement into a party in Poland. As martial law wore on in the course of the 1980s, Solidarity leaders (many of them still in prison) began to reshape their roles from the representatives of industrial workers into political party leaders. When, in 1989, the regime was forced to call meaningful elections, Solidarity emerged with a solid majority in both houses of parliament. That transformation brought the movement into intimate connections with institutions.

Poland's Solidarity was a social movement that produced a change from an authoritarian regime to a democratizing one. The regime change would ultimately have disintegrating effects on the movement, dividing its activists among trade unionists and politicians. Within the latter group, furthermore, it drove a wedge between economic liberals and Catholic populists. New movements would eventually take their place, illustrating the symbiotic relationship between democracy and the form of the social movement. The next section turns to the "new" American women's movement, to examine interactions among social movement bases, political institutions, and contentious politics in a democratic regime.

The New American Women's Movement

Many changes took place in the role of women in American society in the half-century after World War II, but not all were part of "the women's movement." For example:

- Changes in employment brought more women into the workforce.
- Public attitudes regarding the status of women evolved.
- Legislatures passed laws favorable to women—in part because members of Congress wanted women's votes.
- Philosophies and schools of feminism developed that became part of the base of that movement.
- A network of women's social movement organizations developed.

Our concept of social movements recognizes these changes and their relevance to the formation of the new women's movement and especially to its bases. But, as in the Polish case we have just examined, we must distinguish changes in the bases of women's political action from the important movement campaigns that developed in the late 1960s and beyond.

While an early women's movement had emerged in the fight for women's rights (Banaszak 1996), it remained largely dormant during most of the interwar and early postwar years (Rupp and Taylor 1987). The 1960s added a new base to women's resources and opportunities. That base came in part through "spillover" of activists from the civil rights movement (Evans 1979; McAdam 1988; Meyer and Whittier 1994) and in part from autonomous social and political sources. Of course, the new movement drew on both liberal and radical feminist ideas (Freeman 1975), on the increased presence of women in the workforce, and on opportunities in American political institutions. These were part of its movement base. But it started into motion through a series of campaigns that placed it in contentious interaction with other groups, with the government, and against a countermovement that it actually helped to trigger—the antiabortion movement.

The new women's movement produced innovative solutions to all three aspects of our sketch of social movements: campaigns, public representations, and claim-making repertoires:

- The movement consisted of campaigns such as the Equal Rights Amendment (ERA) campaign, which occupied the energies of vast numbers of women activists during the 1970s and early 1980s (Costain 1992: chap. 4; Mansbridge 1986).
- Parts of the movement sought a new self-representation through changes in women's dress, language, manners, and collective activities. Although only representative of one branch of the movement, consciousness-raising was a creative tool for the development of a new representation of women. Such grassroots activities fostered "sisterhood," women who had previously been demure and retiring learned to speak up for themselves, and new frames of meaning emerged.
- In both its associational and action repertoire, the movement innovated equally. Although national groups such as the National Organization for Women (NOW) adopted the increasingly common form of the public interest group, groups such as the Women's International Terrorist Conspiracy from Hell (WITCH) expanded women's action repertoire into theatrical actions, while feminists within professions such as the church and the military quietly organized to advance the status of women within their institutions (Katzenstein 1998).

Not all of these innovations lasted into the new century. Some merged with general changes in the repertoire that arose in the protest cycle of the 1960s and declined with the end of that cycle. Others (e.g., the caricatured image of "bra-burning" feminists) never gained acceptance. In fact, the countermovement appropriated them to roll back feminist gains (Meyer and Staggenborg 1996).

One of the movement's bitter ironies was that its gains helped to crystallize a traditionalist view of women's role. This contributed to the defeat of the ERA and to a powerful antiabortion campaign (McCarthy 1987). It also contributed to the triumph of a raw form of conservative Republicanism in the Reagan and second Bush administrations. Ultimately, these countermoves contributed to a retrenchment of state programs in favor of women, children, and the poor. They rolled back many of the movement's gains (Banaszak, Beckwith, and Rucht 2003).

Like Polish Solidarity, the rise of the new American women's movement offers a prime example of a sustained challenge to power holders in the name of a population living under the jurisdiction of those power holders by means of concerted public displays of that population's worthiness, unity, numbers, and commitment, a social movement. But unlike Polish Solidarity—which had to struggle *against* instituted power for most of its early history—the new American women's movement developed in intimate interaction with institutions.

Movements and Institutions

Remember from chapter 3 what we mean by *institutions*. Within any particular regime, they are established, organized, widely recognized routines, connections, and forms of organization employed repeatedly in producing collective action. Some (e.g., the armed forces) are fairly insulated from contentious politics; others (e.g., political parties and elections) are highly sensitive to such politics; while still others (e.g., legislatures, courts, and executives) are both contention-shaping and contention-responding institutions.

Our way of thinking about social movements denies any rigid boundary between institutionalized and noninstitutionalized politics. We see contentious politics embracing both institutions and social movements. Social movement bases develop both within and outside institutions. Movement campaigns act within, against, and outside institutions. They can contribute to the rise of new institutions. What is more, different institutions harbor, oppose, or stimulate the formation of social movement campaigns.

Boundaries between institutionalized and noninstitutionalized politics are hard to draw with precision. Take the movement coalition that formed around defeating President Ronald Reagan's nuclear arms policy in the 1980s. It bridged the space between institutional groups and protesters outside institutions. Newly formed movement organizations such as the Nuclear Weapons Freeze Clearinghouse (NWFC) combined with established peace organizations, on the one hand, and with congressional Democrats, on the other, to form a coalition that persuaded the government to preempt the movement by starting an arms control process (Meyer 1990). Only by looking at both sides of the formal boundary between institutional and noninstitutional politics and at their interactions can we understand the dynamics of episodes of contentious politics.

Of course, much of the work that political institutions do lies outside the boundaries of contentious politics. Executives sign laws, preside at openings, greet foreign dignitaries, and turn on the Christmas tree lights on the lawn of the White House. Legislators declare days of commemoration, make speeches aimed only at pleasing local constituents, and greet visiting Boy Scout troops. Much of what they do is uncontentious and routine.

Social movement activists also engage in contentious activities only part of the time. To build their bases, and before any action mobilization begins, movement organizations often engage in "consensus mobilization" (Klandermans 1988). To please their members, they organize festivals and ceremonials. To gain a broader following, they engage in educational activities. To broadcast who they are and the nature of their claims, they cultivate the media. Figure 6.2 portrays graphically the intersection of social movements, social movement bases, institutions, and contentious politics.

Do not regard figure 6.2 as the vehicle for our arguments about the dynamics of contention. See it instead as a static road map to the interac-

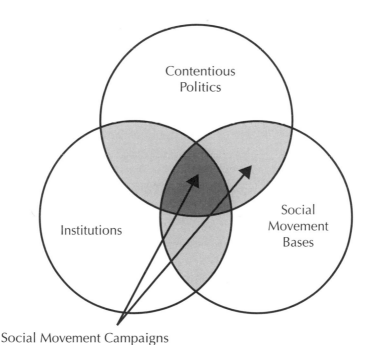

Social Movement Campaigns

Figure 6.2. Contentious Politics, Social Movement Campaigns, Social Movement Bases, and Institutions

tions among our key terms. Any such vehicle would have to put these concepts into motion, asking questions such as:

- When and under what conditions do social movement campaigns arise out of movement bases, what kinds of institutional frameworks offer them opportunities, and which ones suppress their emergence?
- When and under what conditions do institutional actors produce or assist social movement campaigns, by reaction, transmutation, or fractionation?
- When and under what conditions do movement campaigns ignite broader forms of contentious politics, such as civil wars, nationalist episodes, or revolutions, that threaten institutions?
- When and under what conditions do movement campaigns create new institutions and new social movement bases?

From the beginning of social movement politics, political institutions provided opportunities for movement development, found ways to repress them, but also processed movement claims. Remember how the British Parliament and its practice of receiving petitions served as a vehicle for the advance of the British antislavery campaign? And how the struggle against election fraud provided the focal point for the Ukrainian Orange Revolution? And how Congress, with its formula for deciding whether new states entering the Union would be slave or free, actually produced the American Civil War? Institutions serve as an umbrella for social movement activity, a focal point for its campaigns, and the major source of social movement outcomes. The new American women's movement illustrates these points.

From the first, that movement grounded itself within institutions (Katzenstein and Mueller 1987). The first important turning point came with President John F. Kennedy's Commission on the Status of Women in 1961 and with the inclusion of women's rights in the Civil Rights Act of 1964 (Beckwith 2003: 193). Then came executive orders that assigned the task of monitoring wage equality and discrimination in hiring to government agencies and a burst of legislative activity favoring women in the 1970s (Katzenstein 2003: 205-7). Figure 6.3 plots Anne Costain's (1992) time line of legislative enactments in her book *Inviting Women's Rebellion* alongside the activities of major women's organizations such as NOW. It illustrates the general co-occurrence of the new women's movement with congressional activity on behalf of women.

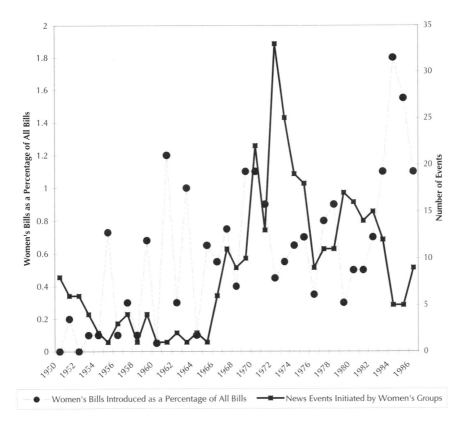

Figure 6.3. News Events Initiated by Women's Groups and Women's Bills as Percentage of All Bills Introduced in the U.S. Congress, 1950–1986
Source: Costain (1992: 108, 113).

One reading of figure 6.3 would see in it evidence that Congress was responding to the pressures of the movement—a direct policy effect of a movement's campaigns. Two other readings are also possible: first, that Congress, or its majority, was responding with electoral motivations to changes in public opinion that were, in large part, independent of the women's movement; second, that members of Congress were ideologically but independently committed to the policy goals they advanced. We cannot, on the basis of the time lines in figure 6.3, decide among these three different readings. But the only partial parallels between NOW's efforts and Congress's legislation suggest that the movement's policy impact was at least indirect and at best partial.

Movement Impacts

Movement impacts do not end with policy change alone. We can distinguish roughly among three kinds of effects, all of them visible in American women's movements: (1) direct impacts of social movement campaigns on public policies, (2) effects of participation in claim-making campaigns on the lives of activists, and (3) outside campaigns, effects of involvement in the social movement base on political contention in general.

As Costain's analysis suggests, the first category—direct effects of campaigns—is difficult to assess. Most scholars now believe that policy impacts are, at best, mediated by political contexts (Meyer, Jenness, and Ingram 2005), while others are even more cautious. Piven and Cloward (1977), focusing on four episodes of contentious politics in the 1930s and the 1960s, conclude that movements seldom succeed, and when they do, success is often followed by failure. Other movement scholars, including Paul Burstein and his collaborators, are even more pessimistic. Referring to a variety of evidence from the United States, they find that collective action on the part of social movement organizations is most often ineffective in influencing public policy (Burstein and Linton 2002; Burstein and Sausner 2005).

Policy changes have a great impact on movements. For example, simple changes in the tax laws can deprive a movement group of its tax-exempt status. More broadly, the retrenchment of the American welfare state since the 1990s has created an entirely new and more constrained opportunity structure for women (Banaszak et al. 2003). That in turn has created the need for women to rethink the mechanisms of worthiness, unity, numbers, and commitment that produced their gains in an earlier generation.

With respect to the second category—the effect of participation on the lives of activists—the impact of the women's movement appears to have been more certain. Nancy Whittier's (1995) study of radical women activists in Columbus, Ohio, shows that well outside public claim-making activity, involved women supported each other and kept each other committed. During the campaign lull of the Reagan years, one woman Whittier interviewed declared:

> Some of these people, I've known them for so long now that we can refer back to a certain event or series of events with just a word or two. It's that kind of communication you can have with someone you've known for a long time, so that we don't really discuss it, we know what we mean. And we get that kind of good feeling that you have with people that you've been through a lot with and you've known for so long. (112)

For her and for women like her, involvement in the movement base had become a defining feature of day-to-day life.

With respect to the third category—movements' effects on future patterns of political contention—the balance sheet for the American women's movement is truly mixed. On the one hand, women's movement support was critical in producing a distinguished cadre of women political leaders such as Senator Hillary Rodham Clinton, Senator Barbara Boxer, and Nancy Pelosi, leader of the Democratic Party in the House of Representatives. On the other hand, the success of such "threatening" women as Clinton and the support of the women's movement for such controversial issues as abortion have helped to polarize American politics.

This countermovement first grouped around the opposition to the ERA, which was defeated in the 1980s (Mansbridge 1986), and it continues to attack the Supreme Court's legalization of abortion in the case of *Roe v. Wade*. As we write, in early 2006, changes in the composition of the Supreme Court at the hands of a "prolife" president, George W. Bush, threaten this signal achievement of the women's movement.

After Mobilization

What happens to movement bases after movement campaigns subside? Building on his research on "new" social movements such as the American women's movement (Kriesi et al. 1995), Hanspeter Kriesi has constructed a typology of movement dynamics that can help us answer this question. Figure 6.4 reproduces his typology. All four of the groups that Kriesi and his collaborators studied emerged from the 1968 period; all relied on loose networks of activists rather than on solid bureaucratic bases. All focused their activities around precise claims rather than on general ideologies. All followed a cyclical trajectory like the one we traced in Italy in chapter 5 (Koopmans 2004; Kriesi et al. 1995). Yet despite their similarities in origins, structure, issue focus, and trajectory, these social movement organizations (SMOs) ended their active period of contention in very different ways.

Starting out from the ideal type of SMO—a formal organization that mobilizes its constituency for collective action with a political goal (Kriesi 1996: 153)—Kriesi deduces four processes of transformation.

First, he sees as one possibility the *institutionalization* of a movement organization, a process we encountered in Italy (see chapter 5). This process combines formalization of an SMO's internal structure,

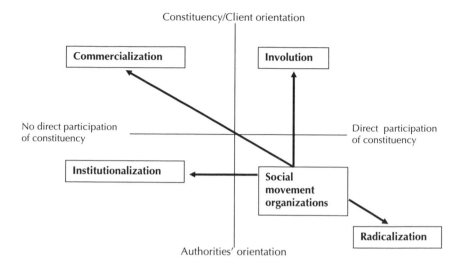

Figure 6.4. Typology of Transformations in Goal Orientations and Action Repertoires of Social Movement Organizations
Source: Kriesi (1996: 157).

moderation of its goals, adoption of a more conventional action repertoire, and integration into established systems of government. Figure 6.4 argues that institutionalization involves a shift from the direct participation of a movement's constituency to delegation to professional organizers. This resembles the familiar pattern of goal displacement detected a century ago by Robert Michels (1962) and after the last cycle of American protest by Theodore Lowi (1971).

Second, Kriesi sees the possibility of *commercialization,* the transformation of a movement organization in the direction of a service organization. This pattern was typical of the autonomous firms and cooperatives that developed out of the new social movements in Germany, and it can also be seen in the United States in what happened to the consumer group Consumer's Research as it went from consumer advocacy to becoming a product-testing and product-endorsing firm (Rao 1998).

Third, Kriesi sees the possibility of *involution,* a path that leads to exclusive emphasis on social incentives. SMOs that experience involution become self-help groups, voluntary associations, or clubs. Many of the communes that developed out of the American 1960s experienced a process of involution from active participation in politics to the cultivation of personal and religious development.

Kriesi's fourth variant, *radicalization*, or "reinvigorated mobilization," we saw in the escalation of collective violence in Italy after 1968 and in the transformation of America's Students for a Democratic Society into the Weathermen.

Kriesi's typology serves as a rough guide to the changes in the American women's movement's base after the height of its campaigns in the 1960s and 1970s. In this largely "liberal" family of movement groups, institutionalization was the dominant process coming out of its phase of mobilization. Its major expression was the large number of public interest groups that grew out of the 1960s (Schlozman 1990). Most of these, such as NOW and the National Abortion and Reproductive Rights Action League (NARAL), became active in lobbying and educational work in Washington, leading to the formation of an array of public interest lobbies. Though their dedication to the women's movement remained strong, their tactics and interactions with others resembled those of conventional business and professional lobbies.

Commercialization occurred less often in American women's groups than it did in Europe's post-1960s autonomous firms and cooperatives. Women's magazines were certainly commercial. Some of them kept their feminist stands after the 1960s, while others—depending on ads from makeup and clothing companies—drifted into lifestyle preoccupations. Women's bookstores developed for a time but soon disappeared within the general expansion of book megastores. Services for women's health, such as Planned Parenthood, inherited some veterans of the new women's movement but could hardly be called "commercial."

We find evidence for involution in the development of women's self-help groups—for example, in the groups formed to counsel women on abortion and to help women who have been raped and those diagnosed with breast cancer (Taylor and Van Willigen 1996). The breast cancer coalition in particular embodied both the new conception of gender that grew out of the new women's movement and an unwillingness to delegate authority to the (mainly male) medical hierarchy (Parthasarathy 2003).

Radicalization shook the movement in the internal struggles that developed between competing philosophies of feminism. Conflict over the admission of lesbians to the ranks of the "straight" feminist community compounded the initial cleavage between liberal and Marxist feminists. Another axis of competition differentiated groups of women of color from mainstream feminism (Roth 2004). But since the most radical groups also tended to involution—especially in the universities—this development had less impact on the movement than its overwhelming institutionalization.

Scholars have sometimes seen movements inexorably turning into interest groups or disappearing into institutions. Kriesi's typology shows how periods of high mobilization give rise to a variety of forms of exit that keep a movement base alive during periods when campaigns are in abatement (Rupp and Taylor 1987). By joining self-help groups, working for women's service organizations, and paying dues to public interest groups, women activists from the 1960s and 1970s kept up their contacts with old comrades, remained available for mobilization at times of stress or opportunity (e.g., when two new Supreme Court appointments threatened the legal protection of a woman's right to choose an abortion in 2005), and kept the flame of activism alive to fight another day.

Conclusion

This chapter's main arguments summarize easily. First, we argued that not all episodes of contentious politics are social movements. The 1956 events in Poland were contentious, at times violent, and, like many of the episodes we have examined, responded to changes in political opportunities. But they did not constitute a social movement, either in our sense of the term or in comparison to what would occur in that country in 1980.

In contrast, Solidarity, like many social movements, emerged from a local episode of contention and, like many of the episodes we have examined in our book, grew through a process of brokerage, certification, diffusion, and scale shift. It qualifies as a social movement campaign because it mobilized an until-then passive social movement base that had grown up after 1956 and because it developed the properties of worthiness, unity, numbers, and commitment that made it a powerful social and political force.

Similarly, in 1960s America, many changes of great interest to women occurred: changes in labor force participation, presence of many more women in colleges and universities, and increasing participation of women in politics. Not all these changes belonged to or resulted from social movement campaigns. Changes in public opinion, vote-seeking members of Congress, judges favoring equal rights, as well as determined women legislators, all affected American public politics. The distinction matters: Only by singling out social movement campaigns can we detect relations between them and other sources of change. Without the distinction, we can't examine transitions between movements and other forms of contention.

Third, movements frequently challenge institutions. Both Solidarity and the American women's movement did challenge their countries' institutions. But movements also work *within* institutions. They often dovetail with parallel changes in institutional politics, as the women's movement did in the 1970s and 1980s. Movements sometimes become institutional actors, as did Solidarity in 1989, when it forced the Polish regime to hold competitive elections. Their very success sometimes defeats them, as institutional logic takes over from the logic of contentious politics.

Movements frequently trigger the formation of countermovements. The American women's movement did so in the failed campaign for ERA and in the struggle over abortion rights. The give and take of institutional politics often reflects a more civilized version of the struggle for supremacy between movements for change and countermovements that attempt to return to a more traditional society. That is why a symbiotic relationship exists between democratic politics and social movements: The successes of broad, alliance-building and consensus-building movements expand the range of democratic politics.

If social movements twin with democratic and democratizing politics, what about other kinds of regimes? If a symbiotic relationship prevails between democratic politics and social movements, do similarly symbiotic relations appear between these other forms and other types of polities? The next chapter turns to more violent forms of contentious politics, looking closely at their relationships to democracy and undemocracy.

In many recent lethal conflicts around the world, child soldiers as
young as nine years of age have been mobilized to fight in civil
wars in places including the Sudan, Sierra Leone, and the Congo.
(UN/DPI Photo)

CHAPTER SEVEN
LETHAL CONFLICTS

Large-scale lethal conflicts occur most often in regimes with intermediate and low levels of governmental capacity, including the unstable intermediate cases that David Laitin and James Fearon (2004) call "anocracies." We will also see them in the type of regime chapter 8 studies—"composite regimes." In this chapter, we move from chapter 6's relatively nonviolent world of social movements into regimes where government agents, popular challengers, and other competitors for political power regularly use armed force to back up their contentious claims. Three forms of lethal conflict provide our primary examples: violent ethnic or religious conflicts, civil wars, and revolutions. To see how those three forms of lethal conflict interact and overlap, let us first turn to Sudan.

Lethal Conflict in Sudan

The independent state of Sudan, due south of Egypt, long lived under Egyptian domination. It occupies the largest territory of any African state. Toward the Egyptian border on the north and the Red Sea coast on the northeast, the Sudanese population is increasingly Muslim in religion and Arab in self-identification. Toward the south and the west, higher and higher proportions speak sub-Saharan African languages, identify with black African tribes, and practice either Christianity or African regional religions. The central government, based in mainly Muslim and Arabic-speaking Khartoum, exercises tight control over the Khartoum metropolitan area and the northeast, but it has an uncertain grip on the rest of the country. Few roads penetrate the poor and mainly agricultural southern and western regions.

Sudan's politically troubled neighbors include not only Egypt but also the Central African Republic, Chad, the Democratic Republic of the Congo,

Eritrea, Ethiopia, Kenya, Libya, and Uganda. From independence in 1956 to the strife-torn year of 2005, Sudan had suffered active civil wars during forty of its fifty postcolonial years. Many of those civil wars spilled over its boundaries into adjacent countries or sprang from conflicts already going on in those countries. During most of that half-century, military officers ran the regime but could not extend their control over the country's entire territory.

Periodically, Sudan's rulers have called their regime Muslim and have tried to install Islamic principles as national law. They have also monopolized substantial revenues from oil exports and Red Sea commercial zones. Southerners and westerners have repeatedly resisted both moves by armed force. With varying degrees of unity, warlord-led armies have often effectively run the south since independence. Under pressure from neighboring states and international organizations, the central state has seesawed between granting the south extensive autonomy and attempting to annihilate or co-opt its rebels.

What Is and Isn't Special about Large-scale Lethal Conflicts

Sudan's struggles feature a variety of contentious politics that previous chapters have only touched in passing: large-scale lethal conflicts in which the violence does not occur chiefly as a by-product of nonviolent claim making but forms part of claim making's central rationale. In this chapter, we enter a realm in which both governments and other political actors regularly use organized armed force as they make claims. Organized armed force ranges from local gangs to disciplined national armies, passing by militias, paramilitaries, private armies, and mercenaries. Sometimes organized armed force remains very one-sided, as when military units attack demonstrators or paramilitaries hunt down labor organizers. But it becomes especially lethal when at least two armed organizations battle each other.

Lethal conflicts have special features that set them off from other forms of contentious politics. Two features in particular make a difference: the high stakes of claim making and the problem of sustaining armed force. Killing, wounding, and damaging affect the survival of participants well after the immediate struggle has ended. They break up families and communities, destroy available labor power, and eliminate means of production. With such high stakes, potential participants in violent encounters commonly flee them unless, as participants, they are likely to prevail or to get away unscathed. But once committed, they exit less easily so long as their organization remains intact.

That brings us to the second point. Large-scale lethal conflicts include interstate wars, civil wars, revolutions, and genocides as well as a significant subset of struggles across religious, ethnic, linguistic, and regional boundaries. Unlike recruiting people for demonstrations or public meetings, creating and maintaining an armed force requires extensive resources. Some military organizations (e.g., the militias formed by Guatemala's peasants) live on their own land, drawing support from their own communities. But they also need weapons, ammunition, information, means of communication, and personnel to replace those they lose.

Occasionally mass killing occurs without much use of high-powered weapons. In the huge Rwandan genocide of 1994, for example, most killers slaughtered their victims with clubs, machetes, and other everyday tools. Even in that extreme case, however, the killing began with a well-trained presidential guard and militias organized by the ruling party (Dallaire 2003; Des Forges et al. 1999; Jones 1995; Mamdani 2001; Prunier 1995, 2001; Taylor 1999). Reproducing a disciplined military organization depends on extensive brokerage and internal coordination. All forms of large-scale lethal conflict involve high stakes and disciplined military organizations.

Those are the differences. Yet we will soon recognize familiar mechanisms and processes within large-scale lethal conflicts. To see them, we must avoid two fallacies that commonly blur people's understanding of such conflicts. We can call them the motivational fallacy and the general law fallacy.

The *motivational fallacy* assumes that we would know the true, fundamental cause of large-scale violence if we could only read the perpetrators' minds: What do they want and feel? Even if we could read their minds, in fact, we would soon discover that participants in large-scale violence want and feel a great many different things at different times; that whether and how large-scale violence occurs depends on such nonmotivational matters as whether weapons, victims, and previous connections among perpetrators are available; and—most important—that large-scale violence is not a solo act but a complex interactive process.

The *general law fallacy* assumes that each type of large-scale lethal conflict has its own distinctive character and therefore follows its own general laws. Genocides, civil wars, revolutions, lethal ethnic or religious conflict, and violent nationalism, in this view, differ dramatically from each other, and each have their own distinctive necessary and sufficient conditions. On the contrary, as we will soon see, these various forms of contention overlap, mutate into each other, and result from similar mechanisms and processes in different combinations, sequences, and initial conditions. Mechanisms and processes do, indeed, conform to general laws; brokerage, for example, operates in essentially the same way across a wide variety of political circumstances. But the laws do not cover whole classes of episodes such as revolutions or civil wars.

As we look at large-scale lethal contention, we revisit the identity mechanisms and processes of chapter 4. We see political actors declaring themselves to be revolutionaries or defenders of the true religion through combinations of mobilization, brokerage, diffusion, certification, and boundary activation. We discover that existing political opportunity structure regularly interacts with established repertoires to shape what sorts and degrees of large-scale violence can occur within a given regime. We recognize again that the overall character of a political regime (especially the capacity of its central government and its degree of democracy) strongly affects the location and the sheer possibility of large-scale lethal conflict.

Central states ordinarily control the largest single concentrations of coercive means within a given regime. Concentrated coercive means identify an organization as a state or something like a state. Because of that fact, large-scale lethal conflict inevitably involves states in one or both of two ways: as direct participants in the conflict and/or as third parties whose own power the conflict threatens. High-capacity states reduce the threat by making it difficult for anyone to create rival concentrations of coercive means within their territories. But (as we will see) they do not always succeed. Low-capacity states more often face precisely the threat that some rival actor will build up a major concentration of coercive means and use it to topple existing rulers.

Struggles for control of concentrated coercive resources grew up with the emergence of centralized states thousands of years ago. But they only started to involve religious, ethnic, racial, and cultural identities more directly with the growth of nationalism in the era of the French Revolution. During the later eighteenth century, American revolutionaries overthrew British rule in the name of an American nation. French revolutionaries upended their old regime in the name of the French nation and then went out to conquer other people in the name of national liberation. The revolutionary era established top-down and bottom-up nationalism. From the top down, rulers say, "We run the state; therefore, we have the right to define the ethnicity, religion, race, and culture of our nation." From the bottom up, people who occupy distinctive religious, ethic, racial, and cultural niches reply, "We are a separate nation; therefore, we have the right to a separate state." A great deal of the world's large-scale lethal conflict within regimes pits the two principles against each other.

In large-scale lethal conflict, two dramatic possibilities loom larger than in social movement campaigns: regime split and transfer of power. The first is that the entire regime will split, so that at least two different clusters of political actors, including agents of government, have broken their alliances and routine interactions with the others. At the extreme, two rival governments or segments of government can contend with each other, as when a rebel army establishes control over a region far from a national capital and acts like a government within that region. This is, of course, a matter of degree. In the United States, for example, antitax rebels, libertarian militias, and Indian tribes sometimes declare their independence from the national government and draw a local following without much shaking the national regime. But the Civil War really did split the entire American polity.

Small transfers of power occur all the time in every regime. One political actor gains greater access to government, another loses access, and a third forms a new alliance with the rising actor. Competitive elections always involve some possibility of a greater realignment. But fundamental transfers of power more often occur in the company of large-scale violence of the kinds this chapter analyzes. Again we are dealing with a matter of degree: from minor, incremental shifts in power to major, rapid overturns of the existing power structure. Figure 7.1 sketches the range of possibilities.

Figure 7.1 makes two valuable points. First, coups, top-down seizures of power, revolts, civil wars, lethal ethnic-religious conflicts, and great revolutions are all cousins; they combine varying extents of split and transfer. The diagram's overlapping circles stress that point. Second, a great revolution is simply the extreme case—a very extensive split followed by a major transfer of power. In fact, as the diagram suggests, a civil war or revolt can become a great revolution if it produces a fundamental transfer of power.

We have already encountered violent conflicts in precariously democratizing Venezuela, in a disintegrating Soviet Union, as well as in certain phases of Italian and German contention. The closest we have come so far to sustained lethal conflict at something resembling Sudanese intensity, however, appears in Charles Brockett's (2005) analysis of Guatemalan politics. In Guatemala, we saw both a low-capacity undemocratic regime

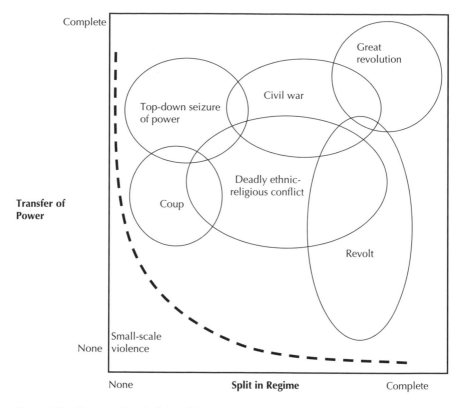

Figure 7.1. Forms of Lethal Conflict

and outright civil war. Summing up his study of El Salvador and Guatemala and putting it in comparative perspective, Brockett comments that levels and sites of collective violence result from the interaction between popular mobilization and state repression:

> Repression generally succeeds in smothering contention if the prior level of mobilization was low. However, if state violence is increased after a protest cycle … is well underway, this repression is more likely to provoke even higher levels of challenge, both nonviolent and violent, rather than deter contention. This provocation is especially likely if state violence is inconsistent. But revolutionary toppling of thrones such as Nicaragua in 1979 are rare events. El Salvador and Guatemala are extreme examples of the more usual outcome: When regimes are willing to repress as necessary and have the capacity to do so, they usually succeed in eliminating popular contention as a threat to their regime and often to their own rule as well. (327)

Let us return to Sudan to see how Brockett's connections between popular mobilization and state repression work.

Back to Sudan

In 1989, Colonel Omar Hassan al-Bashir led a military junta that seized power over Sudan's central government. The new rulers named its new regime the Revolutionary Command Council for National Salvation. At least the junta called their arrival in power a revolution. For ten years, al-Bashir ruled by means of a military-civilian government backed by senior Muslim clerics. In 1999, however, he reacted to the clerics' plan for limiting presidential powers by dissolving parliament, declaring a state of emergency, dismissing the leading cleric from his government post, and calling for elections to validate his own rule. A rigged and widely boycotted 2000 presidential election brought him 86.5 percent of the vote against four token competitors.

By 2005, al-Bashir (now titled president and field marshal) had greatly consolidated his power within the central government. Over most of his rule, nevertheless, al-Bashir pursued a civil war. He faced a formidable southern military force, headed by Dinka leader John Garang (a Sudan-born American economics Ph.D.), that called itself the Sudan People's Liberation Army (SPLA). As the government began moving toward an accommodation with the SPLA in 2003, new rebel groups took up arms in Darfur, in western Sudan. The government sent out the army to put them down. It also armed and supported regional militias—the notorious Janjaweed—that specialized in attacking and burning out civilian populations presumed to support the rebels. The U.S. government called those attacks genocide, thus implying that they involved ethnic or religious conflict. By 2005, civil war had generated four to six million Sudanese refugees (out of a total national population of about thirty-eight million) within the country and in neighboring lands. A huge humanitarian crisis had developed.

At the end of 2004, under rising pressure from the United Nations, the African Union, and the United States, al-Bashir's government signed a so-called Comprehensive Peace Agreement with the SPLA. The settlement granted extensive autonomy to the south and allowed for national elections in 2009 and, in 2011, a referendum that could bring total independence to the southern region. In July 2005, Garang became the country's first vice president as well as president of a new South Sudan Government.

Late that month, Garang went to Entebbe, Uganda, to consult with his sometime supporter Yoweri Museveni, president of Uganda. As Garang returned from Entebbe, his Ugandan helicopter went down in a crash that killed all aboard. Over the next three days:

> Rioting and tit-for-tat killings continued in Sudan's capital, Khartoum . . . as southerners upset with the death of the rebel leader John Garang clashed with northern Arabs and government security forces struggling to restore order. The death toll from three days of unrest in Khartoum and its suburbs approached 100, according to local authorities and relief agencies. There were reports of gangs of people, some carrying clubs, knives and guns, marauding through the streets, even well after a government-imposed dusk-to-dawn curfew.
>
> The imam of a mosque outside of Khartoum was killed, the United Nations reported. Northern Muslims, crying "God is great!" in Arabic, were seen setting upon black African southerners. The ugly scenes represented the worst fears after Vice President Garang's death on Saturday night in a helicopter crash, which the authorities have insisted was an accident caused by foul weather, not an act of sabotage as some southerners claim. (Lacey 2005: 1)

News reports like this one tell stories. Stories usually move quickly from the identities and presumed motives of political actors to their actions without spending much time on political processes. But by now, as students of contentious politics, you should be able to detect familiar political mechanisms and processes at work in Sudan's bloody struggles.

First, behind vague words such as *rioting, marauding,* and *unrest,* we can detect organized attacks on enemies by members of three different groups: southerners, northerners, and government-backed armed forces. The prevailing Sudanese claim-making repertoire does not much resemble performances in the Western social movement campaigns we have just been analyzing. But with lethal weapons widely available and organized political actors regularly deploying them, it has its own local logic of violent competition. Participants called their organizations armies, and their actions, war.

Second, we witness the operation of a fluctuating political opportunity structure with

- multiple independent centers of power within the Sudanese regime,
- openness to new actors (especially those with independent access to arms),

- instability of current political alignments,
- availability of influential allies and supporters (both inside and outside the country) for challengers,
- inconsistent repression and facilitation of collective claim making by the government, and
- day-to-day changes in all these regards.

Together, these circumstances amount to a volatile, open political opportunity structure. They offer huge incentives and opportunities for mobilization on the part of the regime's challengers.

If we looked further into Sudan's day-to-day struggles, we would see four familiar sets of political processes operating repeatedly: mobilization-demobilization, boundary activation-deactivation, new coordination, and polarization. At a dizzying pace, political actors are mobilizing and demobilizing by means of such mechanisms as diffusion and brokerage. External actors such as the United Nations intervene in those processes by certifying some of the domestic actors and decertifying others. Us-them boundary activation occurs repeatedly as agents of a northern, predominantly Muslim government seek to impose their definitions of Sudanese nationality on southern non-Muslims and thus produce temporary unity within a normally fragmented southern population.

The same us-them boundaries often deactivate rapidly, however, when factions begin struggling for priority on one side or the other of the boundary. No permanent division between North and South, Muslim and Christian, or government and opposition defines the lines of struggle. Through combinations of brokerage and diffusion, actors on both sides are creating new forms of coordination, including the terrible destruction wrought by the Janjaweed. Finally, polarization between the two sides scoops out the middle ground between them over and over, most dramatically as the death of John Garang snaps the fragile strands of collaboration that had begun to form in the peace settlement of January 2005.

Behind these processes, notice the signs that we are dealing with a low-capacity undemocratic regime. More so than any other regime we have looked at with any care so far, the Sudanese regime involves a military organization that runs a central state but does not rule consistently and effectively outside its geographic base. Despite the charade of a contested presidential election, nothing like democratic practices and social movements shape contentious politics in Sudan. Civil wars, as chapter 3 pointed out, concentrate disproportionately in low-capacity undemocratic regimes. Sudan provides a salient example. But it also suffers from violent ethnic and religious struggles.

Deadly Ethnic and Religious Conflict

Like civil war, large-scale deadly ethnic and religious conflict concentrates in lower-capacity undemocratic regimes. It concentrates in those regimes for many of the same reasons: because whoever runs the relatively weak governments commonly distribute whatever benefits they gain from ruling to members of their own ethnic and religious networks, because the same governments cannot prevent excluded parties from amassing their own military means, and because informal systems of rule often build on existing relationships of kinship and religion.

But low-capacity democratic regimes face some of the same vulnerability to deadly ethnic and religious conflict for some of the same reasons. Consider Guyana, where roughly half the population claims East Indian descent, a bit more than a third African descent, and about half of the remainder Amerindian descent. In Guyana, political campaigns regularly divide along racial lines, and interracial fighting occurs frequently. Guyana's position as a conduit for Latin American cocaine on its way to the United States provides financial support for gangs and political organizers.

From independence in 1966 until 1992, Afro-Guyanese politicians in the People's National Congress (PNC) dominated the government. In 1992, however, the political balance shifted to the predominantly Indo-Guyanese People's Progressive Party and its coalition partner, the Civic Party. They called their coalition the PPP/C. The PNC formed an opposition coalition with the Reform Party, which accordingly received the name PNC/R. The two coalitions reinforced racial divisions within Guyana's public politics. "From February to September 2002," reports Freedom House,

> nearly a dozen police officers and more than 50 civilians were killed in an outbreak of violent crime that exacerbated uneasy relations between the two main races. In September, the PPP/C-dominated parliament passed four anticrime initiatives. However, PNC/R representatives who boycotted the legislative session claimed that the measures would not solve Guyana's crime problem, but rather were meant "to arm the regime with the draconian powers of dictatorship." (Piano and Puddington 2004: 243)

Both Amnesty International and the World Bank, from very different perspectives, identified a crisis of governance in Guyana. Ethnic divisions rend Guyanese politics. Yet, as in most other democratic regimes, nothing like the levels of armament and armed conflict that prevail in Sudan occur in Guyana. On the whole, the contentious politics of elections, trade unions, and social movements still provide safer, more attractive ways of making collective claims.

Even high-capacity democratic regimes often organize significant portions of their public politics around ethnic and religious divisions. India, the world's largest democracy and a relatively high-capacity democracy at that, recurrently produces deadly confrontations between Hindus and Muslims. In the United States, racial and ethnic divisions continue to inform politics at local, state, and national levels. During the 1860s, the United States fought one of history's bloodiest civil wars over the place of African Americans in its polity, economy, and everyday social life. The days of regular white-on-black lynchings only disappeared during the later twentieth century. On invading Afghanistan and Iraq, furthermore, the United States found itself stirring up large-scale, deadly ethnic and religious conflict.

If deadly ethnic and religious conflict concentrates in low-capacity undemocratic regimes, then, it is not because ethnic and religious divisions are completely absent from high-capacity democracies. High-capacity democracies simply manage to reduce the scale and armament of their domestic ethnic and religious conflicts, channel them into mainly non-violent forms of contention, and thus reduce the levels of death, damage, and destruction that result directly from contention. Their political opportunity structure and prevailing repertoires move them in the direction of social movements.

To see what a large historical effort the pacification of ethnic and religious conflict entails, we can look at Ireland, where for five centuries British-Irish and Protestant-Catholic divisions dominated political struggle. In Ireland, those divisions often organized deadly ethnic and religious conflict, sometimes to the extent of revolution and civil war. In fact, Ireland experienced a series of civil wars ending in a revolutionary transfer of power. By the end of World War I, British-Irish and Protestant-Catholic conflict had been narrowed to the one area of Ireland remaining in the United Kingdom; by 2005, it appeared to have been largely pacified. Box 7.1 provides a crude chronology of Protestant-Catholic struggles in Ireland over the past five centuries.

After assimilation of earlier Anglo-Norman conquerors and colonists, Ireland settled into several centuries of competition among indigenous chiefs and kings. Beginning with Henry VIII, however, Tudor invasions generated a new round of armed resistance. Thus began almost five centuries during which some group of Irish power holders has always aligned with Great Britain, and multiple other power holders have always aligned

Box 7.1. Landmark Dates of Irish Protestant-Catholic Relations	
1520–1602	Tudor invasions, plantations, rebellions, civil wars, establishment of Irish Protestant church.
1610–1640	Stuart dispossessions, English and Scottish settlements in Ireland, especially Ulster.
1641–1650	Rebellions and civil war in England and Ireland, ending with Cromwell's brutal conquest of Ireland.
1689–1691	Glorious Revolution in England, civil war in Ireland, reconquest by William III, sharp abridgement of Catholic political rights, massive seizure of Catholic property continuing to 1703.
1782–1783	Partial restoration of Irish political autonomy, Catholic rights to acquire land and to teach (but Irish Parliament still exclusively Protestant).
1791–1795	United Irishmen (autonomist, increasingly Catholic) and Orange Order (loyalist, Protestant) form.
1798	United Irish risings, civil war, massacres, French invasions, bloody suppression.
1801	Creation of United Kingdom (England, Wales, Scotland, Ireland), abolition of Irish Parliament, incorporation of 100 Irish Protestant MPs into UK Parliament.
1813–1829	Repeated campaigns for Catholic Emancipation in England and Ireland, mass mobilizations for emancipation in Ireland, against it in England, final passage of parliamentary acts expanding (but not entirely equalizing) Catholic political rights, raising property requirements for the Irish franchise, and dissolving Daniel O'Connell's Catholic Association.
1830s–1890s	Numerous antilandlord and antitithe actions, failed agitation for Irish home rule.
1845–1850	Potato famine, leading to large-scale emigration.
1843–	Major Protestant-Catholic violence in Belfast, especially 1843, 1857, 1864, 1872, 1886, 1893.
1848	Young Ireland uprising in Munster.
1858	Founding of Irish Republic Brotherhood (Fenians) in Dublin and New York.
1867	Fenian risings in Ireland, Clan na Gael founded in New York.
1869	Church of Ireland (Anglican) disestablished.
1884	Franchise Act greatly expands rural (and almost entirely Catholic) electorate.
1916	Easter Rising, with German support.
1919–1923	Civil wars, first producing separate governments and parliaments for North and South (1921), then creation of Irish Free State excluding Northern Ireland (1922).

| 1923–2004 | Intermittent Protestant-Catholic struggles in Northern Ireland, frequent involvement of British troops, suspension and restitution of successive Northern Ireland governments. |
| 1949 | Declaration of independent Irish Republic, still excluding Northern Ireland. |

against Great Britain. Between the 1690s and the 1780s, even propertied Catholics lacked any rights to participate in Irish public politics. From the 1780s to the 1820s, they still suffered serious political disabilities. Since the sixteenth century, Ireland has rarely moved far from virulent, violent rivalries. The island has repeatedly careened into civil war.

During the nineteenth century, demands for Irish autonomy or independence swelled. In 1801, largely in response to the Irish rebellion of 1798 and the threat that rebellion posed to Britain's pursuit of its great war with France, Great Britain (England, Scotland, and Wales) incorporated Ireland into a United Kingdom. That move dissolved an exclusively Protestant Irish parliament that had nonetheless at least remained responsive (and linked by kinship, commercial, and professional ties) to Catholic interests. A hundred Irish Protestants joined the House of Commons in distant London. With Catholic Emancipation (1829), propertied Catholics acquired the right to vote and hold most public offices.

These regime changes connected Irish contention more closely to the British political opportunity structure, which was opening erratically as the nineteenth century proceeded; independent centers of power were multiplying, the regime was becoming somewhat more open to new actors, political alignments became a bit more unstable, influential allies and supporters became more available to organized Irish Catholics, and the overall repressiveness of the United Kingdom government declined. But Protestant-Catholic and British-Irish distinctions retained much of their political force.

Over the nineteenth century, conflict between tenants and landlords exacerbated, and public shows of force on either side repeatedly generated street violence in Northern Ireland (Tilly 2003: 111–27). A campaign for home rule brought disestablishment of the previously official Church of Ireland in 1869. Despite the eventual backing of Prime Minister William Gladstone, however, home rule itself failed to pass the UK Parliament. Irish Protestants rallied against such measures to the theme that "Home rule is Rome rule" (McCracken 2001: 262). The Franchise Act of 1884, simultaneous with Great Britain's Third Reform Act, awarded the vote to most of the adult male Irish population and thus greatly expanded the rural

Catholic electorate. By that time, however, each major party had attached itself to a single religious segment. Catholic-based parties had committed themselves decisively to Irish autonomy or independence.

A combination of civil war, deadly ethnic-religious conflict, and revolution was in the making. After multiple anti-British risings over the previous sixty years, the question of military service on behalf of the United Kingdom split Ireland profoundly during World War I. At first Irish people collaborated with the war effort. To be sure, Ulster's Protestants collaborated much more enthusiastically than the rest of the Irish population. The prewar Ulster Volunteer Force, a Protestant paramilitary unit opposing Irish home rule that organized in 1913, joined the British army en masse. Meanwhile, the British maintained twenty thousand troops and police in the rest of the island to contain popular militias of Irish Catholics that started forming in 1914.

By that time, Ireland contained five distinct armed forces: not only the British army and the Ulster Volunteers but also their opponents the Irish Volunteers, the Citizen Army, and the Irish Republican Brotherhood. Still, serious opposition to the British cause did not crystallize until the war had been going on for almost two years. The abortive Easter Rising of 1916—organized in part from New York, supported by German agents, backed by German bombardment of the English coast, and suppressed brutally by British troops—slowed the cause of Irish independence temporarily. Nevertheless, Irish nationalists began regrouping in 1917.

The parliamentary election of 1918 brought a victory for Sinn Féin, a party popularly identified with the Easter Rising and the republican cause. When the UK government decreed military conscription for Ireland in April 1918, all Irish members of Parliament (MPs) except the Protestant representatives of the North withdrew from the UK Parliament. Returned MPs led organization of the opposition back home. In December 1918, Irish nationalists handily won southern Ireland's votes in a parliamentary election, with thirty-four of the sixty-nine successful candidates elected while in prison. The newly elected MPs decided to form their own Irish parliament instead of joining the UK assembly. On meeting in January 1919, they chose New York–born Eamon De Valera, then still in prison, as their parliamentary president. De Valera soon escaped from prison, but after four months of activity in Ireland, he left for the United States.

Soon the British government was actively suppressing Irish nationalist organizations. Nationalists themselves mobilized for resistance and attacked representatives of British authority. By the end of 1919, Ireland reached a state of civil war. As Peter Hart (1998) sums up for County Cork:

Sinn Fein won and guarded its new political turf with the obligatory minimum of street-fighting and gunplay. However, in the course of the revolution the familiar exuberance of party competition turned into killing on an unprecedented, unimagined scale. The political arena was transformed into a nightmare world of anonymous killers and victims, of disappearances, massacres, midnight executions, bullets in the back of the head, bodies dumped in fields or ditches. Over 700 people died in Cork in revolutionary or counter-revolutionary shootings or bombings between 1917 and 1923, 400 of them at the hands of the Irish Volunteers—soon rechristened the Irish Republican Army. (50)

The British painfully established military control but also began negotiating with Irish representatives. Within two years, the negotiations led to an agreement: partition of Northern Ireland (Ulster less Counties Cavan, Donegal, and Monaghan) from the rest, and dominion status similar to that of Canada and South Africa for a newly created Irish Free State outside the North. Although hard-line Irish republicans refused to accept the settlement and raised an insurrection in 1922, the arrangement lasted in roughly the same form until the 1930s.

Within Northern Ireland, anti-British forces never gave up. Although the Catholic third of the region's population remained somewhat more rural, more segregated, and more concentrated toward the South than the Protestant population, it constituted a formidable force. A whole new round of conflicts began with Catholic civil rights marches in 1968, violent confrontations with police, struggles with Protestant counterdemonstrators, and more scattered attacks of each side on the other's person and property. In 1972, British paratroopers trying to break up an unarmed but illegal march through Derry by the Northern Ireland Civil Rights Association fired on the demonstrators, killing thirteen of them. The uproar following that "Bloody Sunday" induced a worried British government to take back direct rule of the province.

After a bilateral cease-fire declared in 1994, raids and confrontations (including some quite outside Ireland) actually accelerated. A further treaty in 1998 (the so-called Good Friday agreement) initiated serious talks among the major parties and terminated most public standoffs between the sides, but it did not end guerrilla action by all paramilitary units or produce full disarmament of those units. Despite rough agreement between the governments of Ireland and the United Kingdom, as negotiations proceeded, paramilitary fractions on both sides repeatedly broke the peace. Support of Catholic militants by the well-armed Irish

Republican Army, based in independent Ireland and extensively supported by Irish overseas migrants, certainly sustained the conflict. But militant Catholics native to Ulster repeatedly challenged equally militant Ulster Protestants. One of Europe's longest runs of large-scale intergroup violence continues.

The toll is serious. Between 1969 and 1982, Northern Ireland's collective violence laid down the following records: 2,268 persons killed, including 491 military, 187 police, and 1,590 civilians; 25,120 persons injured; 29,035 shooting incidents; 7,533 explosions; 4,250 malicious fires; 9,871 armed robberies; 153 tarrings and featherings; and 1,006 kneecappings (Palmer 1988: 2). The numbers bespeak political actors at each other's throats. Although the intensity of violence waxed and waned with the more general rhythms of intergroup struggle in Northern Ireland, mutual attacks continued into the 1990s. Even the tentative settlement of 1998 did not end them:

> In the year of the Good Friday Agreement—1998—fifty-five people died in violence in Northern Ireland. Three Catholic brothers, aged between eight and ten, died on 12 July when loyalists petrol-bombed their home in a predominantly Protestant area of Ballymoney. On 15 August—a traditional Catholic holiday—twenty-eight people were killed in a car-bomb blast in Omagh. The attack also claimed another victim, who died a few days later. A republican splinter group, the Real IRA, had placed a 500–pound bomb in a parked car in a crowded shopping street on a sunny summer Saturday. It was one of the worst outrages of the Troubles. (Keogh 2001: 332–33)

Yet all through the post–World War II conflicts in Northern Ireland, elections continued to be held, Orange (Protestant) supporters marched, the families of victims demonstrated, and political dialogue continued in some forms. Even at the height of the violence, British agents were meeting secretly with representatives of the IRA. By the time of the Good Friday accord, political parties were slowly asserting their power over their paramilitary allies. The 2005 declaration of the Irish Republican Army that it would abandon collective violence may signal the end of lethal conflicts, but we cannot yet be sure.

Ireland's bloody experience clearly illustrates the special features of large-scale lethal conflicts we stressed at this chapter's start: the high stakes of claim making and the problem of sustaining armed force. For centuries, violent Irish-British and Catholic-Protestant struggles pivoted on who was to rule Ireland. For centuries, each side tried to build up sufficient military force for support of its high-stakes claims and to undermine the other side's efforts at building military force. For much of that time, the British maintained the upper hand, partly by drawing on more extensive military resources, partly by allying themselves with Protestant elites. Once the bulk of Ireland became independent, however, Britain's commitment to its Protestant remnant became a serious obstacle to reducing the levels of violence in Ulster. The formidable armed force that had fought its way to Irish independence mutated into an organization devoted to driving the British from their remaining redoubt.

Yet the long history of British-Irish interaction also tells us a different story, a story crucial to the understanding of contentious politics at large. British people, Irish people, and observers of British-Irish conflict have often described relations across the Irish Sea as the outcome of fierce, ancient, irreconcilable hatreds. The actual history of the long conflict, however, reveals that such apparently ancient hatreds are negotiable. Once most of Ireland became independent, the levels of ethnic and religious conflict declined, and the sites of violence concentrated in Northern Ireland. Even the Northern Irish struggle narrowed, became less violent, and showed signs of settlement after 2000, as the Irish Republican Army began to disarm, its leaders became internationally recognized negotiators, and even Northern Ireland's Protestant leaders searched for paths to a longer-term settlement.

The political processes that produced changes in British-Irish relations, furthermore, do not come from a separate realm unique to ancient hatreds and ethnic-religious conflict. On the contrary, the story of Ireland shows us familiar effects of shifting political opportunity structure, mobilization, polarization, brokerage—in short, of contentious politics at large. A similar lesson applies to another phenomenon that at first glance looks distinct and alien: civil war.

Civil War

Civil war occurs when two or more distinct military organizations, at least one of them attached to the previously existing government, battle each other for control of major governmental means within a single regime (Collier 2000a, 2000b; Fearon and Laitin 2003; Ghobarah, Huth, and Russett 2003; Henderson 1999; Hironaka 2005; Kaldor 1999; Licklider 1993; Sambanis 2004; Walter and Snyder 1999). There are many examples of civil wars raging in Colombia, Iraq, Israel/Palestine, Kashmir, Nepal, Peru,

Uganda, Guatemala, and, most recently, Sudan. As part of their effort to analyze and organize peaceful conflict resolution, Scandinavian scholars have made a specialty of cataloging violent conflicts across the world. One group of them does annual tallies of major conflicts, counting as civil wars those armed conflicts between governments and other actors in which at least twenty-five people die during the year.

In 2003 alone, Scandinavia's professional conflict spotters identified civil wars above their twenty-five-death threshold in Afghanistan, Algeria, Burma/Myanmar, Burundi, Chechnya, Colombia, Iraq, Israel/Palestine, Kashmir, Liberia, Nepal, the Philippines, Sri Lanka, Sudan, Turkey/Kurdistan, and Uganda (Eriksson and Wallensteen 2004: 632–35). These cases range from regimes in which the major parties were fighting for control of a single national government (e.g., Nepal) to others in which at least one major party was seeking to escape entirely from a central government's jurisdiction (e.g., the Philippines).

Over the years since World War II, a remarkable change in the world's armed conflicts, including civil wars, has occurred. For two centuries up to the end of that war, most large-scale lethal conflicts had pitted independent states against each other. Colonial conquests and anticolonial resistance constitute the main exceptions to that rule. During the immediate postwar period, European colonial powers faced resistance and insurrection in many of their colonies. Colonial wars surged before subsiding during the 1970s. As the Cold War prevailed between the 1960s and 1980s, great powers—especially the United States, the USSR, and the former colonial masters—frequently intervened in postcolonial civil wars such as those that ravaged Angola between 1975 and 2003 (Dunér 1985). But increasingly, civil wars without direct military intervention by third parties became the main sites of large-scale lethal conflict (Kaldor 1999; Tilly 2003: chap. 3).

Those Scandinavian specialists in the study of armed conflict divide armed conflicts since World War II into these categories:

- *Extrasystemic,* which occurs between a state and a nonstate group outside its own territory, the most typical cases being colonial wars
- *Interstate,* between two or more states
- *Internal,* between the government of a state and internal opposition groups without intervention from other states
- *Internationalized internal,* between the government of a state and internal opposition groups, with military intervention from other states (Strand, Wilhelmsen, and Gleditsch 2004: 11)

The *internal* category includes the purest examples of civil wars. Figure 7.2 (adapted from Eriksson and Wallensteen 2004, using data supplied by Eriksson and Wallensteen) shows trends in the four categories of conflict from 1946 through 2004.

The graph shows colonial wars declining, then disappearing after 1975; interstate wars fluctuating but never predominating; and internationalized civil wars reaching their maximum during the 1980s, then declining after 2000. In terms of sheer frequency of conflict, the big news comes from civil wars without foreign intervention. These internal armed conflicts climbed irregularly but dramatically from the 1950s to the 1990s, only to decline significantly in frequency from the mid-1990s. Soviet and Yugoslav disintegration contributed to the surge of the early 1990s (Beissinger 1998, 2001; Kaldor 1999).

During the later 1990s, despite such sore spots as Chechnya and Kosovo, most postsocialist regimes settled into more stable, less violent forms of rule. Partial democratization of previously divided regimes—South Africa is a case in point—also contributed to civil war's decline from 1994 onward (Piano and Puddington 2004). Despite continuing civil wars in Afghanistan, Algeria, Myanmar, Burundi, Chechnya, Colombia, Iraq, Israel/Palestine, Kashmir, Liberia, Nepal, the Philippines, Sri Lanka, Sudan, Turkey/Kurdistan, and Uganda, the scope of civil war has been shrinking.

Over the longer period since World War II, civil wars have concentrated in two kinds of regimes: (1) relatively high-capacity regimes, however democratic or undemocratic, containing significant zones that escape central control (of recent cases, Israel/Palestine, Kashmir, Peru, Chechnya, the Philippines, Turkey, and Colombia); (2) low-capacity undemocratic regimes (the rest). In both sorts of regimes, armed opponents of central governments range from defenders of regional turfs to activists seeking the overthrow of central governments. They range from warlords and beleaguered peasants, at one end, to outright secessionists or revolutionaries, at the other. All along that continuum, however, they face the dual problems of high stakes and sustaining armed force.

In both types of regimes, furthermore, warlords and revolutionaries alike have the incentives and the means to create their own armed forces and mark out their own zones of territorial control. Arms are widely available on a worldwide clandestine market fed especially by distributors in the United States and the former Soviet bloc (Boutwell, Klare, and Reed 1995). Access to outside support (e.g., of Middle Eastern Islamic activists in Chechnya and of Congo-based militias in Burundi) and availability of

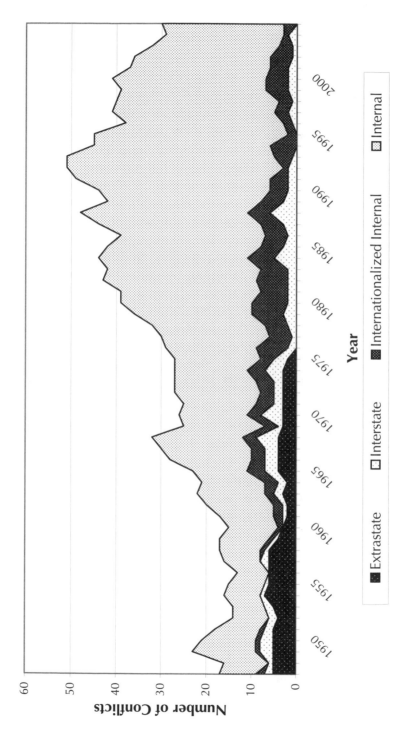

Figure 7.2. Number of Armed Conflicts by Type, 1946–2004
Source: Data supplied by Mikael Eriksson and Peter Wallensteen.

high-value contraband (e.g., diamonds in Liberia and heroin in Afghanistan) makes arming all the easier.

Civil wars, then, illustrate dramatically how the form of a regime generates a political opportunity structure, which in turn interacts with established claim-making repertoires to shape the character of contentious politics. In regimes like that of Sudan, to be sure, contentious politics also proceeds in other modes than civil war. Within regions, local populations still struggle over land, sexual relations, and religious rights. Despite heavy repression, Sudan's university students occasionally manage a peaceful collective statement of dissent. Nevertheless, the low-capacity undemocratic character of the Sudanese regime gives its national-scale contentious politics far greater resemblances to the struggles of Chechnya and Colombia than to those of Italy and Germany.

Revolutions

Revolutions, as we will soon see, share some properties with civil wars. But they also have their own distinctive dynamics. Let us define a *revolution* as a forcible transfer of power over a state in the course of which at least two distinct blocs of contenders make incompatible claims to control the state, and some significant portion of the population subject to the state's jurisdiction acquiesces in the claims of each bloc.

A full revolution combines a revolutionary situation with a revolutionary outcome. A *revolutionary situation* involves a broad split in the regime, with each party controlling some substantial territory and/or instruments of government. Clearly, we are talking about a matter of degree, about a continuum from no split at all to a split that completely divides the regime. A *revolutionary outcome* is different: an extensive transfer of power over the government, such that few of those who controlled it before now hold power. Once again we are dealing with a matter of degree, from no transfer to an utterly complete transfer. Figure 7.1 makes that point by placing great revolutions in its upper right-hand corner: extensive split in the regime followed by a large transfer of power within the regime.

With those insights in mind, let us look more closely at revolutionary situations and revolutionary outcomes. Here are the components of a revolutionary situation:

- Contenders or coalitions of contenders advancing exclusive competing claims to control of the state or some segment of it. This component results from mobilization, which in turn often involves brokerage and boundary activation; it constitutes a revolutionary coalition.

- Commitment to those claims by a significant segment of the citizenry. Again, we regularly see mobilization at work, often accompanied by diffusion, boundary activation, and external certification.
- Incapacity or unwillingness of rulers to suppress the alternative coalition and/or commitment to its claims. This component involves ruler-subject interaction, often with alliances forming between challengers and previous members of the regime.

If all three elements occur together, a significant split has emerged within a previously integrated regime.

A revolutionary outcome has four components:

- *Defections of regime members*: Although sometimes members simply flee from the threat of destruction, often they form new coalitions with segments of the revolutionary coalition.
- *Acquisition of armed force by revolutionary coalitions*: Such coalitions can occur through external support, incorporation of previously separate dissident units, purchase, or mobilization of arms already under control of coalition participants.
- *Neutralization or defection of the regime's armed force*: At times the rank and file melt away as they see a superior force rising and their leaders dividing, but more often military leaders themselves take their units into neutrality or opposition.
- *Control of the state apparatus by members of revolutionary coalition*: Rarely does this happen without some collaboration, however temporary, between revolutionaries and previously loyal agents of the threatened regime.

If all four elements occur together, a major transfer of power has transformed the regime.

Across history, far more revolutionary situations—political splits that cut across whole regimes—have occurred than revolutionary outcomes. Nevertheless, revolutionary outcomes continue to occur in the contemporary world. Dealing only with cases that he considers to qualify as major social revolutions since World War II, for example, Jeff Goodwin (2001: 4) mentions Vietnam, China, Bolivia, Cuba, Algeria, Ethiopia, Angola, Mozambique, Cambodia, South Vietnam, Iran, Nicaragua, and Grenada. Out of this set, box 7.2 offers a time line for the Nicaraguan revolution and its aftermath.

Box 7.2. Brief Chronology of the Nicaraguan Revolution and Its Aftermath	
July 1961	Formation of Sandinista National Liberation Front, beginning of scattered guerrilla activity against dictatorial Somoza regime.
December 1972	Earthquake levels Managua, Nicaraguan capital.
1973	Somoza's National Guard embezzles much of international earthquake aid; widespread disaffection with regime.
1977	U.S. President Jimmy Carter makes U.S. aid conditional on improved human rights situation; Somoza ends state of siege.
January 1978	Assassination of Pedro Joaquín Chamorro, editor of anti-Somoza newspaper; general strikes, urban uprisings, rural attacks on regime begin.
1978–1979	National Guard counterattacks, including aerial bombardment of cities, but gradually disintegrates.
January 1979	Mediation effort led by Organization of American States collapses.
February 1979	Sandinistas form broad National Patriotic Front (NPF); weapons begin to flow from Venezuela, Panama, and Cuba.
May 1979	Front launches major offensive.
June 1979	Regime opponents form government in exile, based in Costa Rica, begin to receive international recognition; Sandinistas gain control of most of country outside Managua.
July 1979	Somoza resigns, flees Nicaragua, Sandinistas enter Managua two days later, form Junta of National Reconstruction, broad coalition of revolutionaries and reformers.
1980	Splits begin to appear in governing coalition; Somoza murdered in Paraguay.
1981	U.S. president Ronald Reagan provides financial and military support for counterrevolutionary forces ("Contras"), including remnants of Somoza's National Guard, imposes trade embargo, and disrupts Nicaraguan shipping.
1981–1989	Contra war, with opposition to Sandinistas strongly supported by United States.
1982	Under congressional pressure, U.S. State Department declares Contra activity terrorism.
1984	National elections, Sandinistas elected overwhelmingly; United States denounces elections as a sham.
1989	End of war in stalemate closely monitored by external powers, with Nicaragua in ruins.
1990	Following peace agreements, election of Violeta Chamorro (non-Sandinista member of NPF) as president.

Nicaragua from 1961 to 1990 shows us the opening of a deep revolutionary situation, creation of a revolutionary outcome, prolonged civil war with uneven external support for both sides, and a settlement that reversed a significant portion of the revolution's earlier power transfer. Whether we count Nicaragua's experience as a "great revolution" in Goodwin's terms therefore depends on the points in time we consider. Certainly the transformations of 1979–1980 undid much of the preceding Somoza regime's corruption and made significant moves toward socializing the national economy. At their height, the Sandinistas provided a model for revolutionaries across Latin America. But U.S.-sponsored Contras, a trade embargo, and attacks on shipping soon started reversing the revolutionary tide.

Let us apply the two checklists of revolutionary elements to Nicaragua. The checkoff for a revolutionary situation looks something like this:

- *Contenders advancing exclusive competing claims to control of the state*: Formation of the Sandinista National Liberation Front (1961) identifies this element; it resulted from polarization, brokerage, and mobilization.
- *Commitment to those claims by a significant segment of the citizenry*: Between the popular reaction to the government's mishandling of the Managua earthquake (1972) and the assassination of Chamorro (1978), this process was clearly under way. More polarization accelerated this process, with diffusion, brokerage, attribution of similarity, and a resulting scale shift powerfully promoting it.
- *Incapacity or unwillingness of rulers to suppress the alternative coalition and/or commitment to its claims*: Jimmy Carter's 1977 decertification of the regime signaled the limits to previously enthusiastic U.S. support for Somoza, but the following disintegration of the National Guard as it failed to suppress the government's growing opposition capped that decertification. Failed repression, signaling spirals concerning the government's vulnerability, and diffusion all contributed to this third element of a revolutionary situation.

Although the three elements of the revolutionary situation reinforced each other as they took shape, somewhat different sets of mechanisms and processes shaped each one of them.

What of the revolutionary outcome, considering the situation in 1979–1980 as the maximum transfer of power from old regime to new? Here is the review:

- *Defection of regime members*: Although a "group of twelve" prominent Nicaraguans early repudiated the regime (1977) and soon fled
into exile, after Chamorro's assassination in 1978, we see massive defections by previous collaborators (however reluctant) with Somoza,
many of whom moved actively into coalition with the Sandinistas.
Defections accelerated as the National Guard vainly tried to restore
its control with massive force. In this regard, polarization and failed
repression played major parts in producing one element of a revolutionary outcome.

- *Acquisition of armed force by revolutionary coalitions*: After a
disastrous defeat of their attempt to produce a mountain uprising in
1967, the Sandinistas concentrated heavily on creating a clandestine
national military organization. They acquired some arms from outside with the help of their international supporters, bought or stole
some from the National Guard, and assembled weapons already held
by individual households, but created much of their insurrection-
ary military organization from scratch, inspired by models already
known elsewhere in Latin America. Mobilization and coordination
were the dominant processes.

- *Neutralization or defection of the regime's armed force*: The Somoza regime provides a spectacular example of this element, as a
once fearsome National Guard melted away. Failed repression and
(now domestic) decertification figured importantly in the regime's
loss of effective armed force.

- *Control of the state apparatus by members of the revolutionary
coalition:* In 1979, Somoza's flight upon the collapse of his army and
the defection of his erstwhile allies produced a double movement,
in which Sandinistas and their collaborators moved quickly into the
principal centers of power and existing officials quickly transferred
their allegiance to a revolutionary coalition now enlarged by the
presence of non-Sandinista reformers. Domestic decertification of the
old regime and international certification of the new one accelerated
the turnover, but top-down coordination within the revolutionary
coalition played the central part.

Notice what we have been doing. The three elements of a revolutionary
situation and the four elements of a revolutionary outcome are true by
definition. When all are fulfilled, they simply tell us that a revolutionary
situation has given way to a revolutionary outcome. Struggle has produced

a significant transfer of power over the government, and a deep split within the regime has first opened and then closed. But distinguishing the seven elements greatly clarifies the work of explaining revolutions. It emphasizes that although the appearance of one element affects the appearance of the others, each element springs from a somewhat different set of causes—of mechanisms and processes.

The distinction also makes clear why revolutionary situations occur so much more frequently than revolutionary outcomes. Actually taking over an existing government depends on even more demanding activities than opening a split within a regime. Among other things, the people who already run the government generally resist being thrown out; even Nicaragua's hapless Somoza regime, after all, held on eighteen years after the Sandinistas' launching and seven years after the disastrous Managua earthquake of 1972. Defections of regime members, acquisition of armed force, neutralization of a regime's armed force, and control of a state apparatus all involve momentous organizational activity, far surpassing the establishment of power at a regional base.

Conclusion

The ethnic-religious conflicts, civil wars, and revolutions examined in this chapter look like quite separate phenomena, a world apart from the politics of the social movements we encountered in chapter 6. Massacres and demonstrations have little in common, even if troops occasionally shoot down demonstrators. Social movement campaigns arise disproportionately in open regimes, such as the United States, or in less open regimes in which cracks are appearing, such Poland in the 1980s. In contrast, the large-scale lethal conflicts analyzed in this chapter took place disproportionately in regimes that did not feature social movements, especially in low-capacity undemocratic regimes. Yet this chapter's look at deadly ethnic-religious conflict, civil wars, and revolutions revealed great affinities among them and substantial connections with less violent forms of contention.

The secret is no secret: Once we take the analysis to the level of mechanisms and processes, we discover that similar causes and effects operate across the whole range of contentious politics, from viciously violent to pristinely peaceful. Much like the main subjects of chapter 6—Solidarity in Poland and the new women's movement in the United States—Ireland's IRA/Sinn Féin and Nicaragua's Sandinista movement took hold through combinations of mobilization, brokerage, diffusion, certification, and boundary activation.

Of course, differences existed, but they were not idiosyncratic or unpredictable. In all these cases, existing political opportunity structure interacted with established repertoires to shape what sorts and degrees of contention occurred within a given regime. In all these cases, the overall character of the regime (especially the capacity of its central government and its degree of democracy) strongly affected the location and the sheer possibility of contention.

That summarizes the two main messages of our book so far: (1) similar mechanisms and processes operate across the whole range of contentious politics, and (2) existing opportunity structures and established repertoires shape the forms and degrees of contention. In mainly democratic regimes, the repertoire of contention leans toward peaceful forms of contention that intersect regularly with representative institutions and produce social movement campaigns; in mainly authoritarian regimes, the repertoire leans toward lethal conflicts and tends to produce religious and ethnic strife, civil wars, and revolutions.

Two additional factors complicate the picture we have drawn. First, not all regimes fit neatly into the simple boxes of our regime typology. Second, contention in national states does not operate in airtight boxes, if it ever did. Globalization and internationalization have created interdependencies between states and peoples. It is logical to ask how these interdependencies affect contentious politics. Chapter 8 turns both to the intersections of social movements with lethal forms of conflict and to linkages between the global and the local in today's contentious world.

8

Jewish settlers in the Gaza Strip display Nazi-
era images to shame the Israeli troops that are
evacuating them from their homes in August
2005. (Roni Schutzer/AFP/Getty Images)

CHAPTER EIGHT

CONTENTION IN COMPOSITE REGIMES

This chapter explores contentious politics in two versions of what we have called composite regimes. We mean regimes in which different systems of rule shape the contentious repertoires of different populations. We saw such a composite regime in Northern Ireland: Even as the British army occupied Ulster and violent conflicts pitted Protestants and Catholics against one another, contained forms of contention typical of democratic states were keeping alive at least a shadow of civil politics. We see it again in two forms in this chapter:

- *horizontally segmented regimes,* like Northern Ireland's, in which lethal and social movement politics coincide;
- emerging *transnationally composite* regimes, in which contention crosses borders and involves actors at different levels of politics—supranational, national, and local.

We first turn to the territories that were once called Palestine and are now governed by the state of Israel. Here, armed struggles for control, guerrilla warfare, and social movement politics have continued from the 1940s onward. In 2006, we find a religious/ethnic conflict interlaced with a continuing near-civil war. But we also find a social movement of Jewish settlers mobilized against the Israeli government.

In 2004, Prime Minister Ariel Sharon, who had masterminded the planting of Israeli settlements among the Arab population in the 1980s, announced the evacuation of some seven to eight thousand settlers from Jewish enclaves in the Gaza Strip, home to over 1.3 million Palestinians. These Israeli citizens responded to Sharon's move with a wide array of actions from what we have called "the social movement repertoire." Their actions intersected with the forms of lethal politics more typical of the authoritarian and semiauthoritarian regimes we studied in the previous chapter. Israel/Palestine is a segmented composite regime.

We then move westward to Spain, where a number of émigrés from Chile were living in the late 1990s and where a magistrate, Balthazar Garzón, was investigating the human rights abuses that drove them out of their homeland. Twenty-six years after democracy fell to a military coup, a group of these exiles informed Garzón that former dictator Augusto Pinochet was visiting London. Garzón immediately issued an extradition request to the British government asking to interrogate Pinochet for torture and other human rights crimes against Spanish citizens during the years when he was Chile's ruler.

The decision electrified supporters of human rights around the world (Davis 2003; Roht-Arriaza 2005). There followed an unusual combination of local and transnational contention and of juridical, parliamentary, diplomatic, and street politics in three different states—Britain, Spain, and Chile. Domestic and international legal traditions clashed. Ancient institutions, such as the British House of Lords, interacted with new transnational groups, such as Amnesty International, which pled for Pinochet's extradition. The British government did send Pinochet home, but the case triggered a cascade of trials of former torturers and authoritarians from several former dictatorships in Latin America (Lutz and Sikkink 2001).

These two vignettes involved different actors, occurred on different continents, combined different forms of contention, and ranged from the very local to the global. The first involved the struggle of two peoples for control of the same handkerchief of land in a corner of the Middle East. The second turned on fundamental issues of human rights, internationalism, and law. Yet they operated through similar mechanisms and processes, and both raise the issue of how mixed regimes affect and are affected by contentious politics. Composite regimes and the forms of contention they foster differentiate subject and citizen populations, but both forms of contention intersect and influence one another.

Homeless in Gaza

Jewish settlements emerged in the West Bank and in the Gaza Strip after 1967 as an extension of the preindependence Zionist practice of "planting Jews" strategically amid the majority Arab population. But private motivations were at play as well: Families who could not afford the high living costs in Israel proper and religious Zionists who were uncomfort-able living in Israel's largely secular society were eager to accept the generous subsidies that the Israeli state offered to take up residence in the territories. Under increasing international pressure and in the face of the ruinous financial and military cost of maintaining isolated settlements, Prime Minister Sharon decided in 2004 to evacuate Gaza's approximately eight thousand Jewish settlers. Box 8.1 summarizes the history of these settlements and the pattern of their evacuation through September 2005, when the Palestinian Authority moved pell-mell into the Gaza Strip.

While the creation of the state of Israel resulted from a policy of "settle-ment" that qualified as a social movement, Gaza was unusual in this respect: Israel wrested the region from Egyptian control in a 1967 war. Israel settled it largely with national-religious families, inspired both by the desire for subsidized housing and by the desire to bring redemption. Most were farm-ers who hired Palestinian labor to produce fruits and vegetables for urban markets along the Mediterranean coast. Israeli authorities surrounded those prosperous enclaves with barbed wire and protected them against the sur-rounding Arab population with a substantial military presence. Periodically, violent Palestinian groups, both secular Marxists and Muslim activists such as Hamas and Islamic Jihad, set off bombs and lobbed mortars into the Jew-ish enclaves, which led to retaliation from the Israeli Defense Force (IDF). These militants also used the southern boundary of the Gaza Strip to bring arms and ammunition across from Egypt.

By the turn of the new century, the Gaza settlements had become a running sore for Israeli rulers and for their relations with Egypt and the Palestinians. Sharon's government sympathized with the settlers' plight. But the government found itself increasingly weighed down by the cost of maintaining their enclaves, by the inability of the military to stop the attacks, and by the desire to preempt Western pressure. As relations with the weak and divided Palestinian Authority stalled and the prospect of a general settlement retreated, the evacuation of a small number of Jewish families from the seething slum of Gaza seemed a sensible way of showing progress in relation to the Palestinians and lowering the tension between Israel and its allies.

The evacuation of the Jewish settlements in the Gaza Strip was embed-ded in a composite regime. Listen to what longtime left-wing critic of the Israeli occupation Uri Avneri had to say about it:

> The present struggle is a kind of civil war, even if—miraculously, again—no blood will be spilled. The Yesha people [i.e., the settler movement] are

Box 8.1. Brief Chronology of the Gaza Evacuation

1947   The United Nations votes in favor of two states, an Arab and a Jewish one, which does not include the Gaza Strip.

1948   The state of Israel is declared. Battles erupt in the south between Egyptian and Israeli forces. Thousands of Palestinians flee and settle in the Gaza Strip. The Strip's population increases more than threefold.

1949   Following the signing of the armistice, the Gaza area comes under Egyptian military rule. Egypt proclaims the Strip held in trust for the Palestinians. The residents of Gaza are not given Egyptian citizenship.

1967   Israel captures the Gaza Strip during the Six Day War. The United Nations Security Council passes Resolution 242, calling for the withdrawal of Israeli armed forces from territories occupied in the war in exchange for an end to the Arab-Israeli conflict.

1970   Kfar Darom—a Jewish community in the Strip evacuated in 1948—is reestablished as a paramilitary Nahal outpost.

1987   First intifada breaks out in Gaza City. Hamas founded in Gaza.

1993   Oslo Accords signed between Israel and the Palestinian Liberation Organization. End of intifada declared. Palestinian Authority created.

1994   Hamas and Islamic Jihad begin suicide bombings. Under the Gaza-Jericho Agreement, Israeli military forces withdraw from Gaza and Jericho and transfer authority to the Palestinian Authority. IDF forces leave most of the Strip's Palestinian inhabited areas. Israel maintains control of the settlements, borders, and other strategic points.

1995   Israel surrounds the Strip with a security fence. Israel and the Palestinian Authority sign the Israeli-Palestinian Interim Agreement on the West Bank and the Gaza Strip. Prime Minister Yitzhak Rabin assassinated in Tel Aviv.

2000   Camp David Summit fails; second intifada erupts, and Gaza settlements suffer constant attacks. IDF recaptures sections of the Gaza Strip in response to Palestinian attacks.

2004   Prime Minister Ariel Sharon presents a disengagement plan from Gaza and the northern West Bank.

2005   July: A nationwide antidisengagement campaign is launched by the settlers and their allies. The Knesset ratifies the disengagement plan. Government announces August 15 as the day disengagement is set to begin. Early August: Finance Minister Netanyahu resigns from the Cabinet. Militant settlers from the West Bank infiltrate the settlements. August 15: Unarmed IDF troops and Israeli police serve eviction notices on the settlers, most of whom leave peacefully. A minority of the settlers refuse to leave on their own and are carried out gently by IDF troops, some of whom collapse in tears. In two settlements, resisters occupy the roof of a synagogue and shower water, oil, and acid on the troops below. August 22: all of the settlers and militants have been evacuated and the settlements are bulldozed. September 12: all IDF forces leave, the Palestinian Authority troops move into Gaza, and Hamas supporters jubilantly celebrate their "victory."

a revolutionary movement. Their real aim is to overturn the democratic system and impose the reign of their rabbis. Anyone who has studied the history of revolutions knows that the role of the army is the decisive factor. As long as the army stands united behind the regime, the revolution is condemned to failure. Only when the army is disintegrating or joins the rebels, the revolution can win. (http://zope.gush-shalom.org/home/en/channels/avnery/1123967824)

Civil wars, revolutionary movements, armies? Avneri's prognosis makes it sound as if Israel had begun to resemble the cases of authoritarian Sudan, divided Northern Ireland, or revolutionary Nicaragua. Yet on Freedom House's rankings, Israel ranks in the highest category for political rights and in the third category for civil rights. Of course, these rankings exclude the occupied territories, where the rankings were as low as six for political rights and six for civil rights. The disjunction reminds us that regimes can vary internally in terms of their degree of democracy. That internal variation leads to contrasts and intersections between their forms of contentious politics. In the Gaza settler's movement we find a social movement campaign overlapping a civil war.

Let's put this analysis in terms of explanations from earlier chapters. Israel/Palestine's political opportunity structures divide sharply between Israeli citizens and Palestinian subjects. (The Arab population of Israel proper stands somewhere in between.) Gaza's settlers occupied an uneasy transition zone between two kinds of politics: the civil politics that regularly produce robust social movement campaigns among Israelis and the uncivil politics that produce lethal conflict both within Israel and in the West Bank and Gaza. If this is not the revolutionary situation that Avneri predicted, it did produce a composite politics of contention in response to the Sharon government's plans to evacuate Gaza in 2004–2005.

In its factual details, the settlers' campaign had little in common with the actors, the performances, and the targets of the social movements we examined in chapter 6. But it embodied many of the properties of social movement politics we have seen elsewhere. The settlers used nonviolent performances from the inherited repertoire of contention. But they innovated around its edges. For example, some of them—notoriously for survivors of the Holocaust—marched out of their settlements wearing yellow stars of David on their clothing. That gesture scandalized most Israelis by hinting that the IDF soldiers accompanying them resembled Hitler's SS.

The stars of David worn by the settlers were no mere costume ornaments. They drew on Israeli's founding myth to activate the boundary between the majority of Israelis who supported Sharon's move and the minority who opposed it. Like the episodes we studied in chapter 5, their campaign followed a trajectory of mobilization and demobilization, first bringing in supporters from outside of Gaza to organize resistance and then losing steam as the IDF and the government combined facilitation of resettlement with repression of those who refused to leave.

Like the movements we saw in chapter 6, the settlers built on a social movement base: the organizations of West Bank settler communities and their religious Zionist supporters in the United States. Their actions could not hope to stop the evacuation, but they were successful in furthering the split in the ruling party. In the midst of the evacuation, Finance Minister Benjamin Netanyahu, Sharon's rival for power, made a dramatic move. Supported by a majority of the Likud Party, Netanyahu resigned from the cabinet and prepared to try to wrest control of Likud from Sharon.

The Gaza movement revealed the same mechanisms we saw working in Solidarity and the new American women's movement. As settlers and their allies demonstrated at the Wailing Wall and used the imagery of the Holocaust to protest their government's actions, they were *innovating in the repertoire of contention.* As their differences from Prime Minister Sharon sharpened, they *activated a new boundary* between religious and realist conservative Zionism. They sought *certification* for their cause by identifying it with the traditions of frontier Zionism and with the horrors of the Holocaust. West Bank militants who filtered into the Gaza Strip *brokered* the settlers' alliance with far right elements in Israeli politics. Their resistance *shifted upward in scale* to Israeli national politics when thousands flocked to the Western Wall to protest the evacuation.

Amid Lethal Conflict

But no social movement operates in a vacuum. Creation of Israel as a state had produced a vast Arab refugee population, part of it living in refugee camps in the West Bank and Gaza. Another part dispersed in a broad diaspora that fed what Benedict Anderson (1998) calls "long-distance nationalism." At first secular Arab leaders, inspired by conventional Marxist and nationalist models, led the liberation movement fed by this double displacement. After the Iranian revolution in 1979, however, Islamist groups became more influential, both at home and in the diaspora. The movement to liberate Palestine took on an increasingly apocalyptic tone. In 1981, militants started using suicide bombing in Lebanon. During the 1990s, it became a preferred tool of religious militants in authoritarian situations (Berman and Laitin 2005; Gambetta 2005; Pedahzur 2005). From that point on, suicide bombers killed increasing numbers of Israelis. In the Gaza evacuation, we see links to the kinds of lethal conflicts we studied in chapter 7.

Lethal politics infested both communities. After the death of longtime Palestinian Liberation Organization leader Yassir Arafat, a new Palestinian Authority government in the West Bank began to seek accommodation with Israel. But the Israeli government demanded more—a retreat from violence to advance the peace process. It was just at this point, in 2006, that the radical Islamist group Hamas came to power in Palestinian elections. Lethal violence also recurred within the Palestinian community, culminating in shoot-outs in Gaza during and after the evacuation (Usher 2005).

The radical fringe of the Palestinian resistance had no monopoly of political violence. In part in reaction to that resistance, but in part as an offshoot of the military nature of the settlement process, a growing strand of apocalyptic religious Zionists had emerged, both in the settlement communities and in Israel proper (Lustick 1998; Sprinzak 1991). In the course of the 1990s, attacks on Palestinians by Jewish militants multiplied. Conflicts sharpened between Jewish militants and the secular majority of Israeli society. This process of radicalization culminated in the assassination of Prime Minister Yitzhak Rabin by a religious fanatic at a Tel Aviv peace rally in 1995 (Peleg 2002; Sprinzak 1999). In the same period, attacks on West Bank Arab farmers increased. Lethal politics migrated from the occupied territories to Israeli society.

By the time Israel evacuated its settlers from Gaza, this double radicalization had hardened relations between Arabs and Jews as well as within both communities. While the majority of Israelis had wearied of living in a state of civil war, the prosettlement minority moved inexorably toward the kind of extremism and isolation we saw in Northern Ireland. Simultaneously, while the Palestinian Authority under Abbas reluctantly accepted the necessity of coexistence with Israel, the religious militants of Hamas and Islamic Jihad intensified their attacks on them. As chapter 3 would have predicted, the composite nature of the Israeli regime produced two kinds of contentious politics: the social movement politics we saw in the Gaza evacuation and lethal politics within and between the two communities.

Given the cleavages within Israeli and Palestinian society and between the Israelis and the Arab militants, it is surprising how little violence actually marked the evacuation. In its course, scattered outbursts occurred on both sides. In an act designed to short-circuit the evacuation process, Israeli militants shot eight Palestinian citizens, four inside Israel and the others in the West Bank. During the evacuation, Hamas militants lobbed a few mortar shells into the Jewish enclaves but failed to trigger the desired military response. Unknown activists tried to sink an American ship in the harbor of the Jordanian port of Aqaba but succeeded only in killing a Jordanian soldier. After the evacuation, a mysterious commando gunned down the brother of late Palestinian leader Yassir Arafat in broad daylight.

As often occurs when the possibility of peace appears, tensions developed within Israeli and Palestinian politics. On the one hand, as the Palestinian Authority prepared to take control of Gaza, Hamas militants were taking credit for the pullout and looking forward to governing the "liberated" territory (Usher 2005). That meant both the creation of a stronger base from which to attack Israeli settlements and the transformation of Hamas into a political party, as was occurring to its sister organization, Hezbollah, in Lebanon. If the former dominated, a lethal military reaction would come from the Israelis. If the latter, Gaza could become the core of a Palestinian social movement politics, vigorous and sometimes violent, but centering on electoral competition. As we go to press at the start of 2006, there has been a radical realignment in both Israeli and Palestinian politics, but Israel/Palestine is still paralyzed between the social movement politics we examined in chapter 6 and the lethal politics we saw in chapter 7.

Transnational Contention

The case of Israel/Palestine reminds us that we cannot detach social movement politics from the broader context of national politics. It also tells us that there are striking similarities and interconnections between the mechanisms and processes that drive lethal politics and social movements. But it tells us something new as well. In concentrating so centrally on political regimes, repertoires, and opportunities, we have implicitly assumed that the arenas of contentious politics are national and local. But if this was ever accurate, it is no longer the case today. At the beginning of the twenty-first century, local, national, and international politics intersect at many points.

Think of foreign policy: High on the priority list of Prime Minister Sharon in evacuating Gaza was the wish to placate the international community that had been insisting, without visible success, that Israel end its occupation. Now think of the links between both communities and their respective transnational allies. Both Jewish activists and Arab militants were deeply embedded in transnational axes of contention. Within the Gaza settlers' movement, numerous foreign settlers—mainly Americans—had left the diaspora to bring up their children in the land of Israel. Solidarity and financial support from the most lethal transnational movement in the world today, political Islamism, animated the Arab militants who were harassing the Gaza settlers. Israel/Palestine's composite regime overlaps with the contentious politics of the wider world.

Students of contentious politics have been slow to adjust their lenses from a close focus on national politics. That focus grew logically both from historical reality and out of pedagogical convenience. But in the real world we seek to understand, large-scale contention rarely takes place entirely within national borders. It seldom has. Thinking back, many of the domestic episodes in our book were linked to other parts of the world, either through militants' transnational ties or through the impersonal diffusion of their claims. British antislavery diffused rapidly to Western Europe and the Americas. The Ukrainian Orange Revolution followed closely on antielection fraud movements elsewhere in the former Soviet bloc and gave rise to copycat movements in Central Asia. Although Solidarity was a Polish national movement, it inspired dissidents throughout Eastern Europe. Even the "shantytowns" that American college students built in the 1980s were part of an international movement against apartheid.

In today's contentious politics, transnational links have taken on a qualitatively new character. Three broad processes mark it off from past epochs of contention: transnational activism, the formation of transnational coalitions, and rapid transnational diffusion.

In *transnational activism,* a new stratum of activists supports the claims of others beyond their own borders in a wide variety of sectors of activity (Keck and Sikkink 1998). When Clarkson went to France to convince that country's revolutionaries that slavery was an affront to the Rights of Man, his effort was almost unique. But today's transnational activists can be in Chiapas or Darfur in a matter of days with help for insurgents or for victims of aggression. These "rooted cosmopolitans" are as comfortable in the halls of international institutions as they are in their own countries (Tarrow 2005: chap. 3).

Second, the World Bank, the International Monetary Fund, the United Nations and the European Union act as "coral reefs" around which activists, advocates, and those simply seeking their own advancement form *transnational coalitions* (O'Brien et al. 2000). International treaties such as the Torture Convention and tribunals such as the International Criminal Court offer focal points for human rights groups to attempt to bring violators to justice. International events and conflicts produce domestic contention, too, as was the case when millions of people around the world protested the U.S. invasion of Iraq in 2003.

Finally, regarding *rapid international diffusion of contention,* we have seen that local contention often has profound effects on contentious politics in other countries. Of course, this was true in the past. The 1848 revolution spread across Europe like an inkblot. But advances in communication and transportation and the links among peoples and groups across borders today hasten and intensify both diffusion and scale shift. Here the role of the Internet is important, but so are cheap and rapid international travel, and the diffusion of similar norms and cultural symbols in many parts of the world (Boli and Thomas 1999).

All three of these processes—transnational activism, transnational coalitions, and rapid international diffusion of contention—combined in the events surrounding the indictment of General Augusto Pinochet of Chile by a Spanish magistrate while he was being treated in a British clinic in 1998.

El Condor No Pasa

"General Augusto Pinochet really wanted to travel," writes Naomi Roht-Arriaza (2005: 1) in her definitive retelling of the Pinochet affair and its aftermaths. His problem, among others, was that thousands of other Chileans had been forced to leave their native land for fear of death or torture during the years when his ruthless regime ruled Chile. These diaspora Chileans formed the core of a social movement to try Pinochet for crimes against humanity when he was arrested in England in 1998.

As one Chilean exile told the story;

> During the dictatorship years, we had created a fabulous support network
> throughout Europe, including artists, unions, politicians and the like. We
> had been organizers in Chile, so we knew how to organize.... We knew
> each other all over Europe because we had either been prisoners together or
> knew someone who had. So as we learned English, got jobs, and developed
> good contacts in British society, we kept in touch with others throughout
> Europe. (quoted in Roht-Arriaza 2005: 38)

Those contacts turned out to be crucial when, in October, Pinochet traveled to London for surgery. It was members of the network of the Chilean
diaspora that located the clinic in which he had checked in under an assumed name. They spread the word to compatriots all over Europe, tipped
off the Spanish magistrates who were investigating torture in Chile and
Argentina, sat in on and demonstrated outside court hearings in London,
took notes on the proceedings, and sent them around the world (Roht-
Arriaza 2005: 39). These exiles fulfilled a classical *brokerage* function in
the sense we have used that mechanism in our book. They helped to put
Chilean human rights lawyers in touch with British civil liberties lawyers
and formed "a key part of the coalition of legal and human rights groups
that eventually formed to press ... for [Pinochet's] extradition" (38).

In contrast to the Chileans living in Western Europe, magistrate
Balthazar Garzón was no cosmopolitan. A man who had spent much of
his career prosecuting Spanish Basque terrorists, he spoke no English. He
was actually investigating human rights abuse in Argentina when word
came through that Pinochet was in London. The link that Garzón established from Argentina to Chile was the secret military intelligence pact
between the two countries and four other Latin American dictatorships.
Called "Operation Condor," this transgovernmental conspiracy took its
name from the giant raptor that traverses the Andes. The pact allowed
the "rendition" of captured militants from any one of these countries to
their home country, where many were tortured and killed. Garzón's case
against Pinochet was based on the ex-dictator's role in coordinating Operation Condor (Roht-Arriaza 2005: 29–31). It was the transgovernmental
conspiracy headed by Pinochet that gave Garzón the legal leverage to seek
his extradition from Britain to Spain.

Operation Condor was only one of the ways in which international
politics affected the Pinochet case. In seeking to extradite the ex-dictator, Garzón was employing a radically new theory in international law—

universal jurisdiction. Traditionally, international law only operates for what are generally recognized as international crimes, such as piracy. It only allows for the extradition of a suspected criminal to his or her own country, not to a third country. But increasingly, magistrates in countries such as Belgium and Spain have been applying the theory of universal jurisdiction to try people for a wide variety of crimes, from genocide to crimes against humanity to war crimes. Garzón based his case on the theory that Pinochet's actions against Spanish and other victims rose to the level of such international crimes. International law was becoming part of the opportunity structure that could enable a Spanish magistrate to seek the extradition of a former Chilean head of state from the United Kingdom.

The Pinochet case and its aftermath had profound diffusion effects. They led to a wave of trials and investigations against suspected torturers and those who gave them their orders. Although Home Secretary Jack Straw of Britain ultimately allowed Pinochet to return home, the events in Madrid and London produced what Ellen Lutz and Kathryn Sikkink (2001) call "a justice cascade." In Argentina, infamous torturer Carlos Guillermo Suarez Mason was arrested for the kidnapping of children of Argentina's disappeared (Lutz and Sikkink 2001: 20–21). In Mexico, authorities arrested retired Argentine navy captain Miguel Cavallo as the plane on which he was traveling stopped in Cancun. In Italy, magistrates advanced a criminal case that had been languishing for years against seven Argentine military officers for the murder of eight Argentines of Italian descent. Rome was also where another Argentine former officer, Jorge Olivera, was arrested in August 2000 while celebrating his wedding anniversary. The cascade came full circle when, in the Chile of 2004, Pinochet came under indictment and a government commission called for reparations for the survivors of his reign of terror.

Globalization, Internationalization, and Transnational Contention

In the Pinochet case, we see all three transnational processes we hypothesized at the outset. First, a group of transnational activists triggered the sequence of events we have sketched here. Second, a transnational coalition formed around the issue. Third, rapid diffusion of contention occurred across national boundaries. (There was even a whiff of scale shift, as the case contributed to the current drive for the creation of the

International Criminal Court.) As we write, Pinochet has been indicted in Chile for both human rights abuses and international money laundering, and the case still moves glacially through the Chilean courts. But it illustrates the partial, ambiguous, and yet insistent move toward a composite global regime of states, international institutions, and nonstate actors. Two major processes lie behind these developments: globalization and internationalization.

Globalization is the increasing volume and speed of flows of capital and goods, information and ideas, people, and forces that connect actors between countries (Keohane 2002: 194). Scholars including Jackie Smith and Hank Johnston (2003) have argued vigorously that globalization sets the stage for transnational contention. Others have derived from this process the idea that something called a "global social movement" is resulting (Evans 2005; McMichael 2005). These writings have an empirical counterpart in the hundreds of thousands of young activists who have flocked to the World Social Forum in Porto Alegre, Brazil, and Mumbai, India. Many thousands of others have participated in regional forums in Western Europe, Latin America, and elsewhere (Pianta 2001, 2002; Pianta and Silva 2003) and taken part in solidarity movements with the insurgent Zapatista movement in Chiapas, Mexico (Olesen 2005).

Globalization takes many forms that affect the mounting and transmission of contentious politics. Here are some of them:

- The growing linkages between the economies of North and South put southern workers at the mercy of market forces controlled by producers, investors, and consumers from the North.
- The same trends have a converse effect in the North: the loss of industrial jobs by workers whose firms move to countries where labor is cheap and trade unions are repressed.
- Improvements in travel and communication make it possible for activists from different parts of the world to travel to the sites of contention, meet others like themselves, and form transnational coalitions. A special vehicle of this convergence is the Internet, which plays a similar role that newspapers and television did in earlier eras (Bennett 2005).
- Cultural and institutional standardization makes it easier for activists to frame issues in similar ways and for modular forms of contention to be understood and adopted in a wide variety of places (Boli and Thomas 1999).

Yes, globalization is having a profound effect on contentious politics (Tarrow 2005: chap. 2; Tilly 1995). But as an orienting concept for understanding transnational activism, globalization on its own says both too much and too little. It says too little because it leaves out the intervening processes and mechanisms that lead people to engage in contentious politics. If earlier chapters have shown us anything, they have demonstrated the value of tracing processes and mechanisms instead of simply correlating big changes with each other. Globalization also says too much: A great deal of the transnational activism we find in the world today doesn't result directly from globalization.

Think of the Islamist militants who lob shells at Israeli settlements, plant bombs on Israeli buses, and occasionally blow themselves up in Israeli cafés and restaurants. While they are certainly prospective actors in the future Palestinian state and part of the transnational archipelago of violent Islamist groups inspired by the Iranian revolution of 1979, what do they have to do with globalization? Although they belong to a profoundly transnational movement—political Islamism—only by a wide stretch of the imagination or a very loose definition are they connected to globalization. Globalization is a threat that inspires many transnational activists, especially those who make claims against the World Bank, the IMF, or the World Trade Organization. But as a "master process" explaining transnational contention, it leaves much to be desired.

The term *internationalization* better summarizes the mechanisms that link domestic political actors to transnational contentious politics. In internationalization, you will find a parallel to our concept of political opportunity structure. Political opportunity structure was introduced in chapter 3 and has appeared at the local, regional, and national levels throughout our book. Internationalization influences opportunity structure through two components: (1) increasing horizontal density of relations among states, governmental officials, and nonstate actors and (2) increasing vertical ties between these and international institutions or organizations (Tarrow 2005: chap. 2).

The logic runs like this: States, nonstate actors, and international organizations and institutions link increasingly within what Anne-Marie Slaughter (2004) calls "a new world order." Think of a few of the factors that were responsible for the extradition request for General Pinochet from Britain by a Spanish judge: a transnational conspiracy between the militaries of Southern Cone dictatorships, transgovernmental cooperation between British and Spanish lawyers and magistrates, and an international legal theory—universal jurisdiction—that permitted Judge Garzón to seek Pinochet's extradition.

As the Pinochet case shows, an important component of internationalization is legalization. As international agreements become more complex and involve larger numbers of actors, they require a legal structure, which in turn requires the creation of international panels and agencies (Goldstein et al. 2001). This development in turn creates focal points, incentives, and threats that lead to the creation and cooperation of transnational groups. When the latter discover one another and their mutual interests, transnational coalitions and movements result. Like domestic institutions that constitute national political opportunity structure, internationalization is like a coral reef around which national governments, firms, and nonstate actors gravitate.

Internationalization triggers a whole array of mechanisms and processes:

- *Internalization* of international controversies manifests itself as domestic contention.
- *Diffusion* of a domestic controversy spreads into the politics of other countries.
- *Brokerage* of transnational alliances is conducted by transnational agents.
- *Boundary activation* and *scale shift* of contention move from the domestic to the international levels.
- *Mobilization* takes the form of transnational protest events, such as the dramatic "Battle of Seattle" that pitted environmental and labor activists against the World Trade Organization.
- The most dramatic innovation, but the most difficult to accomplish, is the creation of sustained transnational social movements from *coalitions* formed among domestic activists.
- To the extent that transnational movements displace domestic contention (and we hasten to add that there is not yet much sign of such a development), they will *deactivate the boundaries* between states and *activate new boundaries* across broader constellations of states.

Nonstate actors in transnational space include nongovernmental organizations (NGOs), professional and service groups, occasional participants in international protest events, and true social movements. Many of these actors feel threatened by globalization and its impact on the poor of the world. But they mobilize within an increasingly complex international opportunity structure. Like domestic opportunity structures, the international one combines opportunities and threats. It operates in the interstices of institutional and noninstitutional politics, offers challengers occasional allies, and rises and falls with broader political changes.

Three factors make this new international opportunity structure especially inviting for activists:

- First, its institutional venues link closely to the threats of globalization—for example, the World Trade Organization has contributed to disadvantages of the global South in international trade.
- Second, it offers a number of domestic and international sites for the "venue shopping" across sympathetic sites that astute activists can use to their advantage. This was clearly the case for the human rights and exile groups from London to Madrid that sought to indict Pinochet.
- Third, these activists can engage in transnational activism without giving up their domestic activities. On the contrary, they often return to their domestic roles invigorated by their experiences abroad, with new models of activism learned in their foreign experiences, and maintain the ties with people they meet at these events (Wood 2004).

Between them, the threats of globalization and the opportunities of internationalization have turned the attention of activists around the world from their domestic regimes to the international system and from domestic opponents to transnational corporations. And given the growing role of international institutions in governing trade, monetary affairs, and development, increasing numbers of advocacy and activist groups have focused their attention on the World Bank, the International Monetary Fund, and the World Trade Organization.

How does transnational contention qualify as part of a composite regime? The answer is that contention at the international level differs fundamentally from contention at the intranational level in a variety of ways.

First, although not all domestic contention targets governments directly, governments structure contention, respond to it, repress actors who go beyond the bounds of tolerated forms, and offer potential allies to those willing to interact with institutions. Although transnational actors find focal points, in individual governments, international institutions, or transnational corporations, in world politics there is no stable focal point like a government around which to organize contention.

Second, building transnational social movements is immensely more difficult than carrying out the same task in domestic politics. Think of our concept of social movement bases: As difficult as these are to build and mobilize in domestic politics, they are immensely harder to assemble in transnational politics. As a result, transnational social movement campaigns are generally fleeting and inconsistent, often leading to tragic failures.

Third—this follows from the second factor—activists who seek to build transnational movements are mainly thrown back on a strategy of federating small cadres of cosmopolitans at the international level with domestic groups in different countries. These face a host of different threats and opportunities, and their claims may only partially coincide with the transnational activists who attempt to coordinate their collective action.

Both the attractions and the difficulties of transnational contention can be seen in the most highly developed composite regime in the world today—the European Union (Hooghe and Marks 2002; Imig and Tarrow 2001). Here contentious action focuses on Brussels, where a host of transnational NGOs cluster and transnational protest events are mounted. But domestic actors, including French farmers, Belgian workers, Italian pensioners, and British environmentalists, have repeatedly protested in their own countries against such policies as reductions of farm subsidies, plant closures, the cutting of pension plans, and the importation of genetically modified seeds. Transnational NGOs from time to time succeed in coordinating collective action among these different national constituencies, but the differences among the institutions of the European Union and the opportunities and threats faced by activists in (now) twenty-five different countries make the task of coordination daunting.

Conclusion

What do the movement of Israeli settlers formed to oppose their evacuation from the Gaza strip and the Pinochet case have in common? Both, of course, combined social movement politics with lethal conflicts. Both also involved institutional elites and ordinary people. And in both, the mechanisms we have emphasized throughout this book—diffusion, boundary activation, brokerage—combined in a few key processes: mobilization, scale shift, and coalition formation. In many ways and in a variety of forms, contention in composite regimes resembles the mechanisms and processes we have seen in "purer" forms of regime.

But just as the social movement politics and the lethal conflicts we studied in chapters 6 and 7 combined with contextual factors to produce very different outcomes, the two composite forms we have examined in this chapter have their peculiar dynamics. For example, segmented regimes like Israel/Palestine exhibit in extreme form a mechanism we have seen before—*polarization*. Polarization involves increasing ideological distance between the wings of a once-unified movement sector, divisions between its leaders, and—in some cases—terrorism. We saw it in Italian contention (chapter 5) and in Sudan's struggles (chapter 7).

Polarization has particularly devastating effects in Israel/Palestine because both the Zionist and Palestinian movements are riven by polarization between moderate and radical factions. Between them, the two movements impede a move to contained contention. While both Israeli institutions and the country's international allies offer incentives for moderation, each time the moderates appear close to a convergence, radicals in one or both of these communities seize the opportunity to repolarize the situation. The same cycles of partial convergence, lethal outrages, and repolarization have impeded the progress of Northern Ireland toward a return to civil politics after the signature of the Good Friday agreement in 1998. Polarization occurs in a variety of settings, but the peculiar property of segmented polities is that the wall between the two segments fosters radicalization on both sides of it.

Transnational politics suffers from a different dynamic. While some have seen international politics moving away from a world of states toward a global civil society, our view is that states are permanent fixtures in world politics. This belief means that while states are drawn increasingly into international agreements, coalitions, and institutions, their alliances and conflicts are fundamentally shaped by their definition of their identities and interests. For example, the British government—which had signed both the Genocide Convention and the Torture Convention—never implemented either one. When push came to shove—and the coalition supporting Pinochet's extradition pushed very hard—Prime Minister Tony Blair's humanitarian instincts and his party's close ties with the Chilean Left were not as strong as the British state's interest in defending the sovereign right of each country to try its own criminals.

The Pinochet case is relevant to other episodes of international politics. When the United States, devastated by the massacres of September 11, 2001, launched a "war on terror," it included a no-holds-barred campaign to arrest, kidnap, and interrogate people suspected of terrorism. That strategy led to the construction of an illegal prison in Guantánamo, Cuba, the abuse of prisoners in Abu Ghraib and elsewhere, and the "rendition" of suspects to countries that routinely torture prisoners. As President Bush continued to proclaim the desire of the United States to advance democracy in the Middle East, a new version of Operation Condor was being secretly launched, with results that so far we can only imagine.

It took more than twenty years for crimes of the Pinochet regime to be publicized and processed by Chilean courts. That delay was in part because its acts were hidden from its own citizens, but in part because they occurred in a world that was less globalized and less internationalized than today's global regime. In 2004, digital photographs of prisoner abuse in Iraq instantly reached the United States as e-mail attachments, and international human rights groups launched inquiries that resulted in international condemnation of Iraq's "liberators." In 2005, word of the Untied States' rendition of prisoners to unknown destinations became known through exposure of the flight logs of the planes that transported them. By the end of that year, the United States' reputation had sunk to new lows around the world, and the U.S. Senate had condemned the abuse of prisoners. In a partially integrated global regime, domestic and international contention intersect.

These observations tell us that globalization and internationalization have mixed results. The same processes that allowed the United States to plant secret detention centers in Eastern Europe and Afghanistan also exposed those abuses to global public opinion. Similarly, the same processes that contribute to the creation of "good" NGOs such as Amnesty International and Human Rights Watch facilitated the formation and mobility of the murderers of September 11, 2001. Transnational politics has no deterministic outcome, just as no single trajectory applies to all of contentious politics. Our final chapter underlines those important conclusions.

In an action soon widely adopted elsewhere, African American students from North Carolina A & T College peacefully occupy seats at the previously whites-only lunch counter of a F. W. Woolworth store in Greensboro, North Carolina (1960). (Copyright © Bettmann/CORBIS)

CHAPTER NINE

CONTENTION TODAY AND TOMORROW

We began our journey though contentious politics with an incident that occurred two centuries ago when future antislavery activist Thomas Clarkson sat down by the side of the road on his way to London. That apparently insignificant event triggered a movement to end slavery that began in Britain, diffused to Western Europe and across the Atlantic, and eventually produced America's Civil War. We will end our book with an equally localized 1960 episode in Greensboro, North Carolina. The episode belonged to the most important American cycle of contention of the twentieth century—civil rights. We will use this movement to recapitulate the lessons of our book and use it as a platform to raise some of the many questions we have addressed and some we have only hinted at.

Sitting In in Greensboro

When four black students sat down at a whites-only lunch counter in Greensboro, sit-ins had already taken place in the American South. But these were mostly set-piece performances mounted by civil rights organizations. Here, four well-dressed black freshmen appeared unannounced at a whites-only lunch counter in the heart of a southern city. Before it was over, the Greensboro sit-in led to what Doug McAdam and William Sewell (2001) would call "a transformative event" (see also Andrews and Biggs forthcoming; McAdam 1999: 138–40). The students staged a deeply transgressive performance, but they carried it out in the most polite, contained manner. They launched a social movement of black college students and their allies.

As in many of the episodes we have studied, contingency and agency played important parts in the Greensboro sit-in. One of the students, Franklin McCain, later recalled:

> The planning process began on Sunday night. I remember it quite well. I think it was Joseph [McNeil] who said; "It's time that we take some action now. We've been getting together, and we've been, up to this point, still like most people we've talked about for the past few weeks or so—that is, people who talk a lot but, in fact, make little action." After selecting the technique, then we said, "Let's go down and just ask for service." It certainly wasn't titled a "sit-in" or "sit-down" at that time. (Raines 1977: 76)

Nor did the current state of the civil rights movement predict that the Greensboro sit-in would occur when it did. African American protests had gone into a holding pattern after the flurry of activity generated by the Supreme Court's *Brown* decision in 1954 (Andrews and Biggs forthcoming). Building on McAdam's (1999) efforts to use the *New York Times* to map the civil rights movement, Craig Jenkins and his collaborators charted events involving the civil rights movement between 1947 and 1997 (Jenkins, Jacobs, and Agnone 2003). As their data in Figure 9.1 figure show, in the wake of the *Brown* decision, the number of both protests and of general civil rights events declined; the 1960 sit-ins reversed both trends.

Right after Greensboro, sit-ins spread rapidly across the South. Kenneth Andrews and Michael Biggs (forthcoming) observe, "The protest was repeated, with increasing numbers of students, on subsequent days. A week later, the sit-ins began to spread to other cities. This typically meant students occupying seats at downtown lunch counters at 'five and dime' stores demonstrating their resistance to public segregation and disrupting the normal operating of business" (1–2).

Scholars have disagreed about the degree of planning versus spontaneity of the student sit-ins and about the role of the media versus civil rights organizations in their diffusion (Andrews and Biggs forthcoming; Killian 1984; McAdam 1983, 1999; Morris 1984; Oberschall 1989; Polletta 1998). But all agree that Greensboro provided a model that was picked up and rapidly diffused across the South. A week after the initial protest, similar sit-ins appeared in other cities, first in proximity to Greensboro but eventually all over the South (Oberschall 1989: n. 4). By April, sit-in campaigns had occurred in more than seventy cities (Andrews and Biggs forthcoming). We can see how far the movement spread from Andrews and Biggs' map of where student sit-ins appeared in figure 9.2.

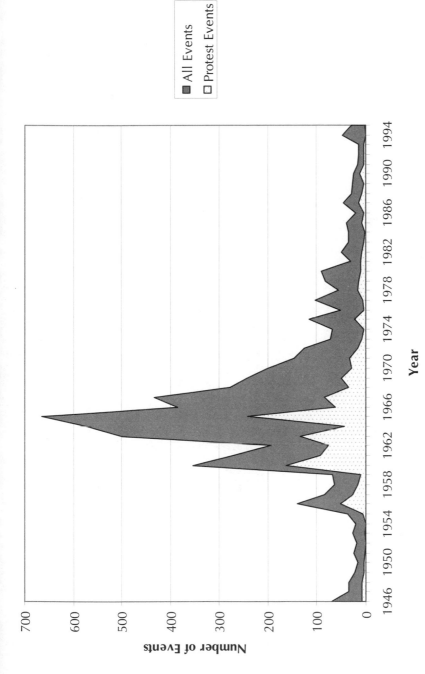

Figure 9.1. African American Total Movement and Protest Events
Source: Courtesy of J. Craig Jenkins.

Figure 9.2. Sit-ins in the American South, February 1 to April 14, 1960
Source: Andrews and Biggs (forthcoming).

The civil rights movement resembled the social movement campaigns that chapter 6 reviewed in a number of ways. All three took advantage of political opportunities offered by their respective regimes and worked their ways through a roughly similar set of mechanisms and processes. All three built on social movement bases—the Catholic Church in Poland, the latent women's rights tradition in the new American women's movement, and the black churches and the NAACP's legal campaigns in the 1950s. All of these had profound effects.

If the title of our book had been *Social Movements,* readers could have relaxed after reading chapter 6. But unlike many fine texts focusing on movements, our aim has been broader. Comparing the two cases in chapter 6 with the ones examined in chapters 7 and 8, you can see that social movements are only one of a wide array of forms of contentious politics. While all the episodes we have studied make claims on authorities, use public performances to do so, draw on inherited repertoires of collective action, forge alliances with influential members of their respective polities, and take advantage of existing regime opportunities while making new ones, the degree to which they use institutional routines to advance their claims varies sharply.

The student sit-ins and other similar actions were not the highest point of African American protests. As figure 9.1 shows, protests reached greater heights during the later 1960s. But the sit-ins forced a wedge into the practice of segregation in the American South and provided a model for other episodes of protest. Other challenges to public segregation followed the lunch counter sit-ins, culminating in the integration of bus terminals, movie theaters, and busses. Both because of its crucial importance for the history of contentious politics and because it has been so well studied, the student sit-in campaign can help us to review the main explanations presented in our book.

What Have We Learned?

Think back to the list of concepts presented in chapter 1. Each of them offers you an orienting point for describing and analyzing the story we have just sketched. The four Greensboro students launched the sit-in movement at Woolworth's, but the movement was actually aimed at a system of segregation created and regulated by state and local *governments.* In doing so, students constituted themselves as *political actors* and assumed the *political identities* of people unwilling to accept the subaltern status assigned to members of their race. As they sat in at a lunch counter, their action became a political *performance,* one with a pedigree in the *repertoire of contention* but that they innovated on like jazz musicians improvising on a theme. As they did so, they engaged with public *institutions*—the press, the police, and, ultimately, the city government. They also involved themselves in the broader conflict brewing between the state and federal governments in the American political *regime.* They mounted a classic social movement campaign.

Using concepts like those we proposed in chapter 2, we can describe the relevant *conditions* at the sites at which contention began (e.g., segregation in Woolworth's). We can then identify and describe the *events and episodes of contention* at those sites (students peacefully sitting in at lunch counters and police, public authorities, and third parties responding to them; the federal government and the courts eventually intervening). We can also describe in a general way the links between these streams of contention and changes in public policy toward equal and integrated access to public facilities (McAdam 1999: 142–44).

But we cannot leap directly to policy outcomes from the actions of the activists. We first need to search the *episode* for the *mechanisms* and *processes* that produced significant changes—in particular, the key mechanism of diffusion. But as we have seen throughout our book, diffusion seldom operates on its own. The sit-in movement spread through the mechanism of *brokerage,* which coordinated the actions of college students across the South; through *certification,* as they sought recognition as legitimate actors to the legislators, judges, and institutions that took up their claim; and through *boundary activation,* as their actions insisted that African Americans had the right to sit on the same side of lunch counters as whites.

Chapter 3's lessons take us one step beyond the actual episode of the student sit-ins. Like the cases we examined there, the sit-ins responded to relations among regimes, repertoires, and opportunities. Remember how contentious politics shifted in close connection with shifts of political power in the unstable political history of Venezuela? Those connections operate in settled democracies like the United States, too. In contrast to authoritarian regimes, in which repertoires are rigid, American politics has always left open opportunities for innovation in the repertoire of contention. This is particularly true during periods of rapid political change. In the history of civil rights, the sit-ins marked a significant shift in the challengers' repertoire, one to which political elites were slow to adapt (McAdam 1983). By the time police and public authorities had learned to respond to them, a new set of opportunities opened up and new kinds of performances emerged to keep them off balance.

Chapter 3 also explained that the causal interaction between regime characteristics and repertoire change runs in both directions. Not only does the character of a regime shape contention, but changes in contention lead to changes in regimes. The broad wave of contention of the 1960s led, first, to the "normalization" of many forms of contention that had previously been considered illegitimate (Piven and Cloward 1992). It also included the spread of contentious politics across new sectors of the population—women, Hispanics, gays, and lesbians (Meyer and Tarrow 1998). It contributed to the most significant democratization of American politics since the passage of women's suffrage after World War I. In both the extent of political rights and in the protection of civil rights, the United States now ranks at the top of Freedom House's rankings of the world's polities (figure 3.3). That ranking owes much to the struggle of African Americans to challenge the running sore of segregation.

The change did not happen at random. As in many of the episodes we have examined, the students were taking advantage of a changing *political opportunity structure.* Chapter 3 pointed out that we can trace political change in any regime through reactions of political actors to six dimensions of opportunity: (1) the multiplicity of independent centers of power within the regime, (2) its openness to new actors, (3) the instability of current political alignments, (4) the availability of influential allies or supporters for challengers, (5) the extent to which the regime represses or facilitates collective claim making, and (6) decisive changes in any and all of these regards. Civil rights protesters took advantage of all of these dimensions of opportunity.

Although it has seldom operated to help African Americans, the multiplicity of independent centers of power in the American regime played to the students' advantage. In 1960, growing concentrations of black college students had become available as a constituency (Andrews and Biggs forthcoming). In communities like Greensboro, where a substantial black middle class was developing, civil rights activists found allies in the local black community and in the churches. The entry of the federal government into race relations in the late 1950s also encouraged contentious politics.

Moreover, police and local authorities hesitated to repress well-dressed college students demonstrating peacefully in the full light of public opinion—especially when whites became involved. Indeed, the sit-ins were literally made for the newly developed media form of television (Andrews and Biggs forthcoming; Oppenheimer 1963). The sit-in movement grew up in the interstices of the complex and changing American political opportunity structure. It helped to change the character of political interaction and shifted the recognized boundaries in American politics. It was a successful social movement campaign.

We cannot judge the outcomes of an episode simply through the programs or policies it produces (Giugni et al. 1998, 1999; Meyer et al. 2005). Chapter 4 explained that challengers make claims along three broad dimensions: identity, standing, and program. *Identity claims* declare that an actor exists. They constitute an answer to the questions "Who am I?" and "How do I relate to you?" *Standing claims* say that the actor belongs to an established category within the regime and therefore deserves the rights and respect that members of that category receive; for that reason, standing claims often imply answers to a further question: "How would I like this relationship to change?" *Program claims* call for the objects of claims to act in a certain way: to do something, to stop doing something, to make someone else do something, and so on.

Although the civil rights movement certainly offered a program for fundamental change in the behavior of American governments, merchants, and citizens at large, it did not simply seek programmatic changes. The sit-ins and other performances also challenged the inherited *boundaries* that allowed African Americans to serve up hamburgers from behind a lunch counter but refused them the right to sit at that counter. That claim fundamentally concerned identity, which became a central issue in the black community during the 1960s. The entire civil rights movement forwarded a process of identity reassessment (Burns 1997: 244).

African Americans were also demanding recognition of their *standing* as citizens with equal rights. Through a variety of boundary-challenging actions, they sought certification from courts, legislatures, committees, and organizations. They also sought changes in the relations between themselves and other Americans through the boundary activation mechanisms examined in chapter 4. But boundary shift is a double-edged sword: As some African Americans struggled up the status ladder through education, geographic mobility, and job change, new boundaries emerged between the well-educated minority who had escaped the ghettoes of the northern cities and those who were left behind.

Big changes in politics connect with broad political processes. Remember our key process of *scale shift,* which chapter 5 introduced? It is a composite process including the mechanisms of *diffusion, attribution of similarity, brokerage,* and *emulation.* Sympathy demonstrations took the movement to the North. Coordination shifted from the local to the regional level in mid-April when students met at Shaw University in North Carolina. The encounter at this meeting eventually led to the formation of the Student Nonviolent Coordinating Committee (SNCC), which went on to play a critical role nationally (Andrews and Biggs forthcoming). The student sit-ins not only diffused horizontally; they produced upward scale shift to the regional and national levels of American politics.

Chapter 5 introduced the broadest processes surveyed in this book: *mobilization* and *demobilization*. We saw them operating in tandem in the occupation of the Church of Saint-Nizier in Lyons and in the Italian cycle of contention. But if we think about it, we realize that we saw these processes in British antislavery, the Ukrainian Orange Revolution, Venezuelan contention, the Zapatista rising, and nationalism in the former Soviet Union. In all these cases, the interactive mechanisms we identified with mobilization included our old friends *diffusion, brokerage, certification,* and *boundary activation.* Through these mechanisms, Italian conflicts over educational reform spread from a few northern universities and factories to the high schools, the urban centers, and the entire economy. In the same way, the Greensboro lunch counter sit-ins began a process of mobilization that took civil rights in this country into a new and more militant phase.

But mobilization is not a one-way process. All cycles of contention eventually decline; what is interesting is their different outcomes. In chapter 5, we saw a number of mechanisms combining to produce demobilization in both Italy and the former Soviet Union. But the outcomes were very different: In Italy a part of the insurgent groups that rose up in 1968 ended up in the terrorist Red Brigades, while a much larger sector entered the party system and the political institutions. In Russia, in contrast, the democracy movement that led the way out of the Soviet Union collapsed when it was overtaken by ethnic strife, and demobilization was more severe. The very same mechanisms took the American civil rights movement from its emergence in the late 1950s and early 1960s to its decline in the late 1960s and after. If our story had moved beyond the period of the sit-ins and the voter registration drives of the mid-1960s, we would increasingly have seen the following:

- *Competition* among different sectors of the movement. Competition was at first healthy, as more moderate organizations strove to keep up with their more radical counterparts. But soon the more progressive Congress of Racial Equality (CORE) and the newly formed SNCC were criticizing the more moderate NAACP and the Southern

Christian Leadership Conference (SCLC) for aligning themselves with Washington.

- *Repression,* both direct, as a broad countermovement of segregation- ists developed in reaction to school desegregation (Andrews 2005), and indirect, as the Nixon administration, which came to power in the late 1960s, shifted the government's focus from assisting African Americans' struggles to a politically divisive war on crime (Button 1978).
- *Defection and disillusionment,* as African Americans saw that the programmatic claims of the movement were not being met and many quit the struggle.
- *Institutionalization,* as the voting rights act shifted the sites of contention from the grassroots to elections and routine politics.

Movement Bases and Movement Campaigns

Chapter 6 first distinguished between episodes of collective action that fail to crystallize into sustained movements (e.g., Poland's response to Khrushchev's "secret speech") and those that do so (e.g., the Polish Solidar- ity movement of 1980). The contrast between the short-lived strike wave of 1956 and the long-lasting Solidarity movement pinpointed that difference and its relationship to changes in the Polish regime and the Soviet bloc more generally. That chapter also introduced the fundamental distinction between social movement bases and social movement campaigns.

If you look at most books on social movements in the United States or elsewhere, you will face a problem. Authors often combine the bases of a movement with its campaigns. *Social movement bases* consist of everything from movement organizations, networks, participants, to ac- cumulated cultural artifacts, memories, and traditions. A *social movement campaign,* however, involves a sustained public and collective challenge to power holders in the name of a population living under the jurisdiction of those power holders.

This book takes that distinction seriously. Using the new American women's movement as our central example, chapter 6 showed that movement bases can be extensive and steeped in tradition (Rupp and Taylor 1987). But absent a process of mobilization and interaction with significant others, they remain inconsequential for political change. For many years, the bases of the women's movement made big differences to their participants' lives but had little impact on American public politics.

Women interacting with legislators, occasionally protesting, forming interest groups, and constructing a new image of themselves constituted this campaign.

Once again, programmatic failures occurred, the most dramatic of them the ill-starred ERA campaign (Mansbridge 1986). But public interest groups such as NOW, lobbying groups such as the National Women's Political Caucus, and professional groups such as the Defense Department Advisory Committee on Women in the Services (DACOWITS) emerged as a new social movement base to carry forward a new identity and a new standing for women in American society.

Chapter 7's lessons about lethal conflict also connect with the trajectory of American civil rights. As we saw in that chapter, in authoritarian and semiauthoritarian regimes, claim makers are more likely to use or be met by lethal methods, triggering spirals of more and more violent interactions, radicalization, and repression. The ruthless resistance of rulers often forces those who aim deliberately at social movement repertoires in such regimes to adopt more radical means. The Russian Revolution of 1905 actually began when a group of hungry citizens, led by a priest, attempted to protest peacefully for food. When a battalion of mounted Cossacks mowed them down, contention turned violent and revolution followed.

Chapter 8 also offers lessons for understanding the Greensboro sit-ins. The American South in the 1950s and 1960s was a *composite regime.* Its governments did not repress so visibly as in the occupied West Bank or as in Ulster under martial law, yet they remained repressive under a patina of representative politics. As we saw in chapter 8, social movement politics and lethal conflicts intersect and feed into one another. Locally, the Greensboro protesters faced Jim Crow laws and customs, white-black segregation, electoral laws skewed to disenfranchise blacks, and a climate of hostility that could explode into physical violence at a moment's notice.

Like Russia's protesters but in a more contained way, civil rights movement leaders adjusted their repertoire to the forms of repression used against them. In his seminal article "Tactical Innovation and the Pace of Insurgency," McAdam (1983) focuses on the interactive dynamics between authorities' repressive tactics and the forms of contention that civil rights organizations developed to respond to them. Each time a new repressive response emerged to meet protesters' performances, civil rights organizers moved elsewhere and designed a new performance. Tactical creativity takes on special importance where claim makers face the truncheons of thugs and the fire hoses of the police.

In a further complication, the civil rights movement triggered a counter-movement, one that had both lethal and nonlethal aspects (Andrews 2002, 2004). On the one hand, as black students entered the public schools under the protection of the federal government, white children were withdrawn from those schools to enter all-white academies, often with the support of state governments. On the other hand, the Ku Klux Klan and other racist groups made life dangerous for civil rights workers and for African Americans who dared to exercise their rights. Social movement politics in a composite regime often becomes a dangerous undertaking.

As the cycle of contention wound down, some black militants chose the path of organized violence, much as the Italian Red Brigades did at the end of the Italian cycle. But not all of them chose armed struggle: As our discussion in chapter 6 would predict, some moved into institutional politics, others used their notoriety to gain commercial success, still others retreated into religious sects and nationalist splinter groups, while the most militant escalated their forms of contention. Partly in response to countermovement threats against racial equality but partly following the logic of militancy to its extreme, some African American groups excluded whites from their ranks, embraced violent rhetoric, and engaged in urban civil conflict with authorities and opponents. These radical groups brought down the armed might of the American state upon them and helped to usher in the end of the period of militancy (Button 1978).

But southern lethal politics operated in a national legal and political context that also encouraged social movement politics. Though civil rights protesters were often abused, frequently attacked, and sometimes murdered, such reactions occurred in a federal system within which the national government provided protected consultation. This composite situation required extraordinary restraint, the use of certified institutions such as the black churches, creative leadership, and allies in Washington and the North. These elements ultimately led to the major reforms in civil and voting rights and to the creation of an African American political class.

Domestic/Transnational Interactions

So far, we have talked about the civil rights movement in strictly domestic terms, as most American observers have done. But although our Greensboro protesters would never have thought of themselves as transnational activists, the civil rights movement was deeply influenced by international politics. In 1960, the United States was engaged in a "cold" but potentially lethal standoff with the former Soviet Union. Both were courting the support of citizens of Africa, Asia, and Latin America. Most of those regions were liberating themselves from the trauma of colonialism. How could the United States claim to lead a campaign for freedom abroad when over 20 percent of its own population lived in segregated neighborhoods, went to inferior schools, and lacked the right to order a hamburger at a public lunch counter? Fighting the international Cold War imposed pressures on U.S. domestic policy that created new opportunities for African Americans (McAdam 1998). At the same time, similar pressures were moving the United States to overturn forty years of racially discriminatory immigration laws (Ngai 2004).

Not all the transnational incentives for civil rights activism came through Washington. While presidents from Truman to Kennedy were attending to foreign policy needs by supporting civil rights at home, black activists were watching closely as third world countries began to strip off colonial rule. Men like Martin Luther King Jr. drew inspiration directly from the nonviolent theories of India's Mohandas Gandhi (Chabot 2003). Black nationalists drew their own inspiration from the success of African liberation movements. Whatever else was true of the country as Greensboro's neat young students sat down at Woolworth's lunch counter, American opportunity structure was influenced both by the United States' role in the world and by transnational influences of liberation movements in Asia and Africa. This transnational effect was mutual: Just as Martin Luther King Jr. regarded himself as a disciple of Mohandas Gandhi, in the years following the 1960s, people as different as Jamaican blacks in Britain, Breton nationalists in France, and Sephardic Israeli immigrants identified their respective struggles with "black power."

Greensboro's protesters were not the only Americans to be influenced by international events. Remember Cornell's shantytown builders from chapter 2? Inspired by the example of the South African blacks who protested against apartheid, Cornell's and other universities' protesters fused the symbol of South African shanties with the well-known performance of the sit-in. As they protested against their universities' investment policies, they were also part of a transnational coalition aimed at isolating the South African regime. In that controversy, governments and activists collaborated in international institutions such as the United Nations and the British Commonwealth, too. The three aspects of transnational contention we observed in the Pinochet case—transnational activism, international coalition building, and transnational diffusion—combined in the struggle against apartheid.

Conclusion

We began our book by comparing the British antislavery mobilization of the 1780s with popular resistance to a stolen election in 2004. We ended with the internationalization of contentious politics over a wide variety of issues. Between the two, we examined a great range of popular contention in Europe, Africa, the Middle East, and the Americas. But much more remains to be done:

- We have neglected Asia because we prefer to write about regions on which we have done research and some of whose languages we know.
- We have said little about the growing (and contested) role of the Internet and the use of new electronic media to perform contentious politics (Bennett 2005; Samuel 2004; Tilly 2004b).
- We have had little to say about the social psychology of contention, a well-studied field in which many specialists know much more than we do (Klandermans 1997).
- We have largely ignored the spread of contentious forms of politics to new sectors of the population and whether this has turned once-transgressive and forbidden means of contention into contained and tolerated ones (Meyer and Tarrow 1998).
- Nor have we attempted systematic empirical demonstrations of our explanations for any of the episodes we have examined. That undertaking would have required another book or expanded this one exponentially.

By now, you can draw your own conclusions about the tools the book has laid out and about the dynamics of contentious politics in general. As a reminder, nevertheless, here are some generalizations and some practical conclusions to take away from your reading.

As generalizations, let us drum away at these:

- Although they generally occur in different sorts of regimes, revolutions, civil wars, lethal ethnic conflicts, social movements, and other forms of contentious politics result from similar causes in different combinations, sequences, and initial conditions.
- We can usefully break those causes into recurrent mechanisms and processes. Explaining contention means identifying the mechanisms and processes that lie behind it.

- In all sorts of regimes, from low capacity to high capacity and from undemocratic to democratic, routine interactions between governments and political actors produce political opportunity structures that greatly limit what forms of contention different potential makers of claims can actually initiate.
- At the same time, governmental action and popular contention interact to form repertoires of contention—limited arrays of known, feasible ways to make collective claims—that also limit possible forms of contention in any regime.
- Nevertheless, all parties to contention are constantly innovating and negotiating, often attempting to persuade, block, defeat, punish, or collaborate with each other. That incessant give and take makes contentious politics a dynamic drama rather than a stale reenactment of old scenarios.

These general features of contention lead directly to some practical conclusions for students of contentious politics:

- Before you try to decide whether some contentious episode is a revolution, a social movement, or something else, describe the episode and its setting carefully. The appendices sum up advice this book has given for the work of describing contentious episodes and their settings.
- Early in the process, sort your description into the elements this book has taught you: governments, political actors, political identities, contentious performances, institutions, and more. Trace how each of them changes, if at all, over the course of the episode.
- When you have made clear what you must explain, turn to the book's explanatory concepts: not only the regimes, political opportunity structures, repertoires, mechanisms, and processes mentioned earlier, but also sites, conditions, streams, events, episodes, and outcomes. Again, the appendices can help you to set up your explanations.
- Instead of trying to explain everything about a contentious episode, close in on its most surprising, interesting, or consequential features—for example, how sit-ins changed the political connections and public image of the U.S. civil rights movement or how Israeli settlers, imbued with a religious vision of Zionism, turned on the Israeli state in a social movement against the evacuation of their settlements.
- Use comparisons—including comparisons with episodes studied in this book—to single out similarities and differences between your

episodes and others in the same general categories. Some of our comparisons would take you far afield—for example, our comparison between British antislavery and the Ukrainian Orange Revolution.

- Armed with a number of mechanisms and processes, do not be afraid to make broad comparisons, but more proximate ones work just as well—for example, Sarah Soule's comparison between American campuses that produced shantytown protests and those that did not. The differences—and the similarities—will be just as revealing.

Even if you don't undertake major investigations of your own, you can still use this book's lessons to better equip you as a citizen who can evaluate the news of political contention that bombards you every day. Almost every daily newspaper and television news broadcast carries reports on contentious politics across the world. By now, you should have a clearer idea what reporters are talking about when they tell you that French people demonstrate, civil wars ravage Africa, and Iraqi insurgents set off bombs under American Humvees. Here are three lessons to apply in judging what they say.

First, beware of the catchall terms that journalists and politicians habitually use to describe contention. Not all displays of violence are "riots," and not all lethal conflict is touched off by rioters. In fact, history teaches that in democracies and semidemocracies, while ordinary people are the sources of most damage to property, the greatest source of violence against persons is the police. Before deciding that a particular performance is a riot, ask yourself who is telling the story—a participant, an onlooker, or an opponent of the claim makers.

Second, use the comparative method in judging the news. If a television broadcaster assures you that masses of Iraqi citizens pulled down the statue of Saddam Hussein following the American-led invasion, ask yourself who was present at that scene. You may be surprised to discover that its organizers were American troops propping up the few Iraqis in attendance. Compare that picture to the exhilarated crowds in Eastern Europe in 1989 that toppled statues of Lenin and Stalin without official assistance.

Third, don't stop with analyzing actually occurring contention. One of Arthur Conan Doyle's major mysteries was called "The Dog that Didn't Bark." In 2003, Americans were falsely assured that their sons and daughters were sent off to Iraq to find and destroy Saddam Hussein's weapons of mass destruction. When word crept out these weapons were nonexistent and that the intelligence that justified the invasion was faked, why did so few people protest? When residents of New Orleans whom Hurricane Katrina had washed out of their homes went without government assistance for days and weeks, why did they not demand better from their rulers?

As our theories and narratives have taught, modern politics contains recurring contentious streams, but it also includes oceans of apathy. We now know a lot about why citizens of authoritarian regimes are normally compliant, rising in resistance only when dramatic windows of opportunity open up. But why do citizens of *democratic* regimes so often sit on their hands when they have the right to resist? And when democracy depends on their active participation? That might well be the next stage in the study of contentious politics. We invite you to take it.

APPENDIX A
CONCEPTS AND METHODS

Box A.1 identifies the book's main descriptive concepts: governments, political actors, political identities, contentious performances, and more. The concepts in box A.1 supply the major terms we use when describing different varieties of contention. Our comparison of British antislavery with Ukraine's Orange Revolution in chapter 1 made it obvious that political actors, political identities, performances, and other aspects of contention vary dramatically from one time and place to another. The concepts specify what sorts of variation and change we have to explain.

As chapters 6 and 7 show, for example, social movements occur mainly in very different circumstances from lethal ethnic and religious conflicts, civil wars, and revolutions. That sets our explanatory problem: What sorts of circumstances favor social movements rather than large-scale lethal conflicts, how, and why? What causes connect contentious episodes with the settings in which they occur? In order to answer that sort of question, we must go on from descriptive to explanatory concepts.

Box A.2 identifies the main explanatory concepts the book employs: sites, conditions, streams, events, and episodes of contention, and so on. We use these terms to identify causal connections among the descriptive elements—for example, by showing which mechanisms bring political actors into social movements. As they differentiate between social movements and large-scale lethal conflicts, chapters 6 and 7 lay out how very different regimes and political opportunity structures underlie the two broad classes of contention. Let us review our major explanatory concepts one by one.

Sites of contention include all human settings that serve as originators, objects, and/or arenas of collective claims. Sites may be human individuals, but they also include informal networks, organizations, neighborhoods, professions, trades, and other settings of social life. Each kind of site has its own peculiarities. Neighborhoods do not behave just like individuals; factories and agricultural communities do not behave like neighborhoods.

Box A.1. Major Descriptive Concepts in the Study of Contentious Politics

- *Government*: within a given territory, an organization controlling the principal concentrated means of coercion and exercising priority over all other organizations within the same territory in some regards. In England of 1785, the organization included a king, ministers, civil servants, Parliament, and a network of appointed agents throughout the country.
- *Political actors*: recognizable sets of people who carry on collective action in which governments are directly or indirectly involved, making and/or receiving contentious claims. In Ukraine, supporters of outgoing president Kuchma, backers of presidential candidate Yushchenko, Interior Ministry troops, and external sponsors on both sides all figured as weighty political actors.
- *Political identities*: as applied to political actors, organized answers to the questions "Who are you?" "Who are they?" and "Who are we?" In late eighteenth-century England, some of those answers included Abolitionists, slaveholders, and Parliament.
- *Contentious politics*: interactions in which actors make claims that bear on someone else's interests, leading to coordinating efforts on behalf of shared interests or programs, in which governments are as targets, the objects of claims, or third parties.
- *Contentious performances*: relatively familiar and standardized ways in which one set of political actors makes collective claims on some other set of political actors. Among other performances, participants in Ukraine's Orange Revolution used mass demonstrations as visible, effective performances.
- *Contentious repertoires*: arrays of contentious performances that are currently known and available within some set of political actors. England's antislavery activists helped to invent the demonstration as a political performance, but they also drew on petitions, lobbying, press releases, public meetings, and a number of other performances.
- *Institutions*: within any particular regime, established, organized, widely recognized routines, connections, and forms of organization employed repeatedly in producing collective action. Eighteenth-century antislavery activists could work with such available institutions as religious congregations, parliamentary hearings, and the press.
- *Social movements*: sustained campaigns of claim making, using repeated performances that advertise that claim, based on organizations, networks, traditions, and solidarities that sustain these activities.

These divide into the following:

- *Social movement campaigns*: sustained challenges to power holders in the name of a population living under the jurisdiction of those power holders by means of public displays of that population's worthiness, unity, numbers, and commitment.
- *Social movement bases*: the social background, organizational resources, and cultural framework of contention and collective action.

Box A.2. Major Explanatory Concepts in Contentious Politics

- *Sites of contention*: human settings that serve as originators, objects, and/or arenas of contentious politics. Example: Armies often play all three parts in contention.
- *Conditions*: characteristics of sites and relations among sites that shape the contention occurring in and across them. *Initial* conditions are those that prevail in affected sites at the start of some process or episode. Example: In Italy of 1966, an array of political organizations and existing connections among them provided the background for the cycle of conflict that occurred over the next seven years.
- *Streams of contention*: sequences of collective claim at or across those sites singled out for explanation. Example: a series of strikes by workers in a given industry against their firm(s).
- *Outcomes*: changes in conditions at or across the sites that are plausibly related to the contention under study, including transformations of political actors or relations among them. Example: During or after a series of strikes, management fires workers, changes work rules, and/or raises wages.
- *Regimes*: regular relations among governments, established political actors, challengers, and outside political actors including other governments; eighteenth-century England and twenty-first-century Ukraine obviously hosted very different regimes.
- *Political opportunity structure*: features of regimes and institutions (e.g., splits in the ruling class) that facilitate or inhibit a political actor's collective action; in the case of Ukraine 2004–2005, a divided international environment gave dissidents an opportunity to call on foreign backers in the name of democracy.
- *Mechanisms*: events that produce the same immediate effects over a wide range of circumstances. Example: Diffusion of tactics from one site to another often occurs during major mobilizations, thus altering action at origin and destination as well as facilitating coordination among the affected sites.
- *Processes*: combinations and sequences of mechanisms that produce some specified outcome. Example: Major mobilizations usually combine brokerage and diffusion with other mechanisms in sequences and combinations that strongly affect the collective action emerging from the mobilization.
- *Episodes*: bounded sequences of continuous interaction, usually produced by an investigator's chopping up longer streams of contention into segments for purposes of systematic observation, comparison, and explanation. Example: We might compare successive petition drives of antislavery activists in Great Britain (each drive counting as a single episode) over the twenty years after 1785, thus not only seeing how participants in one drive learned from the previous drive but also documenting how the movement as a whole evolved.

Yet this book has identified many parallels in the ways that mechanisms, processes, and episodes operate across different kinds of sites. We learn, for example, that repertoires can belong to sets of organizations as well as to sets of informal networks and to sets of individuals.

Conditions are characteristics of sites and relations among sites that shape the contention that occurs in and across them. We might imagine a country, for example, in which one group is a well-established political actor with strong ties to government, while another is an underground opponent of the government currently being harassed by state security forces. The existence of those two groups and of their relations to the government identifies a condition that affects contentious politics within the regime in question.

When looking at mechanisms, processes, and episodes, we have often called attention to *initial* conditions that affect how mechanisms interact, how processes develop, and what outcomes result from those processes. Initial conditions prevail when the stream of contention on which we are concentrating begins. Initial conditions such as the available repertoire of claim-making performances or the organization of the country's government affect how contention actually occurs. Conditions then change during and after contention, as struggle itself alters repertoires, relations among political actors, and other features of the sites.

Streams of contention contain connected moments of collective claim making that observers single out for explanation. We might, for example, treat the entire British antislavery movement from 1785 to 1835 as a single stream on the assumption that throughout the period, earlier mobilizations and their consequences shaped later mobilizations. But we could also focus on antislavery efforts in London alone or on just one intense period of action. A stream may come into view because participants or other analysts already treat it as continuous, as in the mobilization that led to the British parliament's banning of the slave trade in 1807. It may also interest us because of concern with some general process such as democratization. Analysts often line up parallel streams of events that do and don't end up with democratic institutions in order to clarify explanations of democratization in general.

Outcomes consist of changes in conditions at or across the sites under study that are plausibly related to the contention under study, including transformations of political actors or relations among them. In transitions from authoritarian to democratic regimes, previously dominant classes, factions, organizations, or families always lose some of their power. If we ask what happens to former rulers under democratic transitions, we are asking outcome questions. It may turn out that the outcomes we single out did *not* result from the streams of contention we initially observed. In that case, we look for new explanations elsewhere. Part of the adventure comes from determining what actually caused the outcomes in question. For that purpose, we look closely at mechanisms and processes.

Regimes involve regular relations among governments, established political actors, challengers, and outside political actors, including other governments. To identify a regime, we typically begin by locating a *government*: the organization in a given substantial territory that controls the largest concentrated means of coercion—armies, jails, means of shaming people, and so on—within the territory. We then look for political actors outside that government that interact regularly with the government's agents and agencies. We call the actors *members* if they have secure standing in day-to-day politics, *challengers* if they make their presence known collectively but lack secure standing, and *outsiders* if they operate from bases external to the territory under the government's control.

Political opportunity structure figures repeatedly in this book's explanations of contention. Political opportunity structure includes six properties of a regime:

1. The multiplicity of independent centers of power within it
2. Its openness to new actors
3. The instability of current political alignments
4. The availability of influential allies or supporters for challengers
5. The extent to which the regime represses or facilitates collective claim making
6. Decisive changes in items 1 to 5

From the perspective of a whole regime, the instability of alignments and the availability of allies (items 3 and 4) amount to the same thing. Stable alignments generally mean that many political actors have no potential allies in power. By such a definition, however, political opportunity structure varies somewhat from one actor to another. At the same moment, one actor has many available allies; another, few. For all actors, in any case, threats and opportunities shift with fragmentation or concentration of power, changes in the regime's openness, instability of political alignments, and the availability of allies.

Mechanisms are events that produce the same immediate effects over a wide range of circumstances. The mechanism we call *brokerage,* for example, operates in essentially the same way in highly varied situations.

It connects two previously unconnected social sites and thereby lowers the cost of communication and coordination between them. Social movement organizers often employ brokerage, bringing previously unconnected groups or social networks into the same campaign. Contentious politics also frequently involves the mechanism of *identity shift*, as people who formerly thought of themselves in a variety of distinct social roles come together and realize a unified—if temporary—identity such as worker, victim of environmental pollution, African American, or citizen of the world.

Processes assemble mechanisms into different sequences and combinations, thus producing larger-scale outcomes than any single mechanism. This book deals repeatedly with the process called *mobilization*, in which the resources available to a political actor for collective claim making increase. Relevant resources include energy, ideas, practices, and material objects, to the extent that their application would support the making of claims. Brokerage often plays a part in mobilization, but so does identity shift. In fact, brokerage frequently activates identity shift, as people mobilized around the same issue attribute similarity to themselves and their allies.

Mobilization has an equal and opposite process, *demobilization*, or the decline in the resources available for collective claim making. Beyond open contention, political organizers spend a good deal of their effort on mobilization and on fending off demobilization. Governments, too, direct considerable attention to aiding the mobilization of their supporters and to pursuing the demobilization of their enemies. Government forces' massacre of unarmed peasants of Panzós, Guatemala, only aimed in part at the protesters in the plaza; it also aimed at the demobilization of a swelling peasant movement.

Episodes are bounded sequences of contentious interaction. Mapping streams of contention into episodes aids the detection of mechanisms and processes. This appendix shows how to divide complicated streams of contention into episodes, describe those episodes, decompose them into causes, and then reassemble the causes into causal accounts of episodes, of the larger streams of contention to which those episodes belong, and of processes that recur widely in different sorts of contentious politics. A successful circuit from description to decomposition to reassembly leads back to new circuits; improved explanation of one episode, series of episodes, or class of contention offers a starting point for new explanations concerning similar varieties of contention. We call this the *mechanism-process approach* to explaining contentious politics. Box A.3 sums up the steps we take toward explanation in the mechanism-process approach.

Box A.3. Steps in the Mechanism-Process Approach to Explanation of Contention

1. Using the major descriptive concepts in table A.1 (political actors, political identities, institutions, etc.), specify the *site(s)* of contention you are studying.
2. Using the same descriptive concepts, describe relevant *conditions* at those sites when the contention you are studying begins.
3. Identify and describe the *stream(s) of contention* at or among those sites you want to explain.
4. Specify the outcome(s) whose relation to the contention under study you want to determine.
5. Break the streams of contention into coherent *episodes*.
6. Search the episodes for *mechanisms* producing significant changes and/or differences.
7. Reconstruct the *processes* into which those mechanisms compound.
8. Using analogies or comparisons with similar processes elsewhere, combine conditions, mechanisms, and processes into explanations of specified outcomes.

The eight steps of explanation combine the major descriptive concepts of box A.1 with the major explanatory concepts of box A.2. As we have shown, some investigations call for a different order among the steps. If, for instance, you have a promising account of how a certain process works or how a specific initial condition affects such a process, you will start with a theory about the process and then identify streams of contention that will help to verify or falsify the theory. (We have often used this reverse order of explanation in various chapters.) Sooner or later, however, you will ordinarily go through all eight steps on the way to a new, falsified, modified, or better-verified explanation. Interactions among mechanisms, processes, and initial conditions will constitute your explanations.

We can distinguish four variants of mechanism-process explanations, which we might call common process, local process, process generalization, and site comparison.

Common process accounts identify similar streams of contention and ask whether recurrence of a given process helps to explain the similarity among those streams.

Local process accounts take processes whose operation analysts have already established in other settings and apply them to particular instances—often combining more than one well-documented process for a more complete explanation.

Process generalization accounts concentrate on the process itself, asking in general how it arises and what effects it produces under different conditions.

Site comparison seeks to identify significant differences in the frequency, origin, or consequences of certain processes across different kinds of sites.

Following one of these four models, you could adopt a much more systematic procedure than simply browsing Web newswires for the day's contentious events. You could, for instance, do any of these projects:

- Single out a particular form or issue of contentious politics (e.g., suicide bombing or attacks on local officials) for description and explanation, starting with a map of where such events occur most frequently, but moving on to see whether similar processes occur at all the locations, and whether distinctive characteristics of the locales affect how and when this variety of contentious politics occurs. In this case, you might be doing a *common process* study identifying similarities across sites, like those in which Berman and Laitin studied suicide bombing.
- Take an established model of some process in contentious politics (e.g., the simple model of diffusion and brokerage presented in chapter 2), find a series of episodes within the same locale in which that process is occurring, and investigate whether it occurs in accordance with the model. You would be performing a *local process* analysis.
- Even more ambitiously, develop your own model of some contentious process such as mobilization or demobilization, and test it against a variety of relevant episodes. You would be—fanfare, please!—doing your own version of *process generalization.*
- Following Kriesi and his collaborators, you could compare a smaller number of countries (in Latin America, e.g., Colombia, Peru, and Chile) to determine whether other features of those countries such as their political institutions, the place of indigenous people, or involvement in the drug trade help to explain similarities and differences in their contentious politics. You would be conducting a *site comparison* parallel to theirs.

For any of these projects, you would need more information on contention's social and political context than you would find in daily newswire reports. For that information, you might turn to standard reference books such as atlases, encyclopedias, U.S. government country reports, political yearbooks, or the countries' own Web sites. You might also want more evidence on individual events. In that case, you might zoom in on national periodicals from the countries that interest you, which are often available online. No matter how and where you assembled your sources, you would be following the steps of box A.3: describing the sites of contention under study, describing conditions at those sites, and so on, through the mechanism-process routine. You would be identifying important streams of contention, dividing them into episodes, looking for recurrent processes within the episodes, and trying to find the crucial mechanisms within those processes: brokerage, diffusion, emulation, and others.

For other analytical purposes, you could also assemble catalogs of episodes at very different scales from Beissinger, Brockett, Kriesi and his collaborators, Rucht, Soule, Tarrow, Tilly, and others. Drawing on North American newspapers, you could close in on a particular issue or form of action—for example, college campus public meetings on freedom of speech or military service. Comparisons among colleges, cities, states, or provinces coupled with background information about the colleges, cities, states, or provinces would then allow you to start an explanation of the character and relative frequency of those meetings. You could also compare much larger events, including revolutions, military coups, civil wars, or strike waves, across multiple regimes and many years. Box A.3 would still give you guidance for organizing your investigation.

One of the book's many applications of box A.3's procedures occurred in chapter 3. There we looked closely at Venezuelan contention between 1980 and the early twenty-first century. Drawing on Venezuelan researchers' excellent work, we went through these steps:

1. Using the major descriptive concepts from chapter 1 (political actors, political identities, contentious performances, etc.), we specified the *sites* of contention we were studying. López Maya and collaborators divided their attention among three sites: Venezuela as a whole, the population of the Caracas metropolitan area, and the five groups of participants for which they conducted special studies.
2. Using the same descriptive concepts, we briefly described relevant *conditions* at those sites when the contention we were studying began. Supplementing the López Maya account with other historical sources, we sketched the background of Venezuelan contention from the 1980s onward.

3. We identified and described the *stream(s) of contention* at or among those sites we wanted to explain. The Venezuelan researchers identified two streams: the longer run fluctuations of contention in the whole country from 1983 to 1999, and the collective dissent of Caracas's population in 1999.

4. We then tried to specify the outcomes whose relation to the contention under study we wanted to determine. We followed two different outcomes: changing relations between Venezuelan citizens and their regime, and alterations in the regime itself as a result of popular contention.

5. Following the Venezuelan team, we broke the streams of contention into coherent *episodes,* dividing both streams into particular episodes, which the Venezuelan research group called "protests."

6. We searched the episodes for *mechanisms* producing significant changes and/or differences. Here (as we have not shown) the Venezuelan researchers emphasize cognitive mechanisms, especially framing, by which popular understandings of what major actors were doing changed. We have instead combed their accounts for evidence of brokerage and diffusion.

7. We went one step further, reconstructing the *processes* into which those mechanisms compounded. We called attention to the simple process of new coordination. But the story as a whole also involves several other important processes: polarization, democratization, dedemocratization, mobilization, and demobilization. A full analysis of Venezuelan contention from 1983 to 1999 would connect all of these crucial processes.

8. Following López Maya and her collaborators, we presented our analysis of Venezuelan contention primarily in a *local process* mode: taking established models of processes in contentious politics, finding a series of episodes within the same locale in which those processes are occurring, and investigating whether they occur in accordance with the model. Certainly our sketch of Venezuelan contentious politics falls short of a definitive test. Yet it establishes the possibility of assembling solid evidence that bears on the validity of available process models.

STREAMS, EPISODES, MECHANISMS, AND PROCESSES

This appendix identifies the major streams of contention, sets of contentious episodes, causal mechanisms, and causal processes that appear in one part of the book or another. It includes only those streams, episode sets, mechanisms, and processes playing some significant part in the book's descriptions and explanations of contentious politics.

Streams of Contention

As appendix A said, streams of contention contain connected moments of collective claim making that observers single out for explanation. Contentious streams run an enormous range, from a running dispute between you and your neighbor to the coming of the French Revolution. This book's approach makes it possible to analyze streams at either end of the range as well as in between. You get to choose. Most of the book's analyses, however, treat fairly long, large streams in which governments visibly figured as claimants, objects of claims, or third parties to claims. Here are the main streams the book describes:

British Antislavery (chapters 1 and 2): beginning in the 1780s, the series of struggles in which British activists and their allies called for an end to Great Britain's participation in the Atlantic slave trade, next for abolition of slavery throughout British territories and colonies, and then for termination of the slave trade and slavery throughout the Atlantic region.

Ukraine's Orange Revolution (chapters 1 and 2): overturning of a government-stolen election through popular mobilization in 2004.

Repertoire change in the United States, 1955-2005 (chapter 1): general mutations of who was making collective claims—and how—over the country as a whole.

Contention in El Salvador and Guatemala, 1955-1991 (chapters 2, 5, and 7): peasant activism, government repression, and antigovernmental insurgency as analyzed by Charles Brockett.

Opposition to authoritarian regimes in Serbia and Georgia, 2000-2003 (chapter 2): organization and diffusion of protests by students and others against election fraud.

U.S. antislavery, 1820-1860 (chapter 2): struggles between advocates and opponents of slavery up to the Civil War.

Disintegration of the Soviet Union and the Soviet Bloc, 1956-1991 (chapters 2, 4, 5, and 6): breakup of both the multistate Soviet Union and the Soviet-dominated Warsaw Pact countries.

Venezuelan political struggles, 1980-2005 (chapter 3): elite and popular involvement in successive contests over state power.

Zapatista mobilization in Mexico, 1994-2005 (chapter 4): in a poor region of southern Mexico, demands by organizers of indigenous populations for redress and autonomy from the central government, soon receiving support from across the world.

Campaigns of prostitutes in Lyons, France, for recognition and protection (chapter 5): in a series of unusual actions including occupation of a church, a partly successful bid by sex workers for improvement of their political and working conditions.

Italy's political cycle, 1968-1973 (chapter 5): workers, students, and other political activists producing a large series of challenges to the regime, but eventually subsiding.

Antiregime mobilizations in Poland, 1956-1957 and 1980-1989 (chapter 6): failed opposition to the Soviet-backed communist regime during the 1950s contrasting with eventual toppling of the regime during the 1980s.

American women's movements from the 1960s onward (chapter 6): significant fluctuations in the organizational bases, coalitions, issues, and outcomes of women's movement campaigns.

Sudan's Regimes, 1989-2005 (chapter 7): repeated regional rebellions and civil wars against an authoritarian state.

Protestant-Catholic struggles in Ireland, 1529-1989 (chapter 7): recurrent contention ranging from passive resistance to civil war.

Nicaragua's revolutionary situations and outcomes, 1961-1990 (chapter 7): rise and fall of revolutionary changes in a war-torn country.

Israel's withdrawal from Gaza, 2004-2005 (chapter 8): as militant Israelis protest, the Israeli government's removal of its settlers from the Gaza Strip.

International campaign to prosecute Augusto Pinochet, 1998-2005 (chapter 8): a successful effort spearheaded by Chilean exiles to bring the former dictator to justice.

Sit-ins in American civil rights, 1960 onward (chapter 9): an effective new sort of campaign Initiated by African American activists.

Sets of Contentious Episodes

Episodes are bounded sequences of contentious interaction. The book mentions dozens of individual episodes in passing. Here, however, we list only those cases in which some analyst has deliberately broken up a contentious stream into a number of comparable units for disciplined description and explanation. The stream in question only appears in the previous list of contentious streams if the book also offers a more general analysis of changes outside the episodes themselves.

Protests in Germany, 1950-1997 (chapter 1): Dieter Rucht's catalog of different types of public protest events in West Germany (1950-1988) and unified Germany (1989-1997).

Strikes in France, 1830-1968 (chapter 2): multiple catalogs of strikes and contentious gatherings over the country as a whole, drawn by Edward Shorter, Charles Tilly, and their collaborators from official statistics, newspapers, and historical archives.

Protest events in Italy, 1966-1973 (chapters 2 and 5): catalogs of strikes and other contentious events, compiled mainly from Italian newspapers by Sidney Tarrow and his collaborators.

New social movements in France, Germany, the Netherlands, and Switzerland, 1975-1989 (chapter 2): national catalogs of contentious events compiled from national newspapers by Hanspeter Kriesi and his research team.

Shantytown protests on U.S. college campuses, 1985-1990 (chapter 2): Sarah Soule's collection of campus events from NEXIS.

Demonstrations and violent confrontations in the Soviet Union and its successor states, 1987-1992 (chapters 2, 4, and 5): national catalogs by Mark Beissinger and a large research team.

Protest events in Venezuela, 1983-1999 (chapter 3): collection of contentious events from a national newspaper by Margarita López Maya and her collaborators.

Conflicts in Guatemala and El Salvador, 1970-1991 (chapter 5): Charles Brockett's multiple catalogs of strikes, occupations, demonstrations, and "contentious activities."

American women's movement activities and outcomes, 1950-1985 (chapter 6): Ann Costain's counts of legislation affecting women's rights and news mentions of women's organizational activities.

Civil wars across the world, 1946-2004 (chapter 7): catalogs by Scandinavian analysts of war and peace.

African American protests and civil rights activities, 1947-1997 (chapter 9): Craig Jenkins and collaborators' counts of nationally visible contentious events.

The geography of sit-ins, 1960 (chapter 9): Mapping the distribution of sit-ins across the American South by Kenneth Andrews and Michael Biggs.

Mechanisms

Mechanisms are events that produce the same immediate effects over a wide range of circumstances. *Processes* assemble mechanisms into combinations and sequences that produce larger-scale effects than any particular mechanism causes by itself. The distinction between mechanisms and processes, however, depends on our level of observation. We can always look inside any particular mechanism and find smaller-scale mechanisms at work. Examined closely, for example, recognition of parallels between yourself and another political actor—the mechanism we call *attribution of similarity*—depends on smaller-scale cognitive events, moment by moment or person by person. We can also go to the other extreme. At the scale of world history, the complex processes we call revolutions (which chapter 7 analyzes in detail) can operate as mechanisms, with each revolution ending one regime and starting another. In short, whether a causal cluster counts as a mechanism or a process depends on our scale of observation.

The mechanisms and processes identified in this book operate at an intermediate scale. Most of the time, we take the position of an informed observer watching a regime's politics change from week to week, month to month, or year to year. At that scale, we single out mechanisms that contribute to significant shifts in the location, character, or consequences of contention. We then assemble the mechanisms into combinations and sequences that cause the major outcomes we set out to explain. Here are the main mechanisms at work in the book:

Attribution of similarity: identification of another political actor as falling within the same category as your own.

Boundary activation/deactivation: increase (decrease) in the salience of the us-them distinction separating two political actors.

Boundary formation: creation of an us-them distinction between two political actors.

Boundary shift: change in the persons or identities on one side or the other of an existing boundary.

Brokerage: production of a new connection between previously unconnected or weakly connected sites.

Certification: an external authority's signal of its readiness to recognize and support the existence and claims of a political actor. (*Decertification*: an external authority's signal that it is withdrawing recognition and support from a political actor.)

Co-optation: incorporation of a previously excluded political actor into some center of power.

Defection: exit of a political actor from a previously effective coalition and/or coordinated action.

Diffusion: spread of a contentious performance, issue, or interpretive frame from one site to another.

Emulation: deliberate repetition within a given setting of a performance observed in another setting.

Repression: action by authorities that increases the cost—actual or potential—of an actor's claim making.

Processes

Our inventories of the mechanisms and processes identified in this book make clear that we have left plenty of work for future researchers and theorists. The work consists of showing not only (1) exactly how the mechanisms listed activate and produce their effects but also (2) what mechanisms enter complex processes of contention, how they combine, and how they produce their large-scale effects. Here are the main processes the book has discussed:

Actor constitution: emergence of a new or transformed political actor—a recognizable set of people who carry on collective action, making and/or receiving contentious claims.

Coalition formation: creation of new, visible, and direct coordination of claims between two or more previously distinct actors.

Collective action: all coordinating efforts on behalf of shared interests or programs.

Commercialization: shift of an organization toward more extensive sale of its services (Kriesi analysis).

Competition: pursuit of rewards or outcomes in mutually exclusive ways.

Contention: making claims that bear on someone else's interests.

Coordinated action: two or more actors' mutual signaling and parallel making of claims on the same object.

Democratization/dedemocratization: movement of a regime toward or away from relatively broad, equal, and protected binding consultation of the government's subjects with respect to governmental resources, personnel, and policies.

Disillusionment: decline in the commitment of individuals or political actors to previously sustaining beliefs.

Escalation: displacement of moderate goals and tactics by more extreme goals and tactics (usually applied to mutual interactions among political actors).

Framing: adopting and broadcasting a shared definition of an issue or performance.

Globalization: increase in the volume and speed of flows of capital, goods, information, ideas, people, and forces connecting actors across countries.

Identity shift: emergence of new collective answers to the questions "Who are you?" "Who are we?" and "Who are they?"

Institutionalization: incorporation of performances and political actors into the routines of organized politics.

Internationalization: a combination of (1) increasing horizontal density of relations among states, governmental officials, and nonstate actors with (2) increasing vertical ties between these and international institutions or organizations.

Involution: shift of social movement organizations toward increasing emphasis on supply of social services to their constituencies (Kriesi analysis).

Mobilization/demobilization: increase (decrease) in the resources available to a political actor for collective making of claims.

New coordination: coordination produced by the combination of brokerage and diffusion.

Polarization: increasing ideological distance between political actors or coalitions.

Radicalization: shift of social movement organizations toward increased assertiveness (Kriesi analysis).

Scale shift: increase or decrease in the number of actors and/or geographic range of coordinated claim making.

Self-representation: an actor's or coalition's public display of worthiness, unity, numbers, and commitment.

Social appropriation: conversion or incorporation of previously existing nonpolitical groups and networks into political actors.

REFERENCES

Alberoni, Francesco. 1977. *Movimento e istituzione: Teoria generale.* Bologna: Il Mulino.

Alexander, Jeffrey C. 2004. "From the Depths of Despair: Performance, Counter-performance, and 'September 11.'" *Sociological Theory* 22: 88–105.

Alter, Karen, and Jeannette Vargas. 2000. "Explaining Variation in the Use of European Litigation Strategies: EC Law and UK Gender Equality Policy." *Comparative Political Studies* 33: 452–82.

Anderson, Benedict. 1998. *The Spectre of Comparisons: Nationalism, Southeast Asia and the World.* New York: Verso.

Andrews, Kenneth. 2002. "Movement-Countermovement Dynamics and the Emergence of New Institutions: The Case of 'White Flight' Schools in Mississippi." *Social Forces* 80: 911–36.

———. 2004. *Freedom Is a Constant Struggle: The Mississippi Civil Rights Movement and Its Legacy.* Chicago: University of Chicago Press.

Andrews, Kenneth T., and Michael Biggs. Forthcoming. "The Dynamics of Protest Diffusion: Formal Organization, Social Networks, and News Media in the 1960s Sit-Ins." *American Sociological Review.*

Annual Register. 1989. "Venezuela." *Annual Register* 231:75.

Banaszak, Lee Ann. 1996. *Why Movements Succeed or Fail: Opportunity, Culture, and the Struggle for Woman Suffrage.* Princeton, N.J.: Princeton University Press.

Banaszak, Lee Ann, Karen Beckwith, and Dieter Rucht, eds. 2003. *Women's Movements Facing the Reconfigured State.* Cambridge: Cambridge University Press.

Baskin, Gershon. 2005. "This Week in Israel: Behind the News with Gershon Baskin." *Jerusalem Times,* August 19.

Beckwith, Karen. 2003. "The Gendering Ways of States: Women's Representation and State Reconfiguration in France, Great Britain, and the United States." In *Women's Movements Facing the Reconfigured State,* ed. Lee Ann Banaszak, Karen Beckwith, and Dieter Rucht. Cambridge: Cambridge University Press.

Beissinger, Mark R. 2002. *Nationalist Mobilization and the Collapse of the Soviet State.* Cambridge: Cambridge University Press.

Bennett, W. Lance. 2005. "Social Movements beyond Borders: Understanding Two Eras of Transnational Activism." In *Transnational Protest and Global Activism,* ed. Donatella della Porta and Sidney Tarrow. Lanham Md.: Rowman & Littlefield.

Berman, Eli, and David Laitin. 2005. "Rational Martyrs vs. Hard Targets: Evidence on the Tactical Use of Suicide Attacks." Unpublished paper, Stanford University, Department of Political Science, http://dss.ucsd.edu/~elib/RatMartyrs.pdf.

Bernhard, Michael H. 1993. *The Origins of Democratization in Poland: Workers, Intellectuals, and Oppositional Politics, 1976–1980.* New York: Columbia University Press.

Boli, John, and George M. Thomas, eds. 1999. *Constructing World Culture: International Nongovernmental Organizations since 1875.* Stanford, Calif.: Stanford University Press.

Boutwell, Jeffrey, Michael T. Klare, and Laura W. Reed. 1995. *Lethal Commerce: The Global Trade in Small Arms and Light Weapons.* Cambridge, Mass.: American Academy of Arts and Sciences.

Brockett, Charles D. 2005. *Political Movements and Violence in Central America.* Cambridge: Cambridge University Press.

Burns, Stewart, ed. 1997. *Daybreak of Freedom.* Chapel Hill: University of North Carolina Press.

Burstein, Paul, and April Linton. 2002. "The Impact of Political Parties, Interest Groups, and Social Movement Organizations on Public Policy." *Social Forces* 81: 380–408.

Burstein, Paul, and Sarah Sausner. 2005. "The Incidence and Impact of Policy-Oriented Collective Action: Competing Views." *Sociological Forum* 20: 403–19.

Button, James W. 1978. *Black Violence: Political Impact of the 1960's Riots.* Princeton, N.J.: Princeton University Press.

Caporaso, James A., and Joseph Jupille. 2001. "The Europeanization of Gender Equality Policy and Domestic Structural Change." In *Transforming Europe: Europeanization and Domestic Change,* ed. Maria Green Cowles, James A. Caporaso and Thomas Risse. Ithaca, N.Y.: Cornell University Press, pp. 21–43.

Chabot, Sean. 2003. "Crossing the Great Divide: The Gandhian Repertoire's Transnational Diffusion to the American Civil Rights Movement." Unpublished Ph.D. diss., University of Amsterdam.

Chivers, C. J. 2005. "Back Channels: A Crackdown Averted." *New York Times,* January 17, 1.

Collier, Paul. 2000a. "Economic Causes of Civil Conflict and Their Implications for Policy." Paper prepared for United Nations Security Council Global Policy Forum, www.igc.org/globalpolicy/security/issues/diamond/wb.htm.

———. 2000b. "Rebellion as a Quasi-Criminal Activity." *Journal of Conflict Resolution* 44: 839–53.

Collins, Randall. 2004. "Rituals of Solidarity and Security in the Wake of Terrorist Attack." *Sociological Theory* 22: 53-87.

Conant, Lisa J. 2002. *Justice Contained: Law and Politics in the European Union*. Ithaca, N.Y.: Cornell University Press.

Costain, Anne. 1992. *Inviting Women's Rebellion: A Political Process Interpretation of the Women's Movement*. Baltimore: Johns Hopkins University Press.

Dallaire, Roméo. 2003. *J'ai serré la main du diable: La faillite de l'humanité au Rwanda*. Outremont, Québec: Libre Expression.

Davis, Madeleine, ed. 2003. *The Pinochet Case: Origins, Progress and Implications*. London: Institute for Latin American Studies.

della Porta, Donatella. 1995. *Social Movements, Political Violence and the State: A Comparative Analysis of Italy and Germany*. Cambridge: Cambridge University Press.

della Porta, Donatella, Olivier Filleule, and Herbert Reiter. 1998. "Policing Protest in France and Italy: From Intimidation to Cooperation?" In *The Social Movement Society*, ed. David S. Meyer and Sidney Tarrow. Lanham, Md.: Rowman & Littlefield, chap. 5.

della Porta, Donatella, and Sidney Tarrow. 1986. "Unwanted Children: Political Violence and the Cycle of Protest in Italy." *European Journal of Political Research* 14: 607-32.

Des Forges, Alison, et al. 1999. *Leave None to Tell the Story: Genocide in Rwanda*. New York: Human Rights Watch.

Diani, Mario. 1995. *Green Networks: A Structural Analysis of the Italian Environmental Movement*. Edinburgh: Edinburgh University Press.

Diani, Mario, and Doug McAdam, eds. 2003. *Social Movements and Networks: Relational Approaches to Collective Action*. Oxford: Oxford University Press.

Drescher, Seymour. 1991. "British Way, French Way: Opinion Building and Revolution in the Second French Slave Emancipation." *American Historical Review* 96: 709-34.

Dunér, Bertil. 1985. *Military Intervention in Civil Wars: The 1970s*. Aldershot: Gower.

Eriksson, Mikael, and Peter Wallensteen. 2004. "Armed Conflict, 1989-2003." *Journal of Peace Research* 41: 625-36.

Evans, Peter. 2005. "Counter-Hegemonic Globalization: Transnational Social Movements in the Contemporary Global Political Economy." In *Handbook of Political Sociology*, ed. Thomas Janoski, Alexander Hicks, and Mildred Schwartz. Cambridge: Cambridge University Press, pp. 655-70.

Evans, Sara M. 1979. *Personal Politics: The Roots of Women's Liberation in the Civil Rights Movement and the New Left*. New York: Knopf.

Evans, Sara M., and Harry C. Boyte. 1992. *Free Spaces: The Sources of Democratic Change in America*. Chicago: University of Chicago Press.

Favre, Pierre. 1990. *La Manifestation*. Paris: Presses de la Fondation Nationale des Sciences Politiques.

Fearon, James D., and David D. Laitin. 2003. "Ethnicity, Insurgency, and Civil War." *American Political Science Review* 97: 75-90.

Fillieule, Olivier. 1997. *Stratégies de la rue: Les manifestations en France*. Paris: Presses de la Fondation Nationale des Sciences Politiques.

Fish, M. Steven. 1995. *Democracy from Scratch: Opposition and Regime in the New Russian Revolution*. Princeton, N.J.: Princeton University Press.

Franzosi, Roberto. 1995. *The Puzzle of Strikes: Class and State Strategies in Postwar Italy*. Cambridge: Cambridge University Press.

Freedom House. 2000. "FH Country Ratings." www.freedomhouse.org/ratings/index.

Freeman, Jo. 1975. *The Politics of Women's Liberation*. New York: Longman.

Frickel, Scott, and Neil Gross. 2005. "A General Theory of Scientific/Intellectual Movements." *American Sociological Review* 70: 204-32.

Gambetta, Diego, ed. 2005. *Making Sense of Suicide Missions*. Oxford: Oxford University Press.

Garcelon, Marc. 2001. "Colonizing the Subject: The Genealogy and Legacy of the Soviet Internal Passport." In *Documenting Individual Identity. State Practices in the Modern World,* ed. Jane Caplan and John Torpey. Princeton, N.J.: Princeton University Press.

Gavrilis, George. 2004. "Sharon's Endgame for the West Bank Barrier." *Washington Quarterly* 27: 7-20.

Geertz, Clifford. 1973. *The Interpretation of Cultures: Selected Essays*. New York: Basic Books.

Genovese, Eugene D. 1969. *The World the Slaveholders Made: Two Essays in Interpretation*. New York: Pantheon.

Ghobarah, Hazem Adam, Paul Huth, and Bruce Russett. 2003. "Civil Wars Kill and Maim People—Long after the Shooting Stops." *American Political Science Review* 97: 189-202.

Ginsborg, Paul. 1990. *A History of Contemporary Italy: Society and Politics, 1943-1988*. New York: Penguin.

Ginsburg, Faye D. 1989. *Contested Lives. The Abortion Debate in an American Community*. Berkeley: University of California Press.

Gitlin, Todd. 1980. *The Whole World Is Watching*. Berkeley: University of California Press.

Giugni, Marco, Doug McAdam, and Charles Tilly, eds. 1998. *From Contention to Democracy*. Lanham, Md.: Rowman & Littlefield.

———, eds. 1999. *How Social Movements Matter*. Minneapolis: University of Minnesota Press.

Goldstein, Judith, Miles Kahler, Robert O. Keohane, and Anne-Marie Slaughter. 2001. *Legalization and World Politics*. Cambridge, Mass.: MIT Press.

Goldstone, Jack A., and Charles Tilly. 2001. "Threat (and Opportunity): Popular Action and State Response in the Dynamics of Contentious Action." In *Silence and Voice in the Study of Contentious Politics,* ed. Ronald R. Aminzade et al. Cambridge: Cambridge University Press.

Goodwin, Jeff. 2001. *No Other Way Out: States and Revolutionary Movements, 1945-1991.* Cambridge: Cambridge University Press.

Gould, Roger. 1995. *Insurgent Identities: Class, Community and Protest in Paris from 1848 to the Commune.* Chicago: University of Chicago Press.

Grimsted, David. 1998. *American Mobbing, 1828-1861: Toward Civil War.* New York: Oxford University Press.

Hart, Peter. 1998. *The I.R.A. & Its Enemies. Violence and Community in Cork, 1916-1923.* Oxford: Clarendon.

Hellman, Judy. 1999. "Real and Virtual Chiapas: Magic Realism and the Left." In *Socialist Register 2000: Necessary and Unnecessary Utopias,* ed. Leo Panitch and Colin Leys. London: Merlin.

Henderson, Errol A. 1999. "Civil Wars." In *Encyclopedia of Violence, Peace, and Conflict,* ed. Lester Kurtz. San Diego: Academic Press, vol. I pp. 279-87.

Hironaka, Ann. 2005. *Neverending Wars: The International Community, Weak States, and the Perpetuation of Civil War.* Cambridge, Mass.: Harvard University Press.

Hirsch, Eric. 1990. "Sacrifice for the Cause: Group Processes, Recruitment, and Commitment in a Student Social Movement." *American Sociological Review* 55: 243-54.

Hochschild, Adam. 2005. *Bury the Chains: Prophets and Rebels in the Fight to Free an Empire's Slaves.* Boston: Houghton Mifflin.

Hooghe, Liesbet, and Gary Marks. 2002. *Multi-Level Governance in European Politics.* Lanham, Md.: Rowman & Littlefield.

Imig, Doug, and Sidney Tarrow, eds. 2001. *Contentious Europeans: Protest and Politics in an Emerging Polity.* Lanham, Md.: Rowman & Littlefield.

Jenkins, J. Craig. 1986. *The Politics of Insurgency: The Farm Worker Movement in the 1960s.* New York: Columbia University Press.

Jenkins, J. Craig, David Jacobs, and Jon Agnone. 2003. "Political Opportunities and African-American Protest, 1948-1997." *American Journal of Sociology* 109: 277-303.

Jenness, Valerie. 1993. *Making It Work: The Prostitute's Rights Movement in Perspective.* New York: Aldine de Gruyter.

Jones, Bruce. 1995. "Intervention without Borders: Humanitarian Intervention in Rwanda, 1990-1994." *Millennium: Journal of International Affairs* 24: 225-49.

Kaiser, Robert J. 1994. *The Geography of Nationalism in Russia and the USSR.* Princeton, N.J.: Princeton University Press.

Kaldor, Mary. 1999. *New & Old Wars. Organized Violence in a Global Era.* Cambridge: Polity.

Karatnycky, Adrian, ed. 2000. *Freedom in the World: The Annual Survey of Political Rights and Civil Liberties.* New York: Freedom House.

Katzenstein, Mary F. 1998. *Faithful and Fearless: Moving Feminist Protest inside the Church and Military.* Princeton, N.J.: Princeton University Press.

———. 2003. "Re-Dividing Citizens—Divided Feminisms: The Reconfigured US State and Women's Citizenship." In *Women's Movements Facing the Reconfigured State,* ed. Lee Ann Banaszak, Karen Beckwith, and Dieter Rucht. Cambridge: Cambridge University Press.

Katzenstein, Mary F., and Carol M. Mueller. 1987. *The Women's Movements of the United States and Western Europe: Consciousness, Political Opportunity, and Public Policy.* Philadelphia: Temple University Press.

Keck, Margaret, and Kathryn Sikkink. 1998. *Activists beyond Borders: Transnational Activist Networks in International Politics.* Ithaca, N.Y.: Cornell University Press.

Keogh, Dermot. 2001. "Ireland at the Turn of the Century: 1994–2001." In *The Course of Irish History,* ed. T. W. Moody and F. X. Martin, 4th ed. Lanham, Md.: Roberts Rinehart.

Keohane, Robert O. 2002. *Power and Governance in a Partially Globalized World.* London: Routledge.

Kertzer, David I. 1988. *Ritual, Politics, and Power.* New Haven, Conn.: Yale University Press.

Khazanov, Anatoly M. 1995. *After the USSR: Ethnicity, Nationalism, and Politics in the Commonwealth of Independent States.* Madison: University of Wisconsin Press.

Killian, Lewis M. 1984. "Organization, Rationality and Spontaneity in the Civil Rights Movement." *American Sociological Review* 49: 770–83.

Kinealy, Christine. 2003. "Les Marches orangistes en Irlande du Nord: Histoire d'un droit." *Le Mouvement Social* 2002: 165–82.

Klandermans, Bert. 1988. "The Formation and Mobilization of Consensus." *International Social Movement Research* 1: 173–96.

———. 1997. *The Social Psychology of Protest.* Oxford: Blackwell's.

———, ed. 1991. *Peace Movements in Western Europe and the United States.* Greenwich, Conn.: JAI.

Koopmans, Ruud. 2004. "Protest in Time and Space: The Evolution of Waves of Contention." In *The Blackwell Companion to Social Movements,* ed. David A. Snow, Sarah A. Soule, and Hanspeter Kriesi. Malden, Mass.: Blackwell, chap. 2.

Kriesi, Hanspeter. 1996. "The Organizational Structure of New Social Movements in a Political Context." In *Comparative Perspectives on Social Movements,* ed. Doug McAdam, John McCarthy, and Mayer Zald. Cambridge: Cambridge University Press.

Kriesi, Hanspeter, et al. 1995. *New Social Movements in Western Europe: A Comparative Analysis.* Minneapolis: University of Minnesota Press.

Kubik, Jan. 1994. *The Power of Symbols against the Symbols of Power: The Rise of Solidarity and the Fall of State Socialism in Poland.* University Park: Pennsylvania State University Press.

Kuzio, Taras. 2005. "The Opposition's Road to Success." *Journal of Democracy* 36: 117–30.

Laba, Roman. 1991. *The Roots of Solidarity: A Political Sociology of Poland's Working Class Democratization.* Princeton, N.J.: Princeton University Press.

Lacey, Mark. 2005. "Riot Toll Mounts in Sudan after Rebel Leader's Death." *New York Times,* August 4.

Laitin, David D. 1998. *Identity in Formation: The Russian-Speaking Populations in the Near Abroad.* Ithaca, N.Y.: Cornell University Press.

———. 1999. "The Cultural Elements of Ethnically Mixed States: Nationality Re-formation in the Soviet Successor States." In *State/Culture. State Formation after the Cultural Turn,* ed. George Steinmetz. Ithaca, N.Y.: Cornell University Press.

Levi, Margaret, and Gillian Murphy. Forthcoming. "Coalitions of Contention: The Case of the WTO Protests in Seattle." *Political Studies.*

Licklider, Roy, ed. 1993. *Stopping the Killing: How Civil Wars End.* New York: New York University Press.

Linebaugh, Peter, and Marcus Rediker. 1990. "The Many-Headed Hydra: Sailors, Slaves and the Atlantic Working Class in the Eighteenth Century." *Journal of Historical Sociology* 3: 225–52.

López Maya, Margarita. 2002. "Venezuela after the *Caracoza:* Forms of Protest in a Deinstitutionalized Context." *Bulletin of Latin American Research* 21: 199–218.

López Maya, Margarita, David Smilde, and Keta Stephany. 2002. *Protesta y Cultura en Venezuela: Los Marcos de Acción Colectiva en 1999.* Caracas: FACES-UCV, CENDES, FONACIT.

Lowi, Theodore. 1971. *The Politics of Disorder.* New York: Free Press.

Lustick, Ian. 1998. *For the Land and the Lord: Jewish Fundamentalism in Israel.* New York: Council on Foreign Relations.

Lutz, Ellen, and Kathryn Sikkink. 2001. "The Justice Crusade: The Evolution and Impact of Foreign Human Rights Trials in Latin America." *Chicago Journal of International Law* 2: 134.

Mamdani, Mahmood. 2001. *When Victims Become Killers: Colonialism, Nativism, and the Genocide in Rwanda.* Princeton, N.J.: Princeton University Press.

Mansbridge, Jane. 1986. *Why We Lost the ERA.* Chicago: University of Chicago Press.

Mansbridge, Jane, and Katherine Flaster. 2005. "Male Chauvinist, Feminist, Sexist, and Sexual Harassment: Different Trajectories in Feminist Linguistic Innovation." *American Speech* 80:256–79.

Margadant, Ted. 1979. *French Peasants in Revolt: The Insurrection of 1851.* Princeton, N.J.: Princeton University Press.

Martin, Terry. 2001. *The Affirmative Action Empire: Nations and Nationalism in the Soviet Union, 1923–1939.* Ithaca, N.Y.: Cornell University Press.

Mathieu, Lilian. 2001. "An Unlikely Mobilization: The Occupation of Saint-Nizier Church by the Prostitutes of Lyon." *Revue Française de Sociologie* 42: 107–31 (annual English-language ed.).

McAdam, Doug. 1983. "Tactical Innovation and the Pace of Insurgency." *American Sociological Review* 48: 735–54.

———. 1988. *Freedom Summer.* New York: Oxford University Press.

———. 1998. "On the International Origins of Domestic Political Opportunities." In *Social Movements and American Political Institutions,* ed. Anne N. Costain and Andrew S. McFarland. Boulder, Colo.: Rowman & Littlefield, pp. 251–67.

———. 1999. *Political Process and the Development of Black Insurgency, 1930–1970.* 2d ed. Chicago: University of Chicago Press.

———. 2003. "Beyond Structural Analysis: Toward a More Dynamic Understanding of Social Movements." In *Social Movements and Networks: Relational Approaches to Collective Action,* ed. Mario Diani and Doug McAdam. Oxford: Oxford University Press, pp. 281–98.

McAdam, Doug, and William H. Sewell, Jr. 2001. "It's about Time: Temporality in the Study of Social Movements and Revolutions." In *Silence and Voice in the Study of Contentious Politics,* ed. Ron Aminzade, Jack Goldstone, Doug McAdam, Elizabeth Perry, William H. Sewell Jr., Sidney Tarrow, and Charles Tilly. Cambridge: Cambridge University Press, pp. 89–125.

McAdam, Doug, Sidney Tarrow, and Charles Tilly. 2001. *Dynamics of Contention.* Cambridge: Cambridge University Press.

McCarthy, John. 1987. "Pro-Life and Pro-Choice Mobilization: Infrastructure Deficits and New Technologies." In *Social Movements in an Organizational Society,* ed. John McCarthy and Mayer N. Zald. New Brunswick, N.J.: Transaction Books, pp. 49–66.

McCarthy, John D., Clark McPhail, and Jackie Smith. 1996. "Images of Protest: Dimensions of Selection Bias in Media Coverage of Washington Demonstrations, 1982 and 1991." *American Sociological Review* 61: 478–99.

McCarthy, John D., and Mayer N. Zald. 1978. "Resource Mobilization and Social Movements: A Partial Theory." *American Journal of Sociology* 82: 1212–41.

McCracken, J. L. 2001. "Northern Ireland: 1921–66." In *The Course of Irish History,* ed. T. W. Moody and F. X. Martin, 4th ed. Lanham, Md.: Roberts Rinehart.

McMichael, Philip. 2005. "Globalization." In *Handbook of Political Sociology,* ed. Thomas Janoski, Robert Alford, Alexander Hicks and Mildred Schwartz. Cambridge: Cambridge University Press, pp. 587–606.

Mendelson, Sarah, and Theodore P. Gerber. 2005. "Local Activist Culture and Transnational Diffusion: An Experiment in Social Marketing among Human Rights Groups in Russia." Unpublished paper.

Meyer, David S. 1990. *A Winter of Discontent: The Nuclear Freeze and American Politics.* New York: Praeger.

Meyer, David S., Valerie Jenness, and Helen Ingram, eds. 2005. *Routing the Opposition: Social Movements, Public Policy, and Democracy.* Minneapolis: University of Minnesota Press.

Meyer, David S., and Suzanne Staggenborg. 1996. "Movements, Countermovements, and the Structure of Political Opportunity." *American Journal of Sociology* 101: 1628-60.

Meyer, David S., and Sidney Tarrow, eds. 1998. *The Social Movement Society.* Lanham, Md.: Rowman & Littlefield.

Meyer, David S., and Nancy Whittier. 1994. "Social Movement Spillover." *Social Problems* 41: 277-98.

Michels, Robert. 1962. *Political Parties.* New York: Collier Books.

Morris, Aldon D. 1984. *The Origins of the Civil Rights Movement.* New York: Oxford University Press.

Mueller, Carol M. 1999. "Claim Radicalization: The 1989 Protest Cycle in the GDR." *Social Problems* 46: 528-47.

Muir, Edward. 1997. *Ritual in Early Modern Europe.* Cambridge: Cambridge University Press.

Ngai, Mae M. 2004. *Impossible Subjects: Illegal Aliens and the Making of Modern America.* Princeton, N.J.: Princeton University Press.

Norris, Pippa. 2002. *Democratic Phoenix: Reinventing Political Activism.* Cambridge: Cambridge University Press.

Oberschall, Anthony. 1989. "The 1960 Sit-Ins: Protest Diffusion and Movement Take-off." *Research in Social Movements, Conflict and Change* 11: 31-53.

O'Brien, Robert, Anne Marie Goetz, Jan Aart Scholte, and Marc Williams. 2000. *Contesting Global Governance: Multilateral Economic Institutions and Global Social Movements.* Cambridge: Cambridge University Press.

Offe, Claus. 1990. "Reflections on the Institutional Self-Transformation of Movement Politics: A Tentative Stage Model." In *Challenging the Political Order,* ed. Russell Dalton and Manfred Kuechler. Oxford: Oxford University Press, pp. 232-50.

Olcott, Martha Brill. 2002. *Kazakhstan. Unfulfilled Promise.* Washington, D.C.: Carnegie Endowment for International Peace.

Olesen, Thomas. 2005. *International Zapatismo: The Construction of Solidarity in the Age of Globalization.* London: Zed.

Oliver, Pamela E. 1989. "Bringing the Crowd Back In: The Nonorganizational Elements of Social Movements." *Research in Social Movements, Conflict and Change* 11: 1-30.

Olson, Mancur. 1968. *The Logic of Collective Action.* Cambridge, Mass.: Harvard University Press.

Olzak, Susan. 1992. *The Dynamics of Ethnic Competition and Conflict.* Stanford, Calif.: Stanford University Press.

Oppenheimer, Martin. 1963. "The Genesis of the Southern Negro Student Sit-In Movement." Unpublished Ph.D. diss., University of Pennsylvania.

Osa, Maryjane. 2003a. "Networks in Opposition: Linking Organizations through Activists in the Polish People's Republic." In *Social Movements and Networks,* ed. Mario Diani and Doug McAdam. Oxford: Oxford University Press, pp. 77–104.

————. 2003b. *Solidarity and Contention: Networks of Polish Opposition.* Minneapolis: University of Minnesota Press.

Ost, David. 1990. *The Politics of Anti-Politics: Opposition and Reform in Poland since 1968.* Philadelphia: University of Pennsylvania Press.

Palmer, Stanley H. 1988. *Police and Protest in England and Ireland 1780-1850.* Cambridge: Cambridge University Press.

Pape, Robert A. 2004. *Dying to Win: The Strategic Logic of Suicide Terrorism.* New York: Random House.

Parthasarathy, Shobita. 2003. "A Global Genome? Comparing the Development of Genetic Testing for Breast Cancer in the United States and Britain." Unpublished Ph.D. diss., Cornell University, Ithaca, N.Y.

Pedahzur, Ami, and Arie Perliger. 2006. "The Changing Nature of Suicide Attacks: A Social Network Perspective." *Social Forces* 84.

Peleg, Samuel. 2002. *Zealotry and Vengeance: Quest of a Religious Identity Group: A Sociopolitical Account of the Rabin Assassination.* Lanham, Md.: Lexington Books.

Perrow, Charles. 1979. "The Sixties Observed." In *The Dynamics of Social Movements: Resource Mobilization, Social Control, and Tactics,* ed. Mayer N. Zald and John D, McCarthy. Cambridge, Mass.: Winthrop, pp. 192–211.

Perry, Elizabeth J. 1993. *Shanghai on Strike.* Stanford, Calif.: Stanford University Press.

Piano, Aili, and Arch Puddington. 2004. *Freedom in the World 2004: The Annual Survey of Political Rights and Civil Liberties.* New York: Freedom House

Pianta, Mario. 2001. "Parallel Summits of Global Civil Society." In *Global Civil Society, 2001.* Oxford: Oxford University Press, pp. 169–94.

————. 2002. "Parallel Summits Update." In *Global Civil Society, 2002.* Oxford: Oxford University Press, pp. 371–78.

Pianta, Mario, and Federico Silva. 2003. "Parallel Summits of Global Civil Society: An Update." In *Global Civil Society, 2003.* Oxford: Oxford University Press.

Pigenet, Michel, and Danielle Tartakowsky. 2003. "Les Marches." *Le Mouvement Social* 2002 (January–March), entire issue.

Piven, Frances Fox, and Richard A. Cloward. 1977. *Poor People's Movements: Why They Succeed, How They Fail.* New York: Pantheon Books.

————. 1992. "Normalizing Collective Protest." In *Frontiers of Social Movement Research,* ed. Aldon Morris and Carol M. Meuller. New Haven, Conn.: Yale University Press, pp. 301–25.

Pizzorno, Alessandro. 1978. "'Political Exchange and Collective Identity in Industrial Conflict." In *The Resurgence of Class Conflict in Western Europe since 1968,* ed. Colin Crouch and Alessandro Pizzorno. London: Macmillan, pp. 277–98.

Polletta, Francesca. 1998. "'It Was Like a Fever …': Narrative and Identity in Social Protest." *Social Problems* 45: 137–59.

Prunier, Gérard. 1995. *The Rwanda Crisis. History of a Genocide.* New York: Columbia University Press.

———. 2001. "Genocide in Rwanda." In *Ethnopolitical Warfare. Causes, Consequences, and Possible Solutions,* ed. Daniel Chirot and Martin E. P. Seligman. Washington, D.C.: American Psychological Association.

Raines, Howell. 1977. *My Soul Is Rested.* New York: Penguin.

Rao, Hayagreeva. 1998. "Caveat Emptor: The Construction of Nonprofit Consumer Watchdog Organizations." *American Journal of Sociology* 103: 912–61.

Rochon, Thomas R. 1998. *Culture Moves: Ideas, Activism, and Changing Values.* Princeton, N.J.: Princeton University Press.

Rochon, Thomas R., and David S. Meyer, eds. 1997. *Coalitions and Political Movements: The Lessons of the Nuclear Freeze.* Boulder, Colo.: Rienner.

Roht-Arriaza, Naomi. 2005. *The Pinochet Effect: Transnational Justice in the Age of Human Rights.* Philadelphia: University of Pennsylvania Press.

Roth, Benita. 2004. *Separate Roads to Feminism: Black, Chicana, and White Feminist Movements in America's Second Wave.* Cambridge: Cambridge University Press.

Rucht, Dieter. 2005. "Political Participation in Europe." In *Contemporary Europe,* ed. Richard Sakwa and Anne Stephens. Houndmills, UK: Macmillan.

Rupp, Leila J., and Verta Taylor. 1987. *Survival in the Doldrums: The American Women's Rights Movement, 1945 to the 1960s.* New York: Oxford University Press.

Sageman, Marc. 2004. *Understanding Terror Networks.* Philadelphia: University of Pennsylvania Press.

Sambanis, Nicholas. 2004. "What Is Civil War? Conceptual and Empirical Complexities of an Operational Definition." *Journal of Conflict Resolution* 48: 814–58.

Sambanis, Nicholas, and Annalisa Zinn. 2003. "The Escalation of Self-Determination Movements: From Protest to Violence." Paper presented to the Annual Meeting of the American Political Science Association.

Samuel, Alexandra W. 2004. "Hactivism and the Future of Political Participation." Unpublished Ph.D. diss., Harvard University, Cambridge, Mass.

Sawyer, R. Keith. 2001. *Creating Conversations. Improvisation in Everyday Discourse.* Cresskill, N.J.: Hampton.

Schlozman, Kay. 1990. "Representing Women in Washington: Sisterhood and Pressure Politics." In *Women, Politics and Change,* ed. Louise Tilly and Patricia Gurin. New York: Russell Sage Foundation, pp. 339–82.

Scott, James C. 1985. *Weapons of the Weak: Everyday Forms of Peasant Resistance.* New Haven, Conn.: Yale University Press.

Shorter, Edward, and Charles Tilly. 1974. *Strikes in France, 1830-1968.* Cambridge: Cambridge University Press.

Slaughter, Anne-Marie. 2004. *The New World Order.* Princeton, N.J.: Princeton University Press.

Smith, Jackie, and Hank Johnston, eds. 2003. *Globalization and Resistance.* Lanham, Md.: Rowman & Littlefield.

Snow, David A., and Robert D. Benford. 1992. "Master Frames and Cycles of Protest." In *Frontiers in Social Movement Theory,* ed. Aldon Morris and Carol M. Mueller. New Haven, Conn.: Yale University Press.

Soule, Sarah A. 1995. "The Student Anti-Apartheid Movement in the United States: Diffusion of Tactics and Policy Reform." Unpublished Ph.D. diss., Cornell University, Ithaca, N.Y.

———. 1997. "The Student Divestment Movement in the United States and Tactical Diffusion: The Shantytown Protest." *Social Forces* 75: 855-83.

——— 1999. "The Diffusion of an Unsuccessful Innovation." *Annals of the American Academy of Political and Social Science* 566: 121-31.

———. 2001. "Situational Effects on Political Altruism: The Student Divestment Movement in the United States." In *Political Altruism? Solidarity Movements in International Perspective,* ed. Marco Giugni and Florence Passy. Lanham, Md.: Rowman & Littlefield, pp. 161-76.

Spilerman, Seymour. 1970. "The Causes of Racial Disturbances: A Comparison of Alternative Explanations." *American Sociological Review* 35:627-49.

Sprinzak, Ehud. 1991. *Ascendance of Israel's Radical Right.* New York: Oxford University Press.

———. 1999. *Brother against Brother: Violence and Extremism in Israeli Politics from Altalena to the Rabin Assassination.* New York: Free Press.

Strand, Håvard, Lars Wilhelmsen, and Nils Petter Gleditsch. 2004. *Armed Conflict Dataset Codebook.* Oslo: International Peace Research Institute.

Suny, Ronald Grigor. 1993. *The Revenge of the Past. Nationalism, Revolution, and the Collapse of the Soviet Union.* Stanford, Calif.: Stanford University Press.

Tarrow, Sidney. 1989. *Democracy and Disorder. Protest and Politics in Italy 1965-1975.* Oxford: Clarendon.

———. 1995. "Cycles of Collective Action: Between Moments of Madness and the Repertoire of Contention. In *Repertoires and Cycles of Collective Action,* ed. Mark Traugott. Durham, N.C.: Duke University Press.

———. 1998. *Power in Movement.* Rev. ed. Cambridge: Cambridge University Press.

———. 2005. *The New Transnational Activism.* Cambridge: Cambridge University Press.

Tarrow, Sidney, and Doug McAdam. 2005. "Scale Shift in Transnational Contention." In *Transnational Protest and Global Activism*, ed. Donatella della Porta and Sidney Tarrow. Lanham, Md.: Rowman & Littlefield, pp. 121–50.

Tartakowsky, Danielle. 1997. *Les Manifestations de rue en France, 1918–1968*. Paris: Publications de la Sorbonne.

———. 2004. *La Manif en éclats*. Paris: La Dispute.

———. 2005. *La Part du rêve: Histoire du 1 Mai en France*. Paris: Hachette.

Taylor, Christopher C. 1999. *Sacrifice as Terror: The Rwandan Genocide of 1994*. Oxford: Berg.

Taylor, Verta, and Nella Van Dyke. 2004. "'Get Up, Stand Up': Tactical Repertoires of Social Movements." In *The Blackwell Companion to Social Movements*, ed. David A. Snow, Sarah A. Soule, and Hanspeter Kriesi. Oxford: Blackwell.

Taylor, Verta, and Marieke Van Willigen. 1996. "Women's Self-Help and the Reconstruction of Gender: The Postpartum Support and Breast Cancer Movements." *Mobilization* 1: 123–42.

Thompson, Dorothy. 1984. *The Chartists: Popular Politics in the Industrial Revolution*. New York: Pantheon.

Tilly, Charles. 1986. *The Contentious French*. Cambridge, Mass.: Harvard University Press.

———. 1995. "Globalization Threatens Labor's Rights." *International Labor and Working Class History* 47: 1–23.

———. 1998. *Durable Inequality*. Berkeley: University of California Press.

———. 2003. *The Politics of Collective Violence*. Cambridge: Cambridge University Press.

———. 2004a. *Contention and Democracy in Europe, 1650–2000*. Cambridge: Cambridge University Press.

———. 2004b. *Social Movements, 1768–2004*. Boulder, Colo.: Paradigm.

———. 2005a. *Popular Contention in Great Britain, 1758–1834*. 2d ed. Boulder: Paradigm.

———. 2005b. *Trust and Rule*. Cambridge: Cambridge University Press.

Tishkov, Valery. 1997. *Ethnicity, Nationalism and Conflict in and After the Soviet Union: The Mind Aflame*. London: Sage.

———. 1999. "Ethnic Conflicts in the Former USSR: The Use and Misuse of Typologies and Data." *Journal of Peace Research* 36: 571–91.

———. 2004. *Chechnya: Life in a War-Torn Society*. Berkeley: University of California Press.

Usher, Graham. 2005. "The New Hamas: Between Resistance and Participation." www.meronline.org, August 21.

Vasi, Ion Bogdan. 2004. "The Adoption and Implementation of Local Governmental Actions Against Climate Change." Unpublished Ph.D. diss., Cornell University, Ithaca, N.Y.

Verhulst, Joris, and Stefaan Walgrave. 2003. "Worldwide Anti-war in Iraq Protest: A Preliminary Test of the Transnational Movements Thesis." Paper presented to the Second ECPR International Conference, Marburg.

Waismel-Manor, Israel S. 2005. "Striking Differences: Hunger Strikes in Israel and the United States." *Social Movement Studies* 4: 281–300.

Walter, Barbara F., and Jack Snyder, eds. 1999. *Civil Wars, Insecurity, and Intervention.* New York: Columbia University Press.

Walton, John, and David Seddon, eds. 1994. *Free Markets and Food Riots: The Politics of Global Adjustment.* Oxford: Blackwell.

Weingast, Barry. 1998. "Political Stability and Civil War: Institutions, Commitment, and American Democracy." In *Analytic Narratives,* ed. Robert Bates, et al. Princeton, N.J.: Princeton University Press.

Whittier, Nancy. 1995. *Feminist Generations: The Persistence of the Radical Women's Movement.* Philadelphia: Temple University Press.

Williams, Kim M. 2006. *Mark One or More: Civil Rights in Multiracial America.* Ann Arbor: University of Michigan Press.

Womack, John. 1971. *Zapata and the Mexican Revolution.* New York: Knopf.

Wood, Lesley Ann. 2004. "The Diffusion of Direct Action Tactics: From Seattle to Toronto and New York." Unpublished Ph.D. diss., Columbia University, New York.

Young, Michael P. 2006. *Bearing Witness against Sin: The Evangelical Birth of the American Social Movement.* Chicago: University of Chicago Press.

Zhao, Dinxin. 1998. "Ecologies of Social Movements: Student Mobilization during the 1989 Prodemocracy Movement in Beijing." *American Journal of Sociology* 3: 1493–1529.

Zolberg, Aristide. 1972. "'Moments of Madness.'" *Politics and Society* 2: 183–207.

INDEX

Abbas, 169-70
abolitionism, 35. *See also* antislavery
movements
actor constitution, 72-74, 216
Afghanistan, 145
African Americans, 18, 121, 212;
certification of, 190; and domestic
and international interactions,
194-95; protest movements, 183-87;
sit-ins, 18, 19-20, 182, 183-87. *See
also* antislavery movements
al-Bashir, Omar Hassan, 141
Amnesty International, 144
Anderson, Benedict, 169
Andrews, Kenneth, 184
Angola, 152
Annual Register, British, 46
anocracies, 135
antielection fraud campaigns, 32-33
antislavery movements, 6, 7, 9;
American, 121, 212; British, 1-2, 8,
11-12, 32, 43, 58, 61, 95, 115, 126,
171, 191, 196, 211; Clarkson's role in,
1-2, 12; mechanisms appearing in,
34-35; petitions used for, 12. *See also*
African Americans
antiwar protests, 19, 20
appeals, 14-16
Arafat, Yassir, 169, 170
armed conflicts: categories of, 153-55.
See also civil wars; lethal conflicts
armed forces, 136, 144, 150-51;
defections of, 156, 159, 160;
Ireland, 148; Nicaragua, 156, 159,

160; reaction of regimes to, 153;
relationship to revolutions, 167;
resource requirements, 137, 150-51.
See also lethal conflicts; military
organizations
attribution of similarity, 95, 96f5.1, 158,
190, 214, 215
authoritarian regimes, 66, 113
Avneri, Uri, 165, 167

Beissinger, Mark, 38, 41-42, 59, 76,
105-6
Benford, Robert, 102
Biggs, Michael, 184
bin Laden, Osama, 68
Blair, Tony, 180
bookstores, 131
boundary activation, 78, 138, 177, 188,
191, 215; definition, 34; Israel, 168,
179; and lethal conflicts, 143, 156,
161; as reference point for claim
making, 80; separating patriots from
terrorists, 80; Sudan, 143
boundary deactivation, 78, 80, 143, 177, 215
boundary formation, 78, 215
boundary shift, 190, 215
boycotts, 1
breast cancer coalition, 131
Bringing Down a Dictator (film), 33
British-Irish conflicts, 145-52
Brockett, Charles, 28, 102, 139-41; data
on contention, 103-4
brokerage, 11, 35, 188, 190, 191; and
analysis of contention, 30, 31-33, 34;

brokerage *(continued)*
and civic groups, 118; and contention
in Venezuela, 46; definition, 215;
function fulfilled by Chilean exiles,
173; and lethal conflicts, 137, 138,
143, 151, 156, 158, 161; and new
coordination, 74; overview, 205–6;
relationship to internationalization,
177; and scale shift, 95, 96*f*5.1; in
Serbian antielection fraud campaign,
32–33; and struggles in Sudan, 143;
and Ukraine contention, 77; and
Zapatistas, 75
Brown v. Board of Education, 18, 184
Burstein, Paul, 128
Bush, George W., 20, 82, 129

Canada, comparison of political system
with United States, 54–55
capacity, 55–57, 62–66, 67
Carter, Jimmy, 54, 158
Castro, Fidel, 47
catalogs, collecting for analysis of
episodes, 42–43
Catholic Church, 120; Poland, 118;
Protestant–Catholic conflict, 145–52,
212; and workers' rights, 115
Cavallo, Miguel, 174
certification, 11, 75, 81, 118, 188, 191;
of African Americans, 35, 190; by
association with Catholic faith, 115,
120; of cause of contention, 168; and
claims, 85, 86; definition, 34, 75, 215;
and lethal conflict, 138, 156, 158, 159,
161; of union, 121
Chávez, Hugo, 44, 46–47, 53–54, 65
Chiapas, Mexico, actor constitution in,
72–74
Chile, 164, 172–74
Chivers, C. J., 3
churches: occupation of, 89–92, 212.
See also Catholic Church
Civic Party, Guyana, 144
civil liberties, 62–66
Civil Rights March on Washington, 18,
19
civil rights movements, 102; charting

of, 184; concepts involved in, 187–92;
effect on international politics,
194–95; United States, 18, 59, 85–86;
violent methods used in, 20–21. *See
also* sit-ins
civil wars, 151–55, 214; American, 2, 35;
Ireland, 148–49; Sudan, 136, 141. *See
also* lethal conflicts
claimant-object pairs, 16–17
claim making, 6, 80, 90, 115, 136;
and cumulative experiences, 22,
23; effects produced by, 85–87;
and Nicaraguan revolution, 158; as
performance, 12–16; by prostitutes,
90–92; relationship to contention,
4–5; relationship to everyday
social organization, 22, 23; and
repertoires, 16–67; role of regimes
and institutions in, 60–61, 83; and
sources of repertoire changes, 21–23;
Soviet Union, 105; Venezuela, 51, 53.
See also collective claims; identity
claims; program claims; standing
claims
Clarkson, Thomas: as antislavery
organizer, 1–2, 12; and relationship
of regimes and contention, 22–23;
and scale shift, 95; as transnational
activist, 171–72; use of repertoires, 16
Clinton, Hillary Rodham, 129
Cloward, Richard A., 128
coalition formation, 75, 108, 177, 216;
antislavery, 35; Chile, 173; Italy, 92–
94; and lethal conflicts, 144, 156, 159;
relationship to internationalization,
177; Soviet Union, 104–7
coalitions, 9, 124, 177; and lethal
conflict, 144, 155–56, 157*b*7.2,
158, 159; and political actors, 76;
revolutionary, 156, 159; transnational,
172, 173, 174, 175, 177, 195; for
women's health, 131
coercion, 138–39
Coleridge, Samuel Taylor, 2
collective action, 1, 6, 9, 23, 100,
108, 114; by African Americans,
18; as component of contentious

dynamics, 129–31; Ukraine, 2; Venezuela, 54; women's movement, 131, 192; Zapatistas, 73–74. *See also* demobilization
modular identity, 40
modular performances, 12–13
Museveni, Yoweri, 142
Muslims, 135–36, 142, 143

NAACP. *See* National Association for the Advancement of Colored People (NAACP)
NAFTA. *See* North American Free Trade Agreement (NAFTA)
National Abortion and Reproductive Rights Action League, 131, 132
National Association for the Advancement of Colored People (NAACP), 96
nationalism, 11, 30, 138; long-distance, 169; Soviet Union, 42, 104–6, 108, 109, 191; violent, 137
National Organization for Women (NOW), 123, 126–27, 131, 132
Netanyahu, Benjamin, 166*b*8.1, 168
the Netherlands, 37, 59, 63, 213
network of organizations, 113
new coordination, 31, 32*f*2.1, 108; and contention in Venezuela, 46; definition, 217; and scale shift, 94, 95; in Serbian antielection fraud campaign, 32–33; sites of, 32–33; Sudan, 143; Zapatistas, 74–75
newspapers, as data source, 37–39, 50–54, 99–100
new world order, 176
New York Times, 3, 184
NEXIS, 39
Nicaraguan revolution, 156–58, 213
nongovernmental actors, 6
nonstate actors, 177–78
North American Free Trade Agreement (NAFTA), 73
North Carolina A&T College, 182
Northern Ireland, 145–52, 163, 180, 212
NOW. *see* National Organization for Women (NOW)

oil industry, Venezuela, 45, 48–50, 53
Olivera, Jorge, 174
Olzak, Susan, 37
OPEC. *See* Organization of Petroleum Exporting States (OPEC)
Operation Condor, 172–74, 181
oppositional networks, Poland, 116–18
organizational forms, 23
Organization of Petroleum Exporting States (OPEC), 48
Osa, Maryjane, 112, 116
Otpor, 32–33
outcomes, 87, 203*b*A.2, 204–5; and cycles of contention, 102–4; revolutionary, 155, 156, 158–60; and state repression, 140

Palestine, 163–64, 168–70
Palestinian Authority, 165, 169
Panzós massacres, 28
Paris, France, 17, 69–72
People's National Congress (PNC), Guyana, 144
Pérez, Carlos Andrew, 46, 47, 64–65
performances, 12, 188, 202*b*A.1; and civil rights movements, 18; and claim making, 12–16; innovations in, 30; and political actors, 11; residents of Panzós, 28; ritual political, 17
Perrow, Charles, 36
petitions, 12
Pinochet, Augusto, 95, 164, 172–74, 180, 181, 195, 213
Piven, Frances F., 128
Planned Parenthood, 131
pluralism, 113
PNC. *See* People's National Congress (PNC), Guyana
Poland, 111–13, 212. *See also* Solidarity, Poland
polarization, 97, 101, 151, 180; definition, 217; and Nicaraguan revolution, 158, 159; Sudan, 143
police departments, France, 89–90
Polish Communist Party, 112
political actors, 9, 21, 187, 202*b*A.1; activities of, 76; Chiapas, 72–74; and

ABOUT THE AUTHORS

Charles Tilly is Joseph L. Buttenwieser Professor of Social Science at Columbia University and is the author most recently of *Identities, Boundaries, and Social Ties* (Paradigm, 2005) and *Trust and Rule* (Cambridge University Press, 2005).

Sidney Tarrow is Maxwell M. Upson Professor of Government and Professor of Sociology at Cornell University. His latest books are *The New Transnational Activism* (Cambridge University Press, 2005) and (with Donatella della Porta, eds.) *Transnational Protest and Global Activism* (Rowman & Littlefield, 2004).